I0887634

COMPOSING JAPANESE MUSICAL MODERNITY

CHICAGO STUDIES IN ETHNOMUSICOLOGY

A series edited by Philip V. Bohlman, Ronald Radano, and Timothy Rommen

Editorial Board

Margaret J. Kartomi
Bruno Nettl
Anthony Seeger
Kay Kaufman Shelemay
Martin H. Stokes
Bonnie C. Wade

COMPOSING JAPANESE MUSICAL MODERNITY

BONNIE C. WADE

THE UNIVERSITY OF CHICAGO PRESS
CHICAGO AND LONDON

BONNIE C. WADE is professor of music at the University of California, Berkeley. She is the author of many books, including *Imaging Sound: An Ethnomusicological Study of Music, Art, and Culture in Mughal India*, also published by the University of Chicago Press, and, most recently, *Music in Japan: Experiencing Music, Expressing Culture.*

The University of Chicago Press, Chicago 60637
The University of Chicago Press, Ltd., London
© 2014 by The University of Chicago
All rights reserved. Published 2014.
Printed in the United States of America

23 22 21 20 19 18 17 16 15 14   1 2 3 4 5

ISBN-13: 978-0-226-08521-0 (cloth)
ISBN-13: 978-0-226-08535-7 (paper)
ISBN-13: 978-0-226-08549-4 (e-book)
DOI: 10.7208/chicago/9780226085494.001.0001 (e-book)

Library of Congress Cataloging-in-Publication Data
Wade, Bonnie C., author.
Composing Japanese musical modernity / Bonnie C. Wade.
pages cm — (Chicago studies in ethnomusicology)
Includes bibliographical references and index.
ISBN 978-0-226-08521-0 (cloth : alkaline paper) — ISBN 978-0-226-08535-7 (paperback : alkaline paper) — ISBN 978-0-226-08549-4 (e-book) 1. Composers—Japan. 2. Music—Japan—Western influences. 3. Music—Japan—20th century—History and criticism. I. Title. II. Series: Chicago studies in ethnomusicology.
ML340.5.W33 2014
780.952—dc23

2013014448

♾ This paper meets the requirements of ANSI/NISO Z39.48-1992 (Permanence of Paper).

TABLE OF CONTENTS

ACKNOWLEDGMENTS

My first acknowledgment goes to the many individuals in Japan who welcomed me graciously—composers, composer-performers, performers, and the heads of agencies and companies as well as their numerous staff members. They are simply too many to list here. The consistent rapidity of the responses that came to telephone calls, faxes, and letters and the amount of time that individuals were willing to spend with me while I was in Japan for field research was amazing, and I am enormously grateful. The assistance of the staff at the International House of Japan in Roppongi, where I make my home in Tokyo, needs special mention; the number of faxes they sent and received for me every time I was there made them seem rather like part of the project, and they welcomed my visitors cordially.

I wish to acknowledge with affection and gratitude the support of a few people in Japan. The Nakajima family, whom I have known since 1964, is always welcoming and supportive, as is the koto artist Keiko Nosaka, who established a number of important connections for me and in whose home there were always gatherings during my annual sojourns. The musicologist Tokiko Inoue was willing to speak with me about historical European music in Japan, and Fukiko Shinohara responded each time I need translation assistance either for a meeting or at International House, where we worked for hours together with recordings of conversations.

Kimiko Shimbo, whom I met on my first ethnographic foray in 1999 because she was included as a "woman composer" in the *Who's Who* (see the introduction), turned out to be not only a part-time teacher of music but also the full-time assistant to the secretary general of the Japan Federation of Composers. Her cheerful willingness to help with my project—by calling members of the JFC to make introductions that are so valuable in

Japanese life, by giving me invitations to concerts, by taking me along to private receptions after events, by meeting with me to clarify something or explain the significance of things—far exceeded the part of her job description that required her to foster international relations for Japanese composers; I will forever be grateful for her guidance and assistance.

Going to Japan for research is expensive. In this regard (and others), I am blessed to be a professor at the University of California, which afforded me the luxury of multiple sources of funding—specifically the Richard and Rhoda Goldman Chair in Interdisciplinary Studies of the College of Letters and Science at Berkeley; and support from the Center for Japanese Studies for my graduate student research assistants—Marié Abe, and Muyang Chen, Miki Kaneda, Alexandre Youngki Kwon, Sangbec Lee, and Adam Steckler—who helped me mine the considerable resources of the East Asia Library, do translations, and check translations, for example. I wish to thank the staff in the Department of Music, at the Center for Japanese Studies, and at the Institute for East Asian Studies, who guided me through the procedures the university requires for using such funds.

Among my colleagues at Berkeley, I want to thank the historian of modern Japan Andrew Barshay for reading pertinent parts of the draft. The readers of the manuscript for the University of Chicago Press were helpful, as was the editorial associate Russell Damian in the production process. For our conversations during the writing process and her early readings, I give hearty thanks to the editor Elizabeth Branch Dyson. The comments and endorsement of Ronald Radano on behalf of the Chicago Series in Ethnomusicology were greatly appreciated.

Finally, for her patience, encouragement, and lots of help along the way, I especially thank Ann Pescatello.

Bonnie C. Wade

Japanese children sing "God Save the King" in honor of the visit of the Prince of Wales on January 1, 1921. (Bain News Service)

INTRODUCTION

This is a book about composers in Japan, by which I mean musicians who, at least part of the time, create new music. They are professional and amateur, female and male, academic and freelance, innovative and conservative, well-known and ignored, and they work from a base in either European or traditional music. Such a persona as "a composer" has not always existed in Japanese culture; creators of new music have been of two kinds—performer-composers and composers. Who "the creator of new music" is changed during Japan's process of absorbing and normalizing in Japanese culture music from Europe and America—a process that took about fifty years past an initial governmental decision to do so in 1872.

"Composers" in premodern Japanese society were professional performers of one musical repertoire or another who also created new music—that is, they were performer-composers. In the immediate premodern period of Japanese history (the Tokugawa shogunate, 1600–1868), those musicians functioned relationally, in the context of some particular social group such as courtiers, samurai elites, urban populations of merchants and workers, and religious sects. Accordingly, the works they created fit into some particular repertoire such as music for the court, music for private entertainment, music for the popular theater, and music for Zen meditation. While amateur individuals such as wealthy (but low-status) merchants might study an instrument or vocal genre that fit into one of those realms to which they did not belong socially, the right to transmit musical knowledge was limited to professionals, with some spheres of music organized into guilds chartered by the government. While some degree of innovation could and did occur within or across musical spheres, until the nineteenth century "new music" created by performer-composers wandered only so far stylistically from existing music. One might say that new compositions were musically as well as socially relational.

The persona of the performer-composer still exists in modern Japan. I use the term herein to indicate an individual whose musical creativity is informed first and foremost by their competence and situatedness as a performer. Most of them discussed here are based in some sphere of traditional music—players of the *koto* (a kind of long zither, traditionally with thirteen strings) such as Tadao Sawai, for instance. Among performer-composers based in Western-informed music, I think of the pianist Yuji Takahashi, for instance. The style of music newly created by a performer-composer now might still be highly relational—"funded by the tradition" as Charles Seeger would have put it; however, in the context of Japanese musical modernity, the degree of individuality is up to the individual.

The separation of the functions of performing and composing in the creation of new music resulted in the late nineteenth century as needs for different kinds of new music arose. In 1868 the Tokugawa shogunate collapsed. With colonizing forces closing in on Asian cultures close to them and the country experiencing complex power struggles, an oligarchy of leaders emerged who would proceed to set Japan firmly on the path to modernity in the Meiji era (1868–1912). In order to use Western technology and knowledge against Western powers, which were encroaching forcibly on Japan, a systematic process of modernization was initiated. Among other moves, the decision was made in 1872 to adopt Western music along with other technologies; as discussed in chapter 1, composers were initially needed to produce music for the new educational system through which the Japanese would become enculturated into Western culture, including its musical culture.[1] As the decades passed, this new type of creator of new music would contribute to numerous facets of the modernization processes—processes that Japan carried out with astounding rapidity and thoroughness in the late nineteenth and early twentieth centuries. "The composer" was a participant in emergent conditions that I call "Japanese musical modernity"—conditions that I consider to be ongoing.

In this book I will argue that most Japanese composers have continued in some ways to maintain a relational sort of role in their society. Rather than composing music as an autonomous art, most composers have been and are grounded in the social—or, as I will put it several times, they "remain connected to the people." I support my argument by exploring how and why that came to be and for whom and why these composers might create new music. In so doing, I explore those conditions of Japanese musical modernity that afford composers possibilities for supporting themselves and contributing to their culture.

I came to this project by a circuitous path. My first experience with Japan came in the mid-1960s, just after I graduated from college with a degree in music history (naturally, that meant European music history) and, with two friends, set out to explore the world. "The world" was going to be Japan, to which each of us was drawn. To prepare, I convinced the professor in whose course at Boston University I was supposed to learn basic musicological research methodology (naturally, that meant library and archival exploration) to let me develop research tools for the subject of Japanese music. We three also learned what Japanese language we could before setting out.

I owed most of what I learned to William Malm at the University of Michigan, who had very recently, in 1959, published his *Japanese Music and Musical Instruments* (Malm 2000) and who responded to my youthful letter of appreciation by inviting me to get in touch with him when I arrived in Tokyo. There Malm introduced me to the distinguished musicologist Shigeo Kishibe and his wife, the illustrious koto artist Yori Kishibe, who agreed to take me on as her student. For the next eleven months I practiced koto for hours each day and attended as many concerts of traditional music and theater as I could manage with my full-time job teaching English at the YMCA to Tokyo's firefighters, who were preparing for the Tokyo Olympics later that year.

"The world" became much larger for the three of us travelers when we had to find a way to spend millions of unexchangable Japanese yen that we earned during our sojourn in Japan.[2] The solution was to keep traveling, spending our earnings to purchase freighter tickets that would keep us "on the road" headed west from Japan for a total of two and a half years. By the end of that journey, I had decided to become an ethnomusicologist and had applied to UCLA, with the intention of writing my master's thesis on the koto music I had studied, and then to focus my research on North India for the Ph.D. and beyond. All of that came to pass. I returned to Japan periodically to visit friends and continue to learn about traditional music as my teaching career proceeded apace, including courses first at Brown University, then at the University of California, Berkeley, that introduced students to music of Japan (naturally, that meant traditional genres).

In the mid-1980s, with the intellectual flow in ethnomusicology rapidly expanding to encompass postcolonial theory, issues of representation, popular music studies, and other subjects, it seemed time to shift my own intellectual flow, if I could manage it—to really focus on Japan and also to face the reality that I still taught "music of Japan" without acknowledging the fact that most "music of Japan"—not to mention most of my Japanese friends—engaged with instruments, ensemble types, repertoires, and other kinds of musical knowledge that reveal thorough enculturation in the European-derived musical system. This was not a matter of the "influence of Western music"; it was a case of absorption through the modernization processes—and probably indigenization as well. By the early 1990s I could begin to retool with language and other studies of Japanese culture, with the goal of a more comprehensive understanding of music in contemporary Japanese life. I conceived of my project as an ethnographic study of the indigenization of Western music in Japan. In some senses, that is what it remained, although I stopped articulating it in those terms.

The focus on composers came unexpectedly. I had to learn how to read the *kanji* for personal names and came upon a copy of a 1985 *Who's Who of Japanese Conductors and Composers.*[3] Perfect! As I studied the book, I realized that it held a wealth of information about individuals' careers—education, club affiliations, professional affiliations, awards, and personal contact information. A kind of map of musical spheres began to emerge, and I could see choices before me for the directions my research might take. Focusing on composers rather than performers would be a new tack for me. I quickly ruled out the idea of including composers who function primarily in spheres of popular culture because I needed to build on my own interests and experiences in spheres of classical and concert music.[4] Composers in that sphere, I reasoned, are specialists who engage most deeply in intellectual as well as creative terms with music; by investigating what they do and why, I might begin to better understand the music of Japan. The composers of whom I write in the book, then, are composers who function primarily in the sphere of concert music.[5]

To get started, I decided to write (with the help of my tutor) to those individuals in the category of composers least well represented in the *Who's Who*: the twenty-nine female composers among the several hundred listed. I introduced myself professionally and by my previous experience in Japan and asked if I might talk with them about their life in music when I next came to Japan. Expecting little or no response—because in Japan one usually needs to be introduced by a mutual acquaintance—I was astonished when I received welcoming messages from every single one of them. Meet them I did, in 1999—the year from which I date the ethnographic research of this project. The first thing I learned was that none of those women composers wanted to be considered a "female composer"; rather, they were composers, and they set about introducing me to quite a number of other composers, most of them men. Consequently, gender would not be an analytical factor on which I would dwell, although I do bring it into play at some moments in this book.

I also began to adjust in that first ethnographic foray to something that readers of this book might also need to adjust to. While ethnomusicologists often do (and are expected to) investigate musical practices and meanings that are unique to the people whose music we are studying (or are at least somewhat "exotic"), much of what I would learn about in Japan was not in fact unique to that culture. The lines along which musical modernity in Japan has developed are different from those of Europe and the Americas, but only to a certain extent. Nor does most of the music created by Japanese composers "sound Japanese" (i.e., sound different in traditional Japanese musical ways). Indeed, why should it? After all, 141 years have passed since the decision was made to systematically introduce the music of Europe and America in order to create a shared cultural space for all the people of the new nation. This book should not be read as a comparative study in a search for difference.

Nor is this is an ethnographic study of a group of people, as many ethnomusicological studies have been. Composers in Japan do not constitute a group or even a community. While the history of composing in Japan before and a bit after World War II is usually related in terms of small professional groups (see chapter 4), groups are now likely to be professional organizations such as the Japan section of the International Society for Contemporary Music. Consequently, I have made a point in this book to introduce and give voice to a number of individual composers, detailing some opportunities presented to them, some of the decisions they have made, their ideas about what they are doing, and the like. In introducing the composers as creative agents in their chosen spheres, however, I have not devoted much space to biographical information or the analytical exploration of musical works. That mode of presentation would have meant narrowing my coverage to far fewer composers, and probably yielding to the seemingly inexorable pull to focus only on "the great." That I expressly did not want to do. Other sources are cited that can be helpful in those directions.

RESEARCH METHODOLOGY

My methodology for this project was primarily ethnographic in that people led the way, usually to still more people. If I learned in a conversation, for instance, that a composer enjoyed writing music for choruses to sing in competitions, I needed to find people from whom I could learn about the competition system, the stipulations for pieces presented, why a chorus would commission new music from a composer, and how they might select him or her. If I learned in a conversation that teaching did not constitute an individual's primary source of income, I had to understand what else afforded sources of livelihood. Following leads made this project a fourteen-year adventure.

My conversations with individuals are given herein in English, although they were conducted sometimes in Japanese, sometimes in a mixture of Japanese and English, and sometimes wholly in English, depending on the circumstances. I made it a practice to have equipment available, should circumstances and the individuals permit our conversation to be recorded for checking later with a translator.[6] My spoken Japanese was best in the early stages of the project, which followed four challenging years of language study at Berkeley (with undergraduates decades younger than I); once I became an administrator, my opportunity to work on my language skills decreased, and, when during my annual research stints to Japan I considered it wise to take a translator with me to a conversation, I did so regretfully.

Also of methodological importance was the "hanging out" mentioned by so many ethnomusicologists—for instance, at the many concerts I attended. "Collecting music" in this project meant building a large collection of CDs (and learning about the production of them), which will be housed in the Jean Gray Hargrove Music Library at the University of California, Berkeley after publication of this book. I have drawn on that collection heavily to provide citations in the notes of published recordings of works to which I refer. Hopefully the number of online digital sources for works by Japanese composers and performer-composers will burgeon. Print sources such as journal and newspaper articles, concert flyers, program notes, and the like were also crucial; for translation of those items I relied on graduate student research assistants because of the time it would have taken for me to do that work.[7]

ON MODERNITY

"There is no such thing as modernity, you know," Steven Feld asserted to me in a conversation in December 2012. With that I agree: modernity is not "a thing." Yet it exists, and the experiences of being Japanese for the past century and a half have been shaped by the explicit processes of modernization to achieve whatever modernity is for them. Anyone familiar with scholarly work on modernity—and on postmodernity, which has to be understood as something different from modernity—will realize, however, that the ways in which it has been understood are practically equal to the number of scholars who have endeavored to understand it, and important social theories have emerged in the process of doing so.[8]

Because this study focuses on the introduction of Western music to Japan, for a time I considered the possibility that the book might be framed as a study of globalization. I do engage with processes of change that fit into the definition of globalization: namely, those processes, operating on a global scale, which cut across national boundaries, integrating and connecting communities and organizations in new space-time combinations, making the world in reality and in experience more interconnected. The dissemination of "Western music"—here defined as musical practices and knowledge from European and American cultures—is one such process. In the end, however, I considered that focus too much on the globe, when I meant to focus on Japan, and too much on circulation and other processes in general, whereas my subject was the agency of governmental leadership in Japan and their proactive adoption of Western music as a tool in their establishment of a modern united nation-state. Given that both the trend toward national autonomy and the trend toward globalization are deeply rooted in modernity, I chose modernity as my overarching framework.

My understanding of modernity resonates with that of the historian of Japan Carol Gluck: "In my view, modernity is not a trope, theory, project, or destination, or if it sometimes seems to be all these things, it is never these things alone. It is instead a condition, historically produced over three centuries around the globe in processes of change that have not ended yet" (2011: 676). Gluck sees the modern not as unitary or universal, but as possessing commonalities across time and space, however differently it is experienced in different places:

> The common "grammar of modernity" encompasses such elements as the nation-state, whose numbers have proliferated from fifty at the beginning of the twentieth century to nearly two hundred today, and which appears not likely to dissolve, globalization notwithstanding. Other institutional commonalities include social shifts in massified urban and disrupted communal life and the insistence, if sometimes callowly rhetorical, on national political participation. Also global is the subjection to the forces of capitalism and industrialization as well as incorporation into the reigning geopolitical world order, from which

> there appears to be no haven or exit but which also may provide positive inventories such as international human rights. (2011: 676–78)

In this study of Japanese musical modernity, all those grammatical elements come into play: urbanization, disruption, national participation, capitalism, industrialization, and participation in global forces—particularly, in this instance, the cosmopolitan culture of Western musics. In the following chapters, composers are shown to have been called upon or have stepped up to meet the demands of modernity as it was worked out in Japan—the need of the Ministry of Education, for instance, for school songs through which nationalist sentiment could be propagated for the emergence of a new nation-state; the need of the developing music industries for such items as instructional materials by which consumers could learn to play the European instruments that were being newly manufactured domestically; and, in wartime, the demand by the government for patriotic music.

After World War II, when morale as well as the economy needed rebuilding, rather than retreat from the public and avoid emotional expression in their creative work, as a number of prominent Western composers did (taking a high-modernist stance), most Japanese composers responded to the expressive needs of the citizens. That, I suggest, kept composers "connected with the people"—in a different sort of socially relational position from that of the performer-composer in premodern Japan, but socially relational nevertheless. As the historian Thomas Havens observed in his book on artists and patrons in postwar Japan, "Only when cultural life became fully democratic, after World War Two, did most Japanese stop thinking of art as singing, dancing, acting, or painting and start regarding the work as something to be esteemed in itself" (1982: 30).

It is now a commonplace that the modern age gave rise to a new and decisive form of individualism, at the center of which stood a new conception of the individual subject and its identity. The emergence of the composer in Japan can be viewed in this light—a creative individual who would need to "find his own voice."

While contemporary Japanese composers certainly care about finding their own voice (an ever-stronger desideratum through the fourteen years of my research), I will argue that the expectation established in the Meiji era continues: that the composer will be a person who functions for the good of Japanese society. This was evident, for instance, in the representation of Japan by a music critic in *Asian Composers in the 20th Century*, published with reports from thirteen other Asian members and regions of the Asian Composers League: "After the Expo '70, composers began to establish their positions in society and contribute to the development of culture" (Ishida 2002: 233). I respectfully suggest that they began to make that contribution much earlier—from the beginning of the modern era. "Find their own voices" many Japanese composers indeed have done. However, it took some time before the subjectivity of the individual creative artist became an apt way of thinking about a Japanese composer. Because of the particular conditions of Japanese musical modernity, even as they are "finding their own voices," composers tend to be artistically flexible. In addition to writing music that will meet their own needs as artists in the globally shared cosmopolitan space of Western art music, most—including the most distinguished, nationally and internationally—are willing to write music also to satisfy the desires of amateur musicians for new music for their chorus or band, or background music for a television show, or a musical score for *animé*—or whatever is needed.

When I queried Yuji Takahashi about why Japanese composers would write for just anyone, he responded: "Many years ago when I met [John] Cage—in Japan the first time—[I heard him] ask Ichiyanagi how he could live in Japan, writing for kids, film—like Takemitsu and others. An American composer would never do that" (personal communication, May 30, 2011). Takahashi then rephrased my question to ask what he thought was a more interesting question:

> Why do they use a different style for different clients? Like amateur chorus and brass bands. I think it's the difference of the musical market—orchestra here, amateur chorus here, school music (the educational branch), brass band there. Some composers specialize, but others write for all, but using a different language. I knew Tokuhide Niimi as a choral composer, so I thought he wrote in the style of Ravel; then the next time I heard orchestra pieces, and there he's a different man. Perhaps he thinks his most personal expression is in his orchestral pieces. Akira Miyoshi writes for orchestra, women's chorus, children's music. Yes, there's a willingness. That's being a professional composer. (Personal communication, May 30, 2011)

As I undertake to show, neither in their own minds nor in Japanese contemporary music culture is the artistic distinction of even the most renowned professional composers diminished by that stylistic—and relational—flexibility. In this way, professional composers—as well as amateurs and performer-composers—contribute tangibly to the vitality of musical life in their culture.

In a circular manner, that artistic and relational flexibility—which exists because of the particular conditions of Japanese modernity—in turn affords composers multiple possibilities for earning a living. Unlike in the United States, not even professional composers assume that the professoriate will be the primary source of their livelihood; they do not expect to have to devote their careers more or less equally to creativity and to the duties of the academy. Thus, I explore herein what possibilities are afforded them to support their creative activities.

As the Meiji-era leaders hoped it would, the adoption of Western music (European-derived practices and repertoire) resulted in the creation of a shared expressive cultural space for all its citizens. Ironic as it might seem, Western music even created a cultural space in which Japanese participating in spheres of traditional music might connect with musicians in spheres of that music, a space wherein musical tradition and modernity might meet through the creativity of composers and performer-composers.

THE ANALYTIC

I have taken as my analytic the notion of affordance that emerged in the 1970s in perceptual psychology and has since been taken up in several fields, including design (interactive design, for example, with multiple applications such as architectural design and game design) and artificial intelligence.[9] The music sociologist Tia DeNora (2003) found affordance theory useful for suggesting a new empirical research methodology by which musicologists and music sociologists will be able to understand how music "gets into" action—that is, what music affords as a resource for agency (doing, thinking, and feeling "other things"). In DeNora's view, this has not happened in either field of music research. She sees the New Musicology from the 1980s as being focused on music's role as a social medium, pursuing questions about the interrelation between musical works, on one hand, and categories and hierarchies of social structure—identity, power, and the practices of ruling—on the other. But she suggests that even the New Musicology is so strongly committed to the interpretation and criticism of musical texts that the conception and interrogation of the social is constrained; that is, social structure is posited as a backdrop or foil for detailed musical analysis—a resource for musical analysis, but not a topic of sociomusical analysis. To see music as reflecting society, as the New Musicology does, forfeits a theory of dynamism between music and society.

Work on music by sociologists, on the other hand, DeNora finds characterized almost entirely by a focus on how musical activities (composition, performance, distribution, and reception) are shaped socially. It has not been concerned with the reverse— with how music, a dynamic medium, "gets into" social reality.

DeNora's proposed empirical research methodology, based on affordance theory, would provide a corrective for what she sees as shortcomings in work in both sociology and musicology. Explore how music functions in situ, she suggests, not how it is interpreted but rather how it is used. Investigate what music affords its recipients, who may identify with particular aspects of music or see themselves in particular features of compositions. When they do this, music can be said to "do" things, to get into subjectivity. When music comes to serve in some way as organizing material to motivate action, thought, imagination, and so forth, music is getting into action. For example, a marching rhythm affords movement; it does not necessarily cause movement, but it affords movement for the recipient who responds to it in that way.

DeNora's empirical method is organized around the musical event—a specific act of engagement with music. The five core components of the event that would be analyzed in ethnographic research are (1) an actor or actors, composers, listeners, and so on, who (2) engage with or do things with (3) music (4) within specific environments and (5) under local conditions. After the event, the outcome is assessed to consider whether engagement with music afforded anything—whether anything was changed, achieved, or made possible by the engagement.

> For example, if the "act of engagement" is music criticism, of the kind that Adorno . . . engaged in, then the music can be said to afford the ideas that are fashioned in relation to it (e.g., ideas about the music, what it signifies, or ideas about other things that engaging with the music facilitates, exemplifies, or otherwise helps to make possible). To take another example, if the "act of engagement" is listening to music at home, then what the music affords may be mood change, or motivational change or pleasure, or a shifting of ambience, energy levels, or a way of signaling taste/lifestyle issues. It is in how music is drawn into connection with other things, how it is acted upon, that it comes to serve as an affordance structure. (DeNora 2003:50)

DeNora's use of affordance theory, then, permits a functionalist analysis of the reception of music based on ethnographic research. It appears to offer a path along which both musicologists and music sociologists might fruitfully walk together.[10]

The articulation of affordance theory that I find most useful is the originating one of the perceptual psychologist James J. Gibson in his seminal book *The Ecological Approach to Visual Perception* (1979). Gibson was interested in action possibilities—opening a door, for example—and something had to make it possible for a person to carry out that action. That something he termed an affordance. For Gibson, then, an affordance is a quality of an environment that allows an individual or offers him or her an opportunity to perform an action, dependent on his or her capabilities. There are five components of affordance:

1. an environment, in this example, a door;
2. a quality of that environment (affordance), as in this example, the door having a handle or some other mechanism that allows it to be opened;
3. an individual;
4. an action to be performed by the individual; and
5. the requisite capability on the part of the individual.

Gibson was interested in action that is physically possible; the handle on that door is not an affordance for a child who is not yet physically capable of manipulating it.

The action that has interested me is the creation of new music, with possibilities that have been offered to Japanese individuals since the systematic introduction of Western music as a tool for modernization. The individuals who perform this action are composers and performer-composers.

The flexibility of what might defined as an environment turned out to be an enabling element of affordance theory as I thought about the conditions of Japanese musical modernity; an environment is an idea far less confining than a scene, for example. Many different paths had been opened for me and been pursued in the years of this research, and I needed a means of seeing coherence in it all; for me, that is the job of theory. Three environments emerged as significant for the action possibilities in which I am interested: (1) the infrastructures of government, education, industry, and commerce that developed in the processes of modernization;

(2) the shared cultural space for all Japanese that was created by the adoption of Western music; and (3) the presence in Japan of European spheres of musical participation. The book is structured around discussions of each of those environments and its affording quality.

"Capabilities" (which DeNora did not find a useful component of affordance theory) I find crucial. For creators of new music, it is a distinguishing factor between performer-composers and composers, for instance, as it often is for composers who write for different media. Departing slightly from Gibson's articulation, however, I find it pertinent to factor in competences more than capabilities.

To repeat: *An "affordance" is a quality of an environment that allows an individual or offers an individual an opportunity to perform an action, dependent on his or her competency.* In the course of exploring each environment with its affording quality, I offer what I consider to be evidence for the main argument of this book, namely that in some ways most Japanese composers have continued to maintain a relational sort of role in their culture. Rather than composing music as an autonomous art, most composers have been and are grounded in the social—they "remain connected to the people."

In Part I the environment comprises the major infrastructures of Japanese modernity—government, education, industry, and commerce. The affording quality of that environment is the interconnectedness of those infrastructures in the field of music. As elucidated in chapter 1, it is the primary connection of government and education, within which the role of composer emerged as separate from that of performer. Composers are placed in the educational infrastructure as students honing their competencies and as teachers, and as creators of new music for the purpose of education. Chapter 2 adds to that connectivity of government and education the spheres of industry and commerce and explores the connectivities among them all.

The shared cultural space that was created by the systematic introduction of "Western" music in Japan is the environment explored in Part II. The affording quality of that environment is that the cultural space is shared both within Japan and internationally. By adopting Western music as the basis for shared cultural space for all Japanese in the process of modernizing, the government of Japan also situated Japanese musical culture within the global cosmopolitan culture. Chapter 3 focuses on the participation of Japanese composers in the sphere of concert music, especially in the United States and Europe, as the environment of shared cultural space has afforded individual Japanese composers the possibility of participating in, benefiting from, and contributing to international connections and achievements.

Chapter 4 explicates the environment of shared space as it exists internally. Because of the persistence of the small, serious population of persons who pursue and thus preserve the various practices of traditional musics, the environment encompasses the coexistence (however skewed the balance) of two deeply cultivated, historically grounded complexes from which composers make creative choices: traditional Japanese aesthetics, forms, instruments, and practices alongside Western aesthetics, forms, instruments, and practices. Significantly, performer-composers as well as composers share this affordance, depending on their competence. In chapter 4, more than any other, political thought and action must be considered because of the invocation of "tradition," including "traditional music," as part of Japan's cultural essence, as opposed to "the West," in the political tensions of the 1920s through World War II and beyond.

In Part III the environment is the presence in Japan of European spheres of musical participation, and the affording quality of the environment is Japanese audiences' particular reception of the different European ensemble types. Chapter 5 considers composing for European instrumental ensembles types—orchestras, chamber and contemporary-music groups, and wind bands—whose participants are both professional and amateur musicians. The evaluation of competence is a factor of considerable significance in this environment. The focus of chapter 6 is the extremely popular, primarily amateur sphere of singing in choruses that came into being in modern Japan in response to sociopolitical pressures, at times, but also in response to the needs, expectations, and desires for new music on the part of creative individuals and the institutions they formed. For many, many composers, composing choral music is just part of what they do. Because, as in Europe and America, most (but not all) composers put writing for chorus lower on the evaluative musical pecking order than writing for instruments, I explore why some composers have taken advantage of the positive reception to choral singing and what some of the musical results are.

PART I

Composers in the Infrastructures of Japanese Modernity

Among the first steps taken in the process of modernization in many places has been to tend to the education of the populace for national purposes, and Japan was no exception. Universal education was established in 1872 by imperial decree as a tool in the modernizing process. In this case, "imperial decree" actually means that it was done at the behest of an oligarchy of leaders who in 1868 had reinstated the emperor to a position of symbolic leadership not exercised for six hundred years.

Education was but one of the spheres in which infrastructures would emerge to undergird the development of the particular conditions of Japanese modernity. In this chapter and the next I shall address affordances for composers in an environment made up of infrastructures in four spheres of activity—education, government, industry, and commerce. From the beginning of the modernization process, a crucial quality of the environment was the connectivity among those infrastructures in the field of music; it is a connectivity that has continued to afford composers opportunities to engage in the creation of new music. The rewards for composers, I will argue, have been social as well as economic.

In chapter 1 I trace briefly how and why the government put music into the educational infrastructure, and the means by which the new persona of "composer" emerged, might achieve competence, and, in turn, engage in education of others. In chapter 2 I proceed to the consideration of other connectivities.

CHAPTER ONE

The Primary Connection: Music and Education

PUTTING MUSIC INTO AN EDUCATIONAL INFRASTRUCTURE

The new Ministry of Education in the Meiji governmental structure had very clear reasons for deciding to include music in the new educational system. The historian Ury Eppstein (1994) argues convincingly that the educational sector followed the example of the military—that the presence of military bands attached to the embassies of the Western nations that were pushing into Japan for trade in the 1850s and 1860s ultimately led to the official adoption of Western music for Japan's own purposes.[1] Observing the utility of the bands not only for pomp but also for military discipline, the powerful Satsuma samurai clan formed Japan's first brass band in 1869—the year after the founding of the modern nation-state (the Meiji era, 1868–1912). Music could thus be deemed valuable for character formation and discipline, and also for the spiritual and physical health of its practitioners.

The selection of "apt music" for primary school children was not so clear as the choice for military bands, however. Shuji Izawa (1851–1917), a Japanese teacher who had studied in Massachusetts, was asked to submit a statement of options to the Ministry of Education on October 30, 1879. In it he summed up three prevailing opinions:

> [First] that European music has almost reached perfection by means of the contemplations and experience of the last thousand years . . . and it surpasses very greatly oriental music in perfection and beautify, it will, therefore, be far better to adopt European music in our schools

> than to undertake the awkward task of improving the imperfect oriental music. . . ."
>
> The second says . . . we have never heard of any country in which the native music has been entirely supplanted by foreign music, and consequently to introduce European music into our country must, at least, be as useless an attempt as to adopt English as our language; therefore it will be a far wiser plan to take measures toward the cultivation and improvement of our own music.
>
> The third says that the two former opinions are not entirely unreasonable, but they seem to run to the two opposite extremities on the matter and hence, taking a middle course, the proper measure would be to secure the best from both European and oriental music. . . . If, fearing the difficulties, we do not presently undertake the work, when shall we see musical progress in Japan? (Cited in May 1963: 52–53)

Very striking in the statement of the three options is the self-orientalized positioning of traditional Japanese music in the language of the reasoning and the prevailing theory of cultural evolution that it invoked.

The process of introducing Western music into the curriculum of the educational system was carried out in a series of several steps. In 1879 a circular from the Ministry of Education ratified the creation of Ongaku Denshūsho (the Center for Musical Education), which was almost immediately renamed Ongaku Torishirabe Gakari (Music Investigation Committee), the name by which it is commonly known, with Shuji Izawa at its head. Ongaku Torishirabe Gakari had three fundamental objectives: the creation of a new corpus of music using both Western and Japanese elements; the training of musicians in preparation for the new developments to come; and the introduction of music into the national school curriculum at the primary level (Galliano 2002: 29–31). The bottom line was that teachers had to be trained in Western music in order to enculturate others—a tremendous undertaking that would necessarily begin small and gradually extend to every primary school in the nation. In 1889 a national conference on education agreed to introduce music education in secondary schools as well (Galliano 2002: 91), though that would take until well into the twentieth century to manage. Putting the infrastructure for Western music into place was a nearly fifty-year process.

THE EMERGENCE OF COMPOSERS IN THE EDUCATIONAL ENDEAVOR

Before the domestic manufacture of European musical instruments made them widely available, singing was the most affordable musical activity in schools (see frontispiece). The need was pressing for new didactic materials, including a suitable repertoire of songs. While the first books of school songs were made up largely of Western materials such as folk songs, the creation of new songs would soon become a working opportunity for Japanese musicians who needed to become composers in the Western sense. The first book of school songs was produced in 1889–91 by Izawa and Luther Whiting Mason, the music education inspector for Boston, who had come to Japan as an advisor; 90 percent of the songs used Western melodies to which a properly moral and purposefully patriotic Japanese text had been added. In the second collection, only 80 percent of the songs were Western in origin, with the remaining 20 percent contributed by Japanese composers using Japanese scales and melodies (Galliano 2002: 30). The use of borrowed songs would gradually decrease; with the help of Mason, Izawa produced what would become a model genre of *shōka* (children's school songs). While traditional Japanese musical sensibility would remain in some songs in subsequent collections, children learned to read five-line staff notation and to feel comfortable with tonal melodies and harmonizations as they sang together in a shared cultural space, a technology for the expression of the unity and identity of the nation. The school system encourages public-mindedness to this day.[2]

The national government remains in charge of the public educational system under a ministry whose name was changed in January 2001 to the Ministry of Education, Culture, Sports, Science, and Technology. Local boards of education hire teachers and make decisions regarding their conditions of employment, but only under the supervision of the ministry. The ministry establishes curricular guidelines and publishes textbooks—including those for music instruction during regular classroom time. It is also expected that students will participate in school events such as athletic meets, school trips, and outings. Most also participate in after-school clubs such as chorus and wind band, where affective participation in music takes place. Those too are highly structured, as I discuss in chapters 5 and 6.

The periodic revisions of the Monbushō music textbooks have long afforded interested composers the opportunity to create new songs that, if adopted, will circulate widely through the schools. An early example of such a composer was Tsune Matsushima (1890–1985), credited by the musicologist Midori Kobayashi in her book *The Lives of Women Composers* as being the first Japanese woman to primarily pursue a career as a composer (1999: 289). Matsushima convinced her father to allow her to go to music school to conduct musical research only (not performance) under the condition that she would never perform on stage; accordingly, in 1907 she entered the seat of music education, the Tokyo Music School. She would go on to publish a manual for piano technique; works for piano, violin, cello, wind ensemble; and *dōyō* (children's songs that are more artistic than shōka; see chapter 6) and—most pertinent here—shōka. A recent example of a prominent composer who has taken full advantage of this opportunity afforded by the ministry is Akira Yuyama (b. 1932), who graduated from the Tokyo National University of the Arts (previously the Tokyo Music School).

For textbooks, however, music teachers at present have options. Goto, a teacher at the National Elementary School attached to Nara Women's University, explained to me why he did not use the ministry's textbooks:[3] "Public schools use the Monbushō [ministry] textbooks of songs by Yuyama and others; they say 'in April do this, in May do this, etc.' In public schools students mostly sit still and sing from the books. Not in this school. We don't use them" (Goto, personal communication, June 13, 2000). Inspired by the philosophy of that school—founded over a century ago on the principles of the American education philosopher John Dewey, which stress freedom—he was not even using a textbook from among those that are commercially published but approved by the ministry. Goto explained to me what freedom in music instruction meant to him: "I think that moving while singing is important, using their imagination, doing it the way they want—even improvising. It takes a lot of effort to teach that way. Important to have assistance from mothers and other teachers" (personal communication, June 13, 2000). Indeed, I observed his second-grade class, in which a song was being heard for the first time: children had created the poem, mothers composed the melody, and Goto added choreography. Goto was even questioning whether or not students should have to learn to read notation—something that is usually taught to first- and second-graders in Japanese schools; indeed, the children were learning the melody by listening to him play it on the piano.

THE EDUCATIONAL PATH TO COMPETENCE

In the infrastructural environment of Japanese musical modernity, the matter of competence is central to the sphere of education. With regard to composers, it is important to consider the means by which a young person in Japan might gain the competence that will permit him or her to engage successfully in the action of composing.

Private instruction on an instrument or in voice is a huge industry in Japan that I will address later in this chapter, but it is not the only type of instruction that is usually assumed to be necessary for competence. Through several composers who began their systematic study of music at an early age, I learned of two programs in particular that give children a good start. Both are intended to complement, not replace, regular schooling. For Tokyo children whose parents could afford to send them to a school that, from its founding in 1948, has been associated with study of Western "concert music," the program to attend has been Toho Gakuen Music for Children. For more populist training throughout Japan, there is the Yamaha Music School (see below).

As one section of an august private institution for music study, the Toho Gakuen Music for Children program caters to students between the ages of five and fifteen. The general rubric for the instruction they receive is "solfège," and, because composers not only train in it but also are likely to teach it early in their careers, it was important for me to understand what the term encompasses. Introduced and escorted by Kimiko Shimbo, an emeritus instructor, I made a point of observing the instruction there in 2008. The Toho facilities are full of activity in this program, which the children attend for three to four hours on Saturdays; they might also come one other time during the week for private instrumental lessons. Part of Shimbo's response to my question about why parents would involve their child in such an intensive experience reminded me of the rationale for adopting music in the schools in early Meiji: "The children are there because their parents think music education is a good thing. Good training for concentration. Also, if they can play an instrument, they will have an enjoyable life" (Kimiko Shimbo, personal communication, May 31, 2008).[4]

I attended six different classes nonstop from 12:30 P.M. to 6:30 P.M. and recorded the following observations in my field notes:

> First class: Rhythm practice. Five children, three of them five years old. Two teachers: held hands with children, circling and singing an eight-bar melody with syncopation, stopping to demonstrate where not

to take a breath so as not to break a word in the song's lyrics. Now all clapped the rhythm while singing—turning over the palm at the rests. Second song: each sang along, hitting arm/hands to keep beat. Third exercise: children matched the pitch sounded on a small xylophone. Circled, singing and stepping the changing rhythm; teacher down in middle of circle to watch the feet. Next time children sang the melody and teachers sang harmony. Not a problem!

Rhythm notation practice, with a set of cards used in the Kodály training system, each showing a rhythm of a total of two beats. One teacher kept a regular beat, while the other put cards on a stick board in quick succession while the children read/articulated them together. Then all cards were mounted along the bottom of the board and the activity returned to the first song; each child had to put up a card to "notate" the rhythm of the song as the teacher sang.

Second class: Dictation. Eleven students, ten years old (fourth grade in primary school). Notation of an eighteen-bar melody. They were told "E major," and all wrote the key signature (which they knew without being told). Teacher played a melody two times, then worked with them to sing it in pieces, then whole. Then they were told to notate it. Teacher circulated through the class to check on progress. When finished, the teacher went over the chords that underpinned the melody.

Next work: Make a four-part score. Teacher played a long phrase just once. Then they worked with each other to notate it all. Next they were told to turn it into polyphony. It turned out to be Bach.

Third class: Singing class for younger children—third- and fourth-graders in primary school (thirty-five, of whom twenty-five were girls). Started with stretches, then a very few vocalises, then songs—sung in unison—to teach techniques (one with text of "ha ha ha" for diaphragm control, another designed to teach how to control descending melody). They went from one to another in a sheaf of notations; Saburo Iwakama was the composer of several of the songs.

Fourth class: Chorus class for first-, second-, and third-year middle-school students. Most were pianists, one violinist (there was another class simultaneously to which most of the violinists go.) They did Steve Reich's "Clapping Music," then Schubert's "Heidenröslein" in two parts in two languages. The song in German is almost syllabic, so it transfers well for singing in Japanese translation with the usual syllabic setting. The teacher went through the text, trying to make it interesting to the children.

Fifth class: Harmony and polyphony (and dictation). Some of the same eleven- and twelve-year-olds in this class that I had seen in the fourth class. They were turning a melody into a polyphonic score (having captured the melody from dictation, I presume) when we entered, and then sang it—two or three on a part (eleven students, eight girls). They sang beautifully, without problem, in at least four parts.

Then they did harmonic dictation, hearing chords only, not in triadic form. Students got this quickly. Then five children went to the board to write the chords in triadic form and identify them as I, V, etc. They all got it right, except for ii/V, which was a mystery and the new material for the day. Then they sang the chords, in parts. Discussion of resolution: to what pitches does V^7 lead?

Teacher told students to make a score of four measures each on two lines. Gave time signature. Introduced the composer, Bach. Played a theme once through, looked at their notation two more times. She sang it too. This is a tough melody, with chromatics and syncopation. Once they all had it, she gave them the notation of the piece and they sight-read the rest easily. Got them to sing the melody backward and explained that it was a crab canon.[5]

Sixth class: Harmonic dictation (with history). Second-year middle-school students, all girls. Teacher introduced a John Dowland love song in four parts, played a recording, and contextualized it historically. Then (because the teacher had a particular interest in dance), she played a CD recording of a dance—a minuet—and demonstrated the dance. That piece is the project for dictation. She played the top and bottom of four voices—eight measures. Played several times, asked them to sing one of the lines while she played the other. Then they notated it and she replayed the recording.

The study of solfège continues in music high schools and colleges. Unlike students at the Toho Music for Children program, the composer Makiko Kinoshita studied solfège only just before taking the entrance exam for Tokyo Geijutsu Kōkō (music high school), which is affiliated with Geidai, but she was admitted. In our conversation she gave me further evidence of what training in solfège might include:

> In high school an interesting solfège teacher asked us to make a cadenza for a Mozart concerto. I was the only one who did. When I played it in front of classmates, I was applauded. That suddenly changed my dream. "Maybe I have talent. I *know* I have talent. I could make a new thing. Making a cadenza is arranging, not composing, but. . . ." This

> was at age seventeen at the Tokyo Geijutsu Kōkō. I graduated from the piano course and then did the M.A. course in composition. (Makiko Kinoshita, personal communication, June 2, 2004)

Clearly, the rubric of "solfège" is used loosely to encompass training in sight-singing, dictation, and sometimes harmony and even composition. Skills attained in study of solfège are regarded as the basis of competence for a composer.

Testing of the competence of potential composers begins before he or she is admitted to a formal school for specialized training. In keeping with the general practice for school admissions in Japan, admission to the schools of music is by examination at the particular school. A number of composers recounted their experience of preparing for the examinations by arranging for private tutoring with a professor of composition. I gained the sense that such tutoring could be a help in gaining admission to the particular institution not only because of the good training, but also because of the connection. Akira Nishimura's story, for instance, embedded that tutoring in a fuller account of his youthful musical experience:

> In 1953, when I was born, Japan was very poor. Very few children could study Western music. Even though at that time in Osaka there was a symphony orchestra, very few families had a violin or piano. Like most families in Osaka, my family had no equipment for or recordings of Western music.
>
> When I was eleven years old, in junior high school, a teacher organized a broadcasting studio in the school, and one day I touched an LP record for the first time. I had heard marches—Schubert's *Marche militaire*, many marches. At school, during lunchtime we heard Massanet. Like Pavlov's dog, every time I hear this melody [he sings it], I feel hungry for lunch.
>
> When I was twelve years old I heard Beethoven's Ninth, the choral movement, and really "heard" that special chord at the end of the first line. It affected me greatly. I asked my parents for the LP. But they had no record player. Finally they agreed to lay out the huge sum for the player and recording—7,000 and 2,000 yen, respectively. For those times, on a salary of 100,000 yen a month only, it was a big expense for them. [Nishimura's father was a bicycle merchant, his mother a minor official in the Joto-ku area of Osaka.]
>
> My second request was for Dvořák's *New World* Symphony. With the LP came a full score, and for the first time I could look at an or-

> chestral score. It blew me away that so many parts could have been written by one person. I thought: "I must start to study composition. Not instruments—composition." So I asked for a composition teacher. This met with resistance from my parents, but finally I was allowed to study.
>
> During my high school days, from 1970 to 1973, I commuted to Tokyo from Osaka to study French counterpoint and fugue and the harmonic system with Tomojiro Ikenouchi, who was a leading professor of composition at the Tokyo Geidai from 1950 to 1974. The purpose was to enter Geidai, and I was admitted. The entrance examination was very difficult, and some students took five years to pass it. (Personal communications, May 2, 2001, and August 27, 2012)

Whereas some Japanese composers—for instance, Toru Takemitsu and Joji Yuasa in the generation born in the 1930s and, more recently, Yoshihiro Kanno, born in 1953—did not attend a music school, most composers have done so. "Music school" means a conservatory, although that word is not used. Every composer whom I asked gave me the same list of the best music schools for the specialized study of composition in Tokyo and therefore in Japan. The Tokyo National University of Fine Arts and Music (Geidai; from *gei* [arts] and *dai*, short for *daigaku* [university]), with its venerable history, is named as "the top." The next to be mentioned is Tokyo Ongaku Daigaku (the Tokyo College of Music), which, when I began this project in 1999, was consistently said to be "rising," but now is considered to have such an excellent roster of faculty composers who compose in different styles that it challenges Geidai's reputation. Third in the consistent list is Toho Daigakuin. Geidai is a national university, whereas the other two are private institutions. There are other good music schools in the Tokyo area that include one or more composers on the faculty, among them the Kunitachi College of Music, the Musashino College of Music, Tokyo Gakugei Daigaku, and Geijutsu Gakubu (the fine arts section) of Nihon Daigaku. There are, of course, instructors of music in many other institutions.

What is now the Tokyo University of the Arts (Geidai) began as the Music Investigation Committee (Ongaku Torishirabe Gakari), mentioned above. In 1887 it was renamed the Tokyo Music School. Even a decade after its founding, "the education of composers was not yet planned and was completely neglected. . . . The composition department at the Tokyo Music School was founded only in 1932" (Sawabe 1995: 69, 70). The Tokyo University of the Arts was formed in 1949 when the Tokyo Music School merged with the Tokyo School of Fine Arts, which had also been founded in 1887.

The graduate school opened in 1963 and began offering doctoral degrees in 1977. After the National University Corporations were formed on April 1, 2004, the school became known as the Kokuritsu Daigaku Hōjin Tōkyō Geijutsu Daigaku. On April 1, 2008, the university changed its English name from the Tokyo National University of Fine Arts and Music to the Tokyo University of the Arts.[6]

Although the adjective "conservative" is usually the word of choice when Geidai's composition program is the topic of conversation, Geidai is the most desirable school for aspiring Japanese composers to attend, for reasons both tangible and intangible. As a national university, tuition is much less than at a private institution; competition for admission causes it to attract extremely qualified students. Both intangible and tangible is the prestige of the institution: intangible, because of the inestimable and pervasive cultural power it holds owing to its heritage as the instrument of Japan's musical modernization; tangible, because of the networks into which graduates have gained admission through time.

Here the connectivities among the infrastructures of Japanese musical modernity become palpable. In the 1950s the government-supported Japan Broadcasting Company (NHK), for example, hired composers from the government-supported Geidai to provide music for documentary films, social segments, and political segments. In the opinion of the composer Joji Yuasa, it did not afford either himself or Toru Takemitsu the opportunity to create new music for NHK programming until after they received "societal recognition" through their participation in the famous Jikken Kōbō (Experimental Workshop, disbanded in 1957); but even then, he commented, he was hired only by "the less conservative music section" (personal communication, May 3, 2001). The connectivity continues into the present; Reijiro Kuroku, a "popular music specialist" and graduate of Geidai, for example, is writing music for NHK dramas, most especially for the popular series on Sundays at 8 P.M. Geidai composition graduates are now perceived to be getting jobs in the popular music industry—as arrangers, for example (Kimiko Shimbo, personal communications, April 15, 2005, and May 18, 2007).

A student can specialize in composition at the undergraduate level at Geidai, and it has long been the tradition that each student works with a different composition professor each year—the idea being that each would ask for a different style. "Ultimately, however, each student knew he or she had to compose like him- or herself" (Makiko Kinoshita, personal communication, June 2, 2004). The official master of arts course is a two-year program (working with one composer-mentor), but the university permits three-year extensions, which means that the time that students might spend on getting a Ph.D. in the U.S. system has, in the Japanese system, been spent on compositional study—an opportunity of which students such as Kazuko Hayakawa have taken advantage (Kazuko Hayakawa, personal communication, May 13, 1999, unconfirmed).

Founded in 1907, the Tokyo Ongaku Daigaku (the Tokyo College of Music, referred to as To Ondai) was the first private school of music in Japan. In addition to a fine faculty in the composition department, including three women—Tomiko Kohjiba, Keiko Harada, and Noriko Hisada—it now also has other respected composers, such as Shigeaki Saegusa, teaching in a film and broadcasting program that is drawing good composition students. Unlike most of the composition professors at Geidai, who until very recently have been better known as teachers than for their creative work,[7] those at To Ondai are known for being very active as creative individuals as well as teaching. This is no doubt a factor in the program's increasingly positive reputation. The institution includes a music high school as well.

Toho Gakuen is the youngest of the leading music schools with a specialization in composition and, like the Tokyo College of Music, is an expensive private school. Determined to do something cultural that would be helpful for the nation after World War II, Hideo Edo, the president of Mitsui Real Estate, gathered funds from various sympathetic individuals to begin the Toho music program for children. Toho Gakuen opened in 1950 as a music high school for girls but is now coeducational for students from age sixteen up. The institution gradually expanded: in 1964 the Toho Gakuen College of Music was established, then became the Toho Gakuen College of Drama and Music in 1966. The music part, then, consists of five "units": the Music for Children program (see above), Toho Gakuen Ongaku Daigaku (college, established in 1964), Toho Gakuen Daigakuin (graduate school, opened in 1999), and, most recently, an orchestra academy. Toho has from the beginning been associated with Japan's socioeconomic elite. The composer Akira Miyoshi, for instance, who was the dean and president of Toho for fourteen years (he retired in 1995), is very close to the empress, who loves European concert music and plays piano well.[8] I was present at a graduation concert of composition students of the Toho composer and professor Hiroaki Takaha that was attended by the empress herself in the small Tokyo Bunka Kaikan hall in Ueno Park.[9]

The sense of identification with one's institution and of community affiliation is very strong on the part of graduates. Two examples serve to demonstrate this loyalty. In a conversation with a composer who lives in Europe, I asked if that person knew another Japanese composer who lives in the same city. The revealing answer came quickly: "No, not very well. She's Geidai and I'm Toho." Outside Japan, Toho Gakuen is perhaps best known for its most illustrious graduate, the conductor Seiji Ozawa, who, in appreciation of his mentor at Toho, founded the Saito Kinen Symphony Orchestra, made up of Toho graduates (see chapter 5).

COMPOSERS AS TEACHERS

In Japanese musical modernity, the affordances of multiple connected infrastructures provide opportunities by which composers might make a living, to the extent that it is not necessary for them to assume that the academy will be the nearly sole source of their livelihood. Therefore, they do not have to expect to devote their careers more or less equally to creativity and to education to anywhere near the extent that composers do in the United States.

Teaching is, of course, a viable source of income. When young, many composers want to be part-time instructors—rather than full-time—although it means that they will need to supplement their income in other ways. Keiko Harada is one example, despite the fact that she likes teaching. At age twenty-three, after she graduated from Toho, Harada's mentor, Dean Akira Miyoshi, said, "There is a full-time lecturer position available, but I don't recommend you apply for the post. I got a regular job only at age thirty-nine. Until then you can be tough" (Keiko Harada, personal communication, May 25, 2007). At the time we had this conversation, she was thirty-nine, and she had taken his advice. From 1993 to 2010 she had taught regular classes and given lessons as a part-time lecturer at Toho, teaching two days a week. She did not earn enough to live on in this position, but she had time for composing. Harada estimated that she earned around 20 percent of her income from teaching, around 10 percent from producing concerts, and about 70 percent from composition. "Do you want to be a professor?" I asked.

> At Toho the system is problematic. I would have to teach also high school students, five days a week, 8 A.M. to 6 P.M. In the composition department at Toho, only the director, Masahiro Ishijima, and Akio Yasuraoka are regular faculty.[10] It is difficult to find time to compose during school terms. It's the same at Tokyo Ongaku Daigaku for Reiko Arima [now retired] and Tomiko Kohjiba. (Keiko Harada, personal communication, May 25, 2007)

It is not unusual for a composer to hold a post at one institution and teach a course or two at another. Keiko Harada—though a part-time lecturer at Toho Daigakuen (School of Music)—after fourteen years added the teaching of "harmonization" at Tokyo College of Music (personal communication, June 2, 2008). When I spoke with her in 2011, she was still teaching two days a week at Toho, had also agreed to teach individual composition lessons at Geidai, and, in addition, had just begun a full-time professorial appointment at the Tokyo College of Music—too much, she attested (personal communication, May 25, 2011), and when we last communicated she said she now gives major lessons at Toho only if there are students who want them (personal communication, December 13, 2012). In another example of this custom, I was not surprised to see on the business card of Tomiko Kohjiba, head of the composition department at the Tokyo College of Music, the phrase "Instructor at Geidai (Solfège)".

Nor is it out of the question for composers to hold those multiple appointments in different and distant locations. While teaching full-time at Elisabeth University in Hiroshima, Jo Kondo commuted by plane to Hiroshima from his home in Kamakura, near Tokyo, and also commuted to Tokyo to teach at Geidai. His reason: "Quality students are attracted to Geidai, and for many years there was no lecturer/teacher doing twentieth-century music other than Debussy, Ravel, and Schoenberg's early works, such as the 'Five Pieces for Orchestra'" (personal communication, May 13, 2003).[11] Since 2006 Tokuhide Niimi has held a professorship at the distant Toho Gakuen Daigakkuin Daigaku campus, for which he flies to Toyama for regular stints, but he also teaches two classes at Toho Tankidaigaku (a two-year college) in Tokyo. The centrality of Tokyo for contemporary music in Japan has to be a factor in composers' desire to maintain a presence there, and Japan's superb domestic travel systems permit easy mobility. The practice of living in Tokyo and teaching elsewhere is quite common.

Whatever the nature of one's appointments, it appears to be the usual practice to squeeze as much teaching into one day as possible, thereby keeping time free for composing and other creative activities. On May 31, 2000, when I spoke with Tokuhide Niimi over dinner, for instance, he had just taught all day at the Tokyo College of Music—five classes, each an hour and a half long (not private lessons, but harmony and other classes). Keiko Harada explained her teaching schedule to me: she was teaching six subjects in her two days a week at the Toho Gakuen College of Music.

Relatively little time is spent teaching actual composition. Harada's six courses in 2008, for example (1) solfège, (2) harmony class, (3) contemporary-music interpretation for pianists, (4) interpretation coaching for two chamber-music groups, (5) analysis for undergraduate composers, and (6) individual composition lessons. "Interpretation," she explained, "means introducing repertoire with a bit of historical background and a little analysis, that is, information to get performers interested, make them *think* about music, and get them to select music by themselves" (personal communication, June 2, 2008).[12]

One subject that all or—at least most—composers teach at some point or another, or even constantly, it seems—is the ubiquitous solfège. As explained by Keiko Harada, "At Toho there is a solfège department, and students must take at least two years of solfège—two days a week the first year. And if the student earns good marks at the end of the first year, the second year will be at the advanced level. Some teachers in the composition department also teach in the solfège department" (personal communications, June 2, 2008, and September 5, 2012). Just after graduating from Geidai, Akira Nishimura supported himself for six years partly by teaching solfège there. However, senior professors teach it as well: Tomiko Kohjiba not only teaches solfège but has also published a series of solfège textbooks.

Full-time professorial composers are still likely to be men. The very few exceptions include Reiko Arima, now retired; Tomiko Kohjiba and Keiko Harada at the Tokyo College of Music; Hitomi Kaneko at Toho Gakuen; and Kazuko Hayakawa at Ibaragi University.

The strong sense of identification with one's institution carries over into the faculty, because the practice in many schools is to appoint new regular faculty members from their pool of graduates.[13] A national university is likely to appoint as professor a graduate from a national university,[14] and schools are likely to appoint one of their own graduates. Geidai will almost inevitably appoint a graduate of Geidai; likewise, each private school is most likely to appoint one of its own. For example, Masahiro Ishijima, the director of composers at Toho in 2008, was a student of the former dean of Toho, Akira Miyoshi; he became a specialist in the music of Ravel music by doing research with Miyoshi and continues that focus. Hitomi Kaneko, a Toho graduate who studied in Paris, returned to Japan after ten years when "news came from Toho for a chance to teach there. It was particularly difficult in Japan for a woman to find that opportunity" (personal communication, May 17, 2002). For three years she taught part-time, then moved to full-time in 2011. The Tokyo College of Music is unusual in that several graduates of Geidai (Shin-ichiro Ikebe, Tokuhide Niimi, and Akira

Nishimura) are on the faculty, and a graduate of Toho (Keiko Harada) has been appointed for the first time.

In Japanese universities, retirement is mandatory at age sixty-five (though in some cases the age is extended to seventy). However, afterward a former professor can teach as part-time lecturer or guest composer, as Joji Yuasa did at Nihon Daigaku.

As I mentioned above, but from the student's perspective, preparing hopeful applicants for the entrance exam to a music school is another kind of teaching that has been done by composers.[15] I first heard this from Keiko Fujiie, who told me that when she became interested in going to Geidai High School, she was sent by her mother to prepare for the entrance examination by studying harmony and theory privately with a professor at Kobe University (personal communication, March 25, 1999). (Fujiie's family lived in Kyoto, and Kobe was relatively convenient.) While she was in high school in Osaka, Keiko Harada began to prepare for the entrance exam for music college. When her father finally let her go to Tokyo to study, she remarked, she commuted to Tokyo three times a month, preparing for the Geidai exams with Manabu Kanai, who taught both at Geidai and Toho. "He was the 'master of theory'—strict. I learned counterpoint and harmony" (personal communication, May 25, 2007).

For several reasons, then, it makes sense for professional composers in Japan not necessarily to want to devote their careers both to creativity and to an academic institution to anywhere near the extent that composers do in the United States. Among those factors are the possible necessity of teaching students from high school age through the graduate level, if one is full-time, and the onerous administrative duties that are likely to consume even their creative time in a full-time position. Several factors that permit them to avoid having to devote their careers more or less equally to creativity and to an academic institution include the prevalence of the conservatory system for the serious study of music and therefore the number of part-time appointments available that do not come with administrative duties. The customary teaching practice of holding multiple appointments simultaneously, and the acceptability of a composer's presence in an institution on as few days as possible, also provide flexibility.

SUMMARY

In this chapter I traced briefly the connectivity between the spheres of government and education in the field of music, including why the government decided early in the Meiji era to put music study into the curriculum of the new, modern public educational system, and why in 1872 Western music was selected and mandated to become part of the educational infrastructure. As the new persona of "composer" emerged to meet the needs of music instruction in schools—particularly songbooks published by the Ministry of Education—the expectation was established that the work of a Japanese composer might include writing new music for children.

This chapter also suggested how the infrastructure for Western music education developed over approximately fifty years, and it detailed the sort of training considered important in a potential composer's attaining competence. That can happen through instruction in private institutions such as Toho Gakuen and the Tokyo College of Music, and in public institutions such as Geidai, where the connectivity of the spheres of education and government are palpable.

Once competence is achieved, composers may pursue opportunities afforded them in the educational infrastructure to earn a living by teaching, albeit not full-time, especially when they are in the process of establishing their creative reputation.

In the next chapter I move to additional connectivities among the infrastructures of Japanese musical modernity—namely government, education, industry, and commerce—that afford individual composers opportunities for other creative actions. The link to this chapter is another path to competence: the populist systematic music training that is offered all over Japan (and elsewhere) by Yamaha, a Japanese industrial giant of great significance in the field of music.

CHAPTER TWO

Connectivities of Government, Education, Industry, and Commerce

When viewed in terms of economy, Japan has become a world center for the production and consumption of "Western" music in recent decades. Japanese companies have led most sectors of the global music industry, from production of musical instruments (Yamaha, Kawai, Roland, Casio, Korg), to the production, distribution and consumption of recordings (Toshiba/EMI, Sony, Columbia, JVC, Panasonic, Yamaha), and even the world's largest systems for community music education (Yamaha, Kawai, Suzuki, Roland).
—David G. Hebert, *Wind Bands and Cultural Identity in Japanese Schools* (2012)

COMMERCIAL MUSIC EDUCATION

To complement music instruction offered in the public educational system, at age five or six the future composer Keiko Harada went for instruction classes offered commercially by Yamaha.

When I was four to five years old, every day in kindergarten we listened and sang. The teacher played piano. The most interesting thing for me was to imitate the piano playing. I concentrated on it at four—how to move the fingers. I found a small pump organ at home. My mother told me I had to push/pump. But when I imitated the movement of the fingers, my mother recognized the songs and she pumped. So in kindergarten I was memorizing songs.

One day my mother took me to a piano teacher. I didn't like to read music. I asked the teacher to play, and I memorized and imitated. But I had no technical training, so I made something new from what I could

> get. One day I played better, but changed the piece. The teacher said, "Keiko-san, it's not really polite to change the piece by a distinguished composer. Better start from zero."
>
> So from age five to six, I learned to notate, but I cried because I didn't like to do it. Then I went to music school—Yamaha—for keyboard harmony. Not elite. Until age eleven [or] twelve, I was trained in composing and keyboard, solfège and harmony. I composed piano pieces, and I liked improvisation. Then I began to think that improvisation was just a thing and I was stuck, and I started to want to learn something theoretical. (Keiko Harada, personal communication, May 25, 2007)

Yamaha music instruction can be traced to one enterprising individual. Inspired by the informal music making he observed on trips to Europe and Brazil in 1953, Genichi Kawakami, the president of Nippon Gakki (the Yamaha commercial enterprise) began noting that, while many Japanese were buying Yamaha reed organs (the most common home keyboard before the piano), it was rare to walk down a street and hear the sound of one coming out of a house, although this would be expected given the sound-permeating materials from which Japanese homes were constructed. Thus was founded the Yamaha Music School, born of Kawakami's "determination to assume the responsibility for teaching people how to enjoy the instruments they purchased. Opening up the Music School was a social imperative, I thought" (Kawakami 1987: 277). Begun for preschool children in Japan, training initially emphasized the Electone, an early Yamaha organ/synthesizer introduced commercially in 1959.[1]

Beginning in 1966 the nonprofit Yamaha Music Foundation devoted itself to the promotion of music popularization, self-consciously moving education in music beyond formal individual and music-school training. With instruction now extended to all ages in numerous countries and many instruments, the focus remains on popular music. The aim is to provide students a good foundation in "TDS" (tonic, dominant, subdominant chords) and a well-cultivated sense of pitch, thereby giving them the ability to compose their own melodies and to improvise: "Some music for the synchronized swimming in this Olympics [1984] was written by JOC children [performers in the annual Junior Original Concert], and the Canadian ice skating music was written by JOC children from Nagoya. . . . Emi Watanabe, the figure skater, also used music by the Yamaha children" (Kawakami 1987: 270).

Although Kawakami wrote of Yamaha's participation in music education as a "social imperative" and believed he had a "responsibility for people's enjoyment" in keeping with the "serve many people" requirement of the regulations on nonprofit organizations, there is at least one other way of looking at it.[2] In his book *Gakki Gyōkai* [*The Musical Instrument Business World*] (1977), Rikuro Hiyama identifies the development of music classrooms by Yamaha [then Nippon Gakki] as a strategy used by the company in its race for domination over its competitor Kawai. Yamaha and Kawai developed a sort of perfect shared monopolization of the piano market.

Under the rubric of "demand-making activities," Yamaha's marketing strategy nurtured consumers through the promotion of music education, a less direct approach than that taken by Kawai which used direct sales strategies to claim its market share. As of the time of Hiyama's writing, Yamaha's music education system boasted 10,270 classes, with 9,850 instructors, 554,000 students, and 3 million graduates all over the world (Hiyama 1977: 205).

However, the demand extended beyond their own classrooms, Hiyama concludes, drawing attention to connectivity with the governmental educational infrastructure. The companies developed their stranglehold as a result of the unreasonable expense involved in importing pianos to Japan and the demand for cheap, domestically produced pianos among parents, teachers, and schools as a result of the Ministry of Education's encouragement of music instruction.

The connectivity did not stop at pianos. In 1965 Yamaha began producing wind instruments, and the company has strongly supported wind band activity in Japan. Because wind band is an exceedingly popular extracurricular activity in public schools at all levels (see chapter 3) but band instruments are rarely taught as part of the school curriculum, the industrial manufacturing of instruments, the commercial sale of those instruments, and the instruction offered by the Yamaha community music schools are all connected.

COMPOSING NEW INSTRUCTIONAL MATERIAL

With the three infrastructures of school curriculum, instrument manufacturing, and instrument sales thoroughly connected and equally successful, the potential was great for connectivity with a fourth infrastructure in Japanese musical modernity—the publishing industry, for the profitable production particularly of piano instructional material. To contextualize the huge market for piano music for learners—most of whom are presumed to be children—I shall briefly address the status of the piano in Japanese culture. Then I shall comment on how that industrial-commercial-educational connectivity afforded composers the possibility of creating new music for that market.

The piano was associated with elite Japanese culture from early in the Meiji period. Recounting the process of the selection of Western music for the Meiji public school system and the part played by Luther Whiting Mason in it, Ephraim Cutter wrote in the early twentieth century: "As we look over this history, it seems a very wonderful thing that Mr. Mason was given a palace to live in: that he had free access to the homes of the nobility to teach them and tune their pianos" (cited in May 1963: 57). Mason took twelve pianos with him to Tokyo when he went to work for the Ministry of Education, but otherwise they were something only the wealthy could afford to import. Nor could a piano be easily accommodated in the traditional Japanese home. There were few places the heavy instrument could be placed with proper floor support, and few areas of floor that were not covered with relatively fragile *tatami* (straw mats). The piano went into the *tokonoma* (the wood-floored space reserved for especially treasured items), thereby being accorded high status spatially, visually, and emblematically. Thus, not only the instrument itself but the high cultural status it enjoyed in Europe and America was imported into Japan. As Japan's economy improved, the piano became an instrument of aspirations, the instrument that parents were most likely to have their children study for their personal development and upward social mobility.

What undergirded the wide spread of the piano's position as the Western instrument of choice, however, was the successful establishment of domestic manufacturing, which made pianos affordable for the growing urban middle class. Furthermore, the consensus of opinion among everyone with whom I discussed piano music is that the piano became the instrument of choice because of the aggressive sales techniques of the Japanese manufacturers. For competent pianists—graduates of the conservatories—offering piano instruction could become a huge business.

For composers, the materials that teachers select to have their pupils buy is the issue. Non-Japanese piano instructional methods were of course distributed in Japan in the first half of the twentieth century. One of them was the Thompson Method, first published by Willis in 1931 and subsequently by Theodore Presser in the United States. I learned of its use in Japan when, in a conversation with the composer Kikuko Masumoto, she showed me a well-used piano instructional book that had belonged to her mother, a graduate of the Department of Music of Kobe College.

KM: She was a contemporary piano performer at that time. Her repertoire was Albéniz and McDowell.

BW: McDowell—the American composer?

KM: Yes. And her repertoire expanded also to Debussy, who was still contemporary. After getting married, she moved to Tokyo. Her friends and teachers were all in Kobe, so she was alone in Tokyo. She had to look for a piano teacher. I studied piano and musicianship with my mother at the beginning. Ear training, et cetera. [She goes to get something.] This is the first book from which my mother taught me. You have seen this kind of thing, have you?

BW: It's from America!

KM: You recognize it, don't you? Most Japanese bought Beyer, but Beyer doesn't introduce the F clef. At the beginning, just G clef, so children would learn G clef, but not F clef. So it's very hard to make the transition from G clef to F clef. Theodore Presser [sets out] high C, middle C, low C, and you can understand easily. This [book] is very old and worn-out. So that's how you can start from [either clef.] It's very convenient. My mother's teacher from Kobe told her, "You ought to use this book."

BW: An American book!

KM: We were already in the Second World War. . . . And that book has many American songs, like "Yankee Doodle Doo" [*sic*]. So when one unthinkingly played that music, the policeman came around and said you are a bad person. That's the way policemen scolded music students. However, ear training was done as much as one wished. So I did a lot of ear training. After the Theodore Presser book, I used Beyer, *Sonatine*. In Showa 19 [1943], every day, every day there were air attacks. It was the same as in Europe. We ran away from them as if it were a game. So I did not have time to play piano. (Kikuko Masumoto, personal communication, May 4, 1999)[3]

The Zen-On Music Company, founded in Tokyo in 1931, pulled off a publishing and commercial coup when the company began to publish what is referred to as the "Beyer method," named for Ferdinand Beyer (1803–1863). The title of Beyer's original textbook was *Vorschule im Klavierspiel* (*Preparation for Playing the Piano*). Because he has been dead for more than a hundred years, his works are in the public domain, and now most of the major publishing companies in Japan, namely Ongaku no Tomosha, Zen-On, and Yamaha publish Beyer instructional books. The name of the original composer is not shown in any of those publications. "Beyer" is "Beyer" in Japan, it seems (Ryogen Kihara, personal communication, June 16, 2000).

The first real crack in the hegemony of the Beyer method came in the 1960s with the entrepreneurship of a performer-composer. Adapting a French method book known as *Methode Rose*, the respected pianist Kazuko Yasukawa wrote new music to which the method could be applied. Emphasizing exercises less than Beyer, it was thought to be more attractive to children. That method became known in Japan when Yasukawa did a piano-teaching series on the government-supported educational NHK television channel. It is now known in Japan as the "French method" (Yasuko Fukuda, personal communication, June 2, 2000; Reiko Arima, personal communication, June 1, 2000). The graded instructional books are published by Ongaku no Tomosha, another of Japan's major music-publishing houses.[4]

In the ensuing decades, the connectivity of the industrial-commercial-educational infrastructures in music publishing has flourished, affording opportunities for Japanese composers. A series of piano instructional books for young children that is being published and sponsored by Ongaku no Tomosha is particularly interesting to me. It has been composed (and the whole series of video and print materials developed) by Lioko Kihara, who is a piano teacher first and a composer second—but a composer nevertheless. Called *Pianoland*, Kihara's method springs from a sense of play and teaches by interaction between the child and a teacher, mother, or some other adult. Notably, it incorporates the solfège skills that are so important in musical instruction in Japan. Kihara's method is a two-step process: a set of activities are to be done before the child ever touches the piano; then, what they have learned is taken into playing the piano. The activities fall into four categories: listening, singing, moving, and seeing. With respect to listening, for example, the distinction is made between listening and hearing, as one listens in order to hear. At first the teacher plays and the child gets used to the sound, gets interested in it. The basic I–V^7–I chord progression is introduced in what the teacher plays, and the child bows when he or she hears the chord change. The aim is not only to hear the function of the chords, but also to feel it in the body. As to singing: the first three volumes of the *Pianoland* method books make no distinction between song and piano music. At first the teacher plays and the child and teacher both sing. The child is sensitized at first to tempo, rhythm, and pitch, and then to elements that create artistry—phrasing and articulation. When the child finally plays the piano, he or she sings while playing. The aim is to have the children play like they sing—with artistry. Kihara's method provides an utterly thorough enculturation into the Western music system.

Lioko Kihara sent me to Akira Yuyama, perhaps the most prolific of Japanese composers of music for children (and who was then vice chairman of JASRAC, explained below). He asked if I was interested in education for children, and I said yes:

AY: Piano methods. In Japan. I composed the first piano method in Japan. The method's name is Children's Cosmos.

BW: When?

AY: About ten years ago. In Japan, the Beyer method was very popular. Japanese composers didn't make a method for children in Japan. I felt very strange about that situation.

BW: They really needed to create a new method?

AY: *So, so, so.* There were (and are) many children who learned to play the piano, but they used the foreign method—only the foreign method.

BW: Is Beyer still used?

AY: Still Beyer! It is still famous and has authority in Japan for children's education. What American method do you know?

BW: Thompson.

AY: And more? *Methode Rose*—a French method. From Hungary, Kodály. And Bartok's *Mikrokosmos.* All of them are foreign methods. I thought it was very bad, and I wrote music. Here are the first volume and the second volume, but I don't have volume 3. [He showed them to me.]

BW: How did you get interested in children's music?

AY: My character is very childlike. Many, many years ago I found my character. On NHK I had an important program every week, on the radio. On those occasions I composed many children's songs.

BW: What was the name of the show?

AY: *Asobimashoo—Let's Play.* This program was on every week for five years. I composed a lot of music and songs. So many Japanese, from children to adults, sing my melodies. Then I intended to compose, to write music for children's education—a piano method.

BW: But . . . Yuyama-san, you are a graduate of Geidai. Won those prizes. To do a radio program for children is so different.

AY: Yes, it is, isn't it!

BW: What was the relationship?

AY: When I entered the university—Tokyo University of Fine Arts—I was eighteen. But I had no piano. When I was twelve the Second World War ended—my first year of middle school. After that . . . in Japan . . . many houses and many pianos were destroyed by bombs. Pianos were very expensive. Many Japanese had to find a way to survive . . . get a little money and buy rice, food. Now I thank America. American aid . . . food, medicine. I'm grateful. Middle school three years and high school three years. When I was seventeen [a senior in high school], I intended to enter the composition class at Geidai. My teacher said to my mother: "Your son must go to Geidai." But I had no piano. I entered a chorus club, and I conducted, but I wanted to play piano. If I entered the chorus club, I could play the piano. Then, with that piano I studied the theory of composition very hard. I studied only seven months in order to enter Geidai. In my freshman year at Geidai I had no piano. In the spring and summer and fall of my sophomore year I had no piano. At the end of my sophomore year, I could have a piano. So I wrote a violin sonatina.

BW: Without knowing how to play the piano well?

AY: I played the piano passionately. I composed a sonatina for violin and a piano sonata. After that, I entered the competition.

BW: Truly amazing. You had it in your ear.

AY: The piano is my lover! But I didn't meet my lover for over ten years. I was twenty-one before I was able to meet that piano. (Akira Yuyama, personal communication, April 7, 1999)

Looking at his piano instruction book, I found that the left-hand part was printed separately, then the right-hand part, then the two parts together. I commented that there seemed to be fewer exercises than in Beyer. He agreed and added that in Beyer there are many pieces that have harmony, but none is written in counterpoint, as some of his are.

Most telling in this modern Japanese connectivity of infrastructures in the sphere of music, however, is that the piano manufacturers Kawai and Yamaha themselves each established a music-publishing enterprise, which afforded Japanese composers an opportunity to create new music. Around 1976, when the Piano Teachers National Association (PTNA) began holding competitions for child pianists, Edition KAWAI (Kawai Shuppansha) began in earnest to publish Japanese works for children; the company considered it important that Japanese children who were learning to play piano should play Japanese composers' works. To build the Japanese repertoire for recitals and competitions—that is, to create a body of music that went beyond instructional materials—they began to commission works from composers who were well established in other spheres of creative endeavor. From Haruna Miyake, who is best known in the sphere of jazz and improvisation, for instance, Kawai commissioned *Nihon no Uta Henso Kyokushu: Variations on Theme of Japanese Songs* (1981). The variations are indeed varied: variation 2 was written in a scale characteristic of traditional koto music, variation 3 was written "with a bit of a modern touch," while the last (composed when she was twelve years old) was based on the beloved song "Aka tombo" ("Red Dragonfly"), by Kosaku Yamada. In 2000 the volume was still selling well, and "adults play the pieces as encores" (Haruna Miyake, personal communication, June 2, 2000).

Karen Tanaka, an established composer for orchestra and chamber ensemble as well as for solo instruments, composed for Edition KAWAI a collection of piano pieces titled *The Zoo in the Sky* (1995), based on animal constellations; they are intended to be learned between Beyer's *Vorschule im Klavierspiel* and Czerny's *Studies of Mechanism*, Op. 849, with each successive piece increasing slightly in difficulty. For each piece Tanaka gives instructions to guide the playing of the piece, such as this one.

> 14. Dragon. Draco (the Dragon) is a constellation surrounding Polaris in summer. Fast passages in the chromatic scale describe the Dragon. The left hand should always keep on beating 3/4 time, with the right hand always on the beat. Keep an accurate beat, as the left-hand rhythm is the very foundation of the piece.[5]

In order to compete with Beyer (in the public domain but primarily published by Zen-On) and the imported American Thompson method, Edition KAWAI decided to offer a commission for a piano instruction series to a composer who was not only distinguished but domestically influential. From among several considered, they selected Akira Miyoshi because he was (then) the dean of Toho Gakuen, which, as detailed above, was deeply involved in musical training for even very young children. Although Miyoshi was not the head of that particular Toho program, he had started piano at age four or five and was known to be a good player as well as a serious and established composer of piano music (Yoshiaki Hayakawa, personal communication, May 28, 2007). The result was the Miyoshi Piano Method (1997).[6] Beating the competition was apparently an uphill battle for all publishers of piano methods in Japan up until 2007, according to

Hayakawa, Edition KAWAI's editor-in-chief, because "piano teachers continue to use what they learned from."[7]

Edition KAWAI is helpful to composers of piano music in another way. Since 1985, in cooperation with the Japan Federation of Composers (JFC), an organization that functions on behalf of composers, Kawai has published two volumes each year of new piano pieces for children written by JFC members. Each year the JFC requests, by either general announcement or request, new pieces from its members. A committee of six members of a range of ages looks at the scores and selects those for publication. With support from Kawai, a concert called Kodomotachi e (To Our Children) is held each year as well, the idea being that composers will play their pieces and also talk about them. The audience for the concert is made up mostly of piano teachers who want to find new pieces for their students. According to Kimiko Shimbo, "a lot of the audience comes from outside of Tokyo every year" (personal communication, May 26, 2004). Publication of selected pieces by Edition KAWAI expedites this means of encouraging Japanese composers to write for children and for Japanese piano teachers who wish to introduce their students to music by domestic composers.

Among the renowned composers whose pieces have been included are Yasushi Akutagawa, Reiko Arima, Shin-ichiro Ikebe, Tokuhide Niimi, Akira Nishimura, Shigeaki Saegusa, and Akira Yuyama. One extremely well-known piece that was an early result of the JFC program was the celebrated composer Ikuma Dan's "Zoo-san" ("Mr. Elephant").[8] It appears that in recent years composers at the earlier stages of their careers tend to contribute more, unless the composer is particularly interested in composing for children. But the practice is alive and well.

The government's presence is palpable in all this activity on the part of composers, industry, and commerce. I asked the assistant to the secretary general of the JFC why the largest association for composers in Japan (with approximately 550 members in 2002) would be involved in creating, performing, and publishing music for children. It turns out that the impetus has been a national governmental policy and the fact that the JFC holds nonprofit status. Article 1 of the present law, passed in 1998 and amended in 2003, states the law's purpose: "to promote the sound development of specified nonprofit activities in the form of volunteer and other activities freely performed by citizens to benefit society, through such measures as the provision of corporate status to organizations that undertake specified nonprofit activities, and thereby to contribute to advancement of the public welfare."[9] Thus, the nonprofit status encourages and facilitates activities that benefit and serve many people: of the seventeen specific types of activities, "promotion of science, culture, the arts, or sports" is the pertinent official category for the JFC, as in cultural foundations and orchestras, for example. The legal force of nonprofit status, then, is an important force for keeping the creativity of Japanese composers socially relational.

At the time the JFC applied for nonprofit status, one of its directors suggested that members volunteer to compose for children so that Japanese children would have Japanese music to play. This suggestion was in keeping with the practice established at the beginning of the modernizing project in Japan in terms of composers creating new music for children. That this action is received well by "the public" can be measured partly by the fact that the annual concerts are so profitable financially that the income underwrites other federation concerts (Kimiko Shimbo, personal communication, May 26, 2004). The composers ultimately benefit as well because, while they of course write the pieces of their own volition, they retain copyright and will potentially receive royalties.

OTHER INFRASTRUCTURAL SUPPORT FOR COMPOSERS

Additional instances of the affordance of connectivity of industry, commerce, government, and the sphere of music bear mentioning. One is the support of foundations of major and smaller Japanese industries and companies—not only Yamaha and Kawai, but also Suntory Holdings, Asahi Breweries, Nippon Steel, Nomura Securities, Saison, Mitsubishi, Mainichi Shimbun, and a number of others. Each has been extremely important in selected ways.

Facilities for Cultural Events

One cooperative project in support of the arts that I particularly want to highlight here is Tokyo Opera City. Its official pamphlet provides an enticing description:

> Tokyo Opera City is one of the greatest theater complexes in the world. It consists of six theaters/halls and two art museums, together with a wooden-walled Concert Hall, that has a first-class sound effect, and the New National Theatre Tokyo, where opera, ballets, modern dance, and drama are performed.
>
> With about fifty company offices and fifty restaurants and commercial outlets located on the premises, the immense city block, the

first of its kind in Japan, combines business, shopping/eating and cultural entertainment.

Planning to build a New National Theatre for opera and ballet in the Hatsudai area of Tokyo, government agencies conceived the possibility that a huge complex might be built on land owned half by them and half by nine private companies, some of which might build cultural facilities at the same time. Six of the private owners of the property agreed to support cultural facilities and activities: Nippon Life Insurance, the Dai-ichi Mutual Life Insurance, Nippon Telephone and Telegraph (NTT), the Urban Development Group, Odakyu Electric Railway, Yamadai Tetsusho (construction), and Sogo Bussan (minerals and chemicals). NTT, for example, not only has its offices in the complex but also opened an art gallery—the NTT InterCommunication Center—which mounts four exhibitions each year.

With a basic fund of 500 million yen from the Agency for Cultural Affairs of the Ministry of Education, Culture, Sports, Science and Technology, the Tokyo Opera City Cultural Foundation was established on December 13, 1995, "for the purpose of planning and performing musical concerts, and holding exhibitions on the stages at cultural facilities such as the Concert Hall (1,632 seats), the Recital Hall (286 seats), and the art gallery" (TOC Cultural Foundation pamphlet); it also rents the cultural facilities to, for instance, Tokyo Concerts (see below) or to orchestras. The Foundation has a close relationship with the Tokyo Philharmonic Orchestra, which has its office in the complex.[10]

The Tokyo Opera City Cultural Foundation organizes and promotes twenty to thirty concerts each year. For composers, the Foundation's support is a clear instance of an affordance, both individually and collectively. Individual composers offer guidance and advice, following for the most part guidelines established by the Foundation's first artistic director, Toru Takemitsu, with the advice of seven world-renowned conductors and composers.[11] Akira Nishimura, nominated by Takemitsu in 1996, has been a councilor on programming for the Foundation; the composer Shin-ichiro Ikebe is presently the musical director. The support of the Foundation specifically for contemporary music is significant, most particularly through the annual Toru Takemitsu Composition Award competition, initiated by Takemitsu himself (see chapter 5).

While industrial and commercial giants have established practices in support of cultural activities in Japan, many, many smaller businesses and also banks, for example, are often very generous when approached by an individual or organization to support a particular event. Seeking such support is a constant, necessary effort. As in other countries, advertisements in concert programs benefit both the sponsor and "the arts."

One driving reason behind the necessity for the support by industry, commerce, and government for even smaller-scale, nonsubscription performances is a practice with regard to the sale of tickets that cannot help but negatively impact on income:[12] the sociocultural system of awarding complimentary tickets to concerts in numbers that seem to me astounding. In her practical way, composer Keiko Fujiie commented on this in one of her columns in the *Nagasaki Shimbun*:

> One more thing I want to problematize here is the system of complimentary tickets. In Japan, in many public performances, a fair number of complimentary tickets are circulated, but in Europe and North America, they are generally very restricted in number and, except to people in very special positions, are not given out. At New York's shrine to music, Lincoln Center (home of the Metropolitan Opera), there are businesspeople who have contributed large sums of money, perhaps millions of dollars. When they go to watch opera and so on, the Metropolitan Opera House definitely does not provide complimentary tickets. I've heard that they are only presented with free vouchers for drinks during intermission. If a person in a Japanese business that supported culture were to hear this, I'll bet they would be very surprised, and would also think it unfair. However, it is essential to try and think about the actual situation in Japan, where, for one reason or another, concerts are bloated with large numbers of complimentary tickets, and, furthermore, are filled with the socially unconnected, which is unfair to those who buy tickets and attend. However that may be, the current situation in all societies won't change in one fell swoop, since culture, history, the economic situation, and other factors are inextricably intertwined. If private performances before the premieres of experimental works and open rehearsals were to infiltrate Japan, a rational adjustment of invited guests would be made.
>
> By the way, I have also heard that in the above-mentioned Lincoln Center, a businessperson may receive an honor of a completely different nature: a new hall is named for him or her. (Fujiie 2005: 149–50, translated by Miki Kaneda)

It appears that Keiko Fujiie was unaware of the system in fund-raising in the United States whereby free admission to concerts or other special events is part of the package for attracting donors. In that instance, the package is publicly announced. What Fujiie seems to be commenting on is qualitatively different, namely, an individual presentation of complimentary tickets by persons performing or having a work performed on a scale I found to be quantitatively grand.

Production Companies

Production companies are a surprisingly underdeveloped type of enterprise for concert music in Tokyo. While there might be more, the May Corporation and Tokyo Concerts were the only two production companies mentioned in my conversations with composers.

The necessity of the support from the commercial sector led the composer Shigeaki Saegusa to found his own production company, the May Corporation, one purpose of which is to raise funds. Saegusa is an energetic, entrepreneurial individual involved in many spheres in the world of contemporary music, some of which are enumerated on the back of his business card. As of April 2013 they included guest professor at the Tokyo College of Music, president of the Japanische Mozart Gesellschaft, member of the board of directors of Wako University, vice director of the Japan Composers and Arrangers Association, committee member of the Japan Symphony Foundation, committee member of the Japan Society for Contemporary Music (JSCM or Gen On), music producer for Toyota Community Concert, music producer of Shiroishi City White Cube Concert Hall, and representative of ENJIN 01 (Encourage Japan Intelligent Network). The front of the card simply identifies Saegusa as "Composer."[13]

"Why do you do the business—May Corporation?" I asked Saegusa.

"It gives me an office from which to make operas. We produce concerts—mostly classical." A smart businessman, he produces some concerts that he knows will sell tickets, such as the year-end performance in one event of all nine Beethoven symphonies, the profits from which enable him to maintain the office.[14] Saegusa's taste definitely leans toward the spectacular, and he has extremely high standards. The production of his opera *Chushingura*, for instance, the first "fully Japanese opera"—Japanese cast, Japanese orchestra—to be presented in Italy, cost about 30 million yen.

"Why do you produce your own operas?" I inquired of him.

"Because I want to listen to my own operas. Three years ago the National Theatre wanted to produce *Chushingura* and did so. But since I produce my own, the National Theatre doesn't need to do it. I have a plan. By the time I am eighty, I will write certain operas—for parts of the *Heike monogatari*:[15] by 2013 (when I will be seventy-one), by 2016 (when I will be seventy-four), by 2019 (when I will be seventy-seven), and by 2022 (when I will be eighty)" (Shigeaki Saegusa, personal communication, May 16, 2006).

Saegusa is very successful at fund-raising, getting support from such diverse sources as breweries and hotels. His contacts in the spheres of commerce and government are also musical: he organized the Roppongi Men's Chorus in the Roppongi area of Tokyo, where the May Corporation office is located. With members aged from thirty to over seventy, the group performs both locally and abroad, with a repertoire both Japanese—including works by Saegusa—and foreign. The chorus is sometimes even used for commercials (Kimiko Shimbo, personal communication, May 9, 2006).[16] Significantly, Saegusa's success at fund-raising benefits more than just himself: the May Corporation has attracted other musical clients, including composers, for concert production.

Tokyo Concerts was founded in 1970, the year of the Osaka Expo, in which Toru Takemitsu, Maki Ishii, Joji Yuasa, and Toshio Ichiyanagi participated and which led to composers' needing production assistance. Tokyo Concerts manages some of the leading Japanese composers:

> When a composer receives a commission from a group or organization, Tokyo Concerts works out the complete project, trying to work out the things that the composer wants. Ichiyanagi was invited to a book fair in Germany. He went with the ensemble Time. The ensemble was founded for this, and Tokyo Concerts helped to find artists and generally organize the ensemble. Hosokawa founded the *gagaku* [music for court orchestra] group Yusei, which often performs his music. Tokyo Concerts organizes their tours to foreign countries. (Tokyo Concerts staff, personal communication, May 26, 2008).

SARAH, SARVH, AND JASRAC

Other organizations offer further evidence of the connectivity of industry, commerce, and government in the sphere of music. The Society for Administration of Remuneration for Audio Home Recording (SARAH) is an organization established in 1993 for the purpose of collecting remuneration for private copying on audio media and devices and distributing the monies to copyright holders, performers, and record producers.[17] The remuneration is also used to support incorporated groups for artistic projects. SARAH accumulates funds through a small amount taken from the price of blank media and sound-recording devices. The funds are distributed when either an artist or record producer or a member institution such as JASRAC, applies directly to SARAH (see below).[18] Appropriate projects include the publication of scores and recordings as well as concerts, in the form of domestic concerts throughout Japan such as memorial concerts. The amount of funding available through SARAH, of course, depends on the commercial sales of audio media and devices which the government designated for remuneration.

A second organization, the Society for the Administration of Remuneration for Video Home (SARVH), is responsible for collecting remuneration for private copying on audiovisual media and devices. SARVH distributes the monies to the interested parties and helps fund cultural activities in the same way SARAH does.[19]

The Japan Society for Rights of Authors and Composers (JASRAC) has received funds from SARAH since 1995. A nonprofit public-service corporation, JASRAC functions under the Agency for Cultural Affairs (Bunkachō) of the central government's Ministry of Education, Culture, Sports, Science, and Technology; its purpose is to administer musical copyright.

Compared to France, whose copyright law dates from 1899, Japan has less of an understanding of rights. In 1939, when JASRAC was founded, war was coming. It was late to have Japanese people learn about copyright.

> After the war, we saw to the administration of performance rights—concerts, nightclubs, bars. [People involved in concerts] brought lawsuits against JASRAC; most Japanese citizens couldn't understand. If JASRAC asked for a copyright fee, the response would be, "Why do I have to pay? It's not a thing." You can't see the copyright, and they didn't want to pay for something they can't see. We have that kind of copyright history—sometimes people don't want to pay for the rights. (JASRAC officers, personal communication, May 1[5], 2006)[20]

Most people are now aware that they have to clear copyright when they play copyrighted music (Satoshi Watanabe, personal communication, August 9, 2012).

While composers in Japan hold the copyright on their own intellectual property (i.e., their works, including music composed for TV dramas and other broadcast programs), they are likely to entrust their copyrights either directly or indirectly to an organization such as JASRAC, which has writer (composer or lyricist) and publisher memberships. To become a member of JASRAC, a writer might entrust his or her copyrights directly to it. In practice, however, most composers assign their copyrights to publishers, who in turn entrust the copyrights to JASRAC. In Japan copyright protection extends for fifty years, unlike the seventy-year protection in most of Europe and America; JASRAC has been working for some time to improve Japanese copyright protections.

The royalty system seems to work well for composers. I consistently heard praise and gratitude from composers for the vigilance with which JASRAC tracks domestic performances, publications, and sales of recordings of their copyrighted works. Furthermore, as a signatory to the Berne Convention and the Universal Copyright Convention and a member of such international bodies as the World Trade Organization, Japan enjoys a mutual copyright protection relationship "with almost every country on the planet"; JASRAC has reciprocal representation agreements with 109 copyright societies covering 79 countries and 4 territories around the world (*A Guide to JASRAC* [n.d.], given to me in 2006).

Internally, JASRAC is overseen by a board made up of of composers, publishers, and authors, each group forming a third of the membership; there is an election of directors from among the membership every three years. Outside board members consist of such persons as university professors and representatives of member organizations. In my meeting with officers, a point was made of telling me that the board does not include anyone from the broadcast industry. The thirteen member organizations, with the JFC and also the Japan Society for Contemporary Music (Gen On), include groups for pop composers, arrangers, and lyricists.

As a nonprofit organization, JASRAC distributes the monies it collects and otherwise receives to support the activities of member organizations and ultimately the individual members thereof. To the JFC, for example, JASRAC grants funding for the publication of scores (see chapter 3), for the costs of the annual concert of new piano music for children mentioned above, and for "independent" concerts. "JFC Independent" concerts showcase between forty and fifty members' pieces in a year; the opportunity is available to any member, funding permitting (Kimiko Shimbo, personal communications, March 31, 1999, and May 9, 2006).

In 2001 the enactment of the Law on Copyright and Neighboring Rights Management Businesses caused the first major change in musical copyright administration since JASRAC assumed that task in 1939. Requirements for obtaining permission to conduct a copyright administration business were relaxed, making it possible for many commercial enterprises to enter the business of musical copyright management by simply registering with the Agency for Cultural Affairs. For the first time, JASRAC was forced to operate in a competitive environment. Their philosophy remains unchanged, however; JASRAC continues to administer musical copyrights as a nonprofit public-service corporation.[21]

OTHER COMMERCIAL SUPPORT FOR COMPOSERS

Recording Companies

Primarily, contemporary music CDs are released by three Japanese companies—Camerata, Fontec, and ALM RECORDS (neither Sony nor Japan Victor has been interested). The three companies share one operating reality: sales of contemporary music are so low that the production and sale of recordings of other, more popular musics such as European concert music and jazz are necessary to support it. Nevertheless, composers benefit greatly from the enterprise of these three companies.[22]

Of the three firms, Fontec is the one most focused on contemporary music. Fontec was founded by Shoichi Shimizu in 1971 "before the oil/gasoline shock in 1973" that caused recording prices to rise—a financial turning point that was mentioned to me by a variety of people as affecting the course of contemporary music in Japan.[23] Major recording companies in Japan were forced to evaluate their priorities in terms of salable repertoires and to effectively cease production in all recording formats other than CD. Other companies stopped making contemporary-music recordings, but Fontec persevered (Akira Matsuda, personal communication, June 9, 2004). The company was a recording production company, uninvolved in the retail sales end of the business; the top recording person was the highly respected Yukio Kojima. Akira Matsuda, with whom I spoke, joined the company in 1982 to record, edit, and master recordings. Afterward, Fontec gradually added sales as well to their production business, and contemporary music gradually took on higher priority.

"Why contemporary music?" I asked Akira Matsuda. He replied:

> To fill in a gap. We must do this in a small company. We like to foster Japanese music. Also, we want to document and preserve. If we don't record Japanese music, people in the future will forget it. So we make CDs. We don't make any money on contemporary music. If we make ten CDs, perhaps two or three will sell. So we sell other CDs to support contemporary music—classical music, especially violin and piano

lesson CDs for study, and choral music. (Akira Matsuda, personal communication, June 9, 2004)

Fontec management is advised by composers who select what to record. In 2004 they were Nishimura Akira, Michio Mamiya, Yori-aki Matsudaira, and Isao Matsushita. "They really know about Japanese contemporary music, talk among themselves and decide" (Akira Matsuda, personal communication, June 9, 2004). As well as theme CDs featuring works by several composers, portrait CDs featuring works by leading composers have been produced, invariably titled "Works by. . . ." An outstanding example is a series of nine albums of works by Toshio Hosokawa that for a time followed his career in more or less chronological order. Another category of production focuses on one type of work by a single composer, such as "Choral Works by Hikaru Hayashi" or "Orchestral Works by Michio Kitazume."

In 1974—the year after the oil shock—Yukio Kojima, the top producer of recordings for Fontec, founded ALM RECORDS/Kojima so that he might produce CDs of music of his own choosing and also freelance as a recording engineer. I first met him when I needed to have recorded excerpts of a Nō drama for my textbook on music in Japan (Wade 2005), and it became clear that the only way to get them was to commission the recording. He continues to do freelance recording projects, being very much in demand.

One of Kojima's interests has been contemporary music, although his perspective is that the liveliest period for *gendai ongaku* was in the 1970s and early 1980s—with Jo Kondo, Haruna Miyake, Somei Satoh, and Yuji Takahashi; recordings from that time of the works of Kondo, Miyake, and Takahashi are still available on ALM RECORDS. In his opinion (and that of others), what began to erode gendai ongaku in the 1980s was that young people lost interest in avant-garde music; possibly due to economic conditions, they no longer found Japanese music interesting or fun (Yukio Kojima, personal communications, June 2, 2008, and December 27, 2012). Whereas Fontec has focused on more established composers, through the years Kojima has continued to be interested in new Japanese music—that is, in young composers whose works were or are not being heard on many concerts, such as Tetsuji Emura, Atsuhiko Gondai, Keiko Harada, Kishio Hirao, Hidemi Ishida, Makiko Kinoshita, and Hifumi Shimoyama. CDs featuring some of those are listed in the catalog of contemporary works on Kojima's ALM RECORDS label (http://www.kojimarokuon.com/engendai.html). While it is not possible to quantify the effect on those composers' success of the availability of their music on CD, the names of most are now familiar to a wide swath of the Japanese public.

Kojima is very supportive not only of Japanese composers but also of Japanese performers. Works by non-Japanese composers performed by Japanese artists include Chie Sato Roden playing Charles Ives's Piano Sonata No. 2, *Concord, Mass., 1840–60*, and Aki Takahashi performing works by Morton Feldman. The same performers are featured on CD playing works by Japanese composers—Takahashi playing works by Mamoru Fujieda, for instance. Yukio Kojima is an example of a successful Japanese entrepreneur who is part of the infrastructural support for Japanese contemporary music.

Founded in 1978, Camerata Tokyo is another example of successful Japanese individual entrepreneurship. The founder, Hiroshi Isaka, was active as a choral conductor and arranger while still a student at Doshisha University. He went into the recording business, first as a salesman from 1964 for the Japan Victor Company. Moving up quickly through the ranks of JVC, in 1966 he became A&R manager for concert music and a producer of pop records for the Philips label, a part of JVC. In 1968 JVC made him their classical producer, setting him on the path he would follow from then on. Working with eminent musicians in Japan and beyond, from 1968 to 1972 he produced more than 150 LPs from the European classical repertoire for the JVC. In 1972, when the RCA label set up its own distribution independent of JVC, Isaka joined that label as classical producer and also became A&R manager for the classical Erato label (distributed in Japan by RCA)—his final position as a corporate employee. Significantly, this provided him with the opportunity to produce in Vienna as well as Japan, and he signed an exclusive contract with the Vienna String Quartet (http://www.camerata.co.jp/eu/e_prof_a.html; accessed August 17, 2009).

What led Isaka to leave RCA in 1978 and start his own company, Camerata Tokyo, was frustration with the purely financial aims of big companies, coupled with a desire to introduce abroad Japanese musicians such as the pianist Aki Takahashi and the kotoist Keiko Nosaka, and also contemporary music by Japanese composers (Hiroshi Isaka, personal communication, May 27, 2004). Isaka used his connections with European musicians to introduce his new company. From the Vienna String Quartet, he expanded his contacts to members of the Vienna Philharmonic and gradually to young and new artists from Europe. Isaka has no editorial board; rather, he decides what he wants to record and then promotes it to acquaintances—publishers and personnel in other mass-communication media. In order to introduce his choice of performers, Isaka made Camerata a production company for live concerts as well as recordings. In 2005, when I met with him, he was inviting early music instrumentalists from Vienna to Japan.

Isaka's international connections are strong and purposefully cultivated. The cost of producing recordings in Japan keeps him in Europe (Vienna and elsewhere) for much of the year, and he continues to record European works and European musicians. (Recordings of European music by European musicians are more attractive to the Japanese buying public than recordings by Japanese performers of Western music.) If one browses Amazon.com: Camerata: Music, the full catalog is available for international sales.

From our conversation, I had the impression that Isaka takes his collaborations with Japanese composers and musicians very personally, and very seriously. There are of course other factors that affect his decisions about what and whom to record—requests from cultural foundations or other sponsors of special events such as a premiere of a major work, for instance. Isaka keeps tabs on whose careers are particularly successful. "Toshiro Saruya is the featured composer this year. While there is not a featured composer every year, most leading ones have been featured" (Hiroshi Isaka, personal communication, May 27, 2004).

For those Japanese composers and artists whose work has been recorded by Camerata Tokyo and for Japan's musical presence in the world, the benefits have been enormous. In 2003 the Nippon Steel Arts Foundation acknowledged this by awarding Isaka a Special Music Prize for his work in the world of music.

Music Publishers

For professional composers of concert music, of course, access to their works through the publication of scores is crucial. As in many other countries, the number of publishers of scores for widespread sale (or rental) in Japan is small, and certainly insufficient for the number of composers. Unable to or preferring not to rely on a publisher, some composers will make a score available to anyone who requests it; this is the case with Yuji Takahashi, for example. There is no risk in this, because the composer holds the copyright and can be confident that JASRAC will track performances of the work. A few composers are able to find a publisher outside of Japan (see chapter 4).

In Japan two commercial publishers deal only with major works in a "composer's oeuvre" manner. (For the composers, the contract is not exclusive; the composer can publish with other houses as well.) I discuss Schott Japan in chapter 3 on international connections because it is a German company with a Tokyo branch. For contemporary music, Zen-On is Schott Japan's competitor, but it is a very different company, as its name, "All Music," suggests.

When Akira Tanaka moved to Zen-On from Boosey and Hawkes and became director of publishing, he chose to focus mostly on a select few composers—a "quartette," to be precise. This put some older composers such as Minoru Miki (1930–2011) and Michio Mamiya, who had already been published by Zen-On, at a disadvantage. For some years the quartette comprised Keiko Fujiie, Shin-ichiro Ikebe, Tokuhide Niimi, and Akira Nishimura. Fujiie and Tanaka came to a parting of the ways for business reasons, and the fourth composer became Hitomi Kaneko.

The net result of the Schott Japan and Zen-On practice of focusing on a few composers was and is an even greater paucity of opportunities for the many other Japanese composers. This makes the publication by the Japan Federation of Composers of scores of new works by their members all the more important. There are also discrete projects, such as the publication by Shunjūsha of works commissioned by the National Theatre for gagaku ensemble or for Edo-period instruments (see chapter 4).

In the introduction I addressed the flexibility of Japanese composers, which permits them to create new music in a variety of styles, for a variety of musical spheres. The publishing of new music "for the people," as I think of it—music for chorus, wind band, and pianists particularly—presents additional opportunities for composers to earn their livelihood. As already demonstrated in the case of Yamaha and Kawai, the publishers make choices therein. Zen-On, for instance, publishes piano and choral music but does not publish wind band music "because each year the bands all play the same piece and if you don't choose the piece they choose and print huge [numbers of] parts, then you lose lots of money" (Akira Tanaka, personal communication, April 25, 2005). Ongaku no Tomosha, the oldest music publisher in Japan, does publish music for wind band; along with the All-Japan Band Association (see chapter 5), it is credited with the promotion of Japanese composers of band music (Hebert 2012:40). While Japanese wind band composers have good reason to feel poorly supported by the educational system, many of their needs are being met by the private sector (Hebert 2012:167).

Ongaku no Tomosha also publishes a series of scores called "Contemporary Music of Japan" that comprises mostly piano music by Japanese composers, selected by the publisher's copyright section. To keep costs down, they publish manuscript facsimiles in the composer's hand. I was told that "the situation is difficult, and such publications are possible because core classical music supports them" (Horiuchi Kumio, personal communication, April 27, 2005). Indeed, what Schott Japan, Zen-On, and Ongaku no Tomosha have in common is that they publish European music—contemporary or historical—in order to support the publication of new Japanese music of whatever kind they choose.

The bottom line for Ongaku no Tomosha, however, is that its focus has always been primarily on European music in Japan and abroad—whether the publication of scores or the several journals they publish. It is worthy of note, therefore, that the May 2002 issue of the journal *Ongaku no tomo* had a large section devoted to interviews with "Japanese Composers, U-50"—composers of gendai ongaku, many of whom, the reading public is assured, write surprisingly accessible music: "Gendai ongaku doesn't have to be difficult music. If you are a music specialist, great. If not, dive right in!" (2002: 65).[24] The composers Toshio Hosokawa, Akira Nishimura, Takashi Yoshimatsu, and Joji Yuasa were each introduced in a three-page "special close-up." Ten more composers—Mamoru Fujieda, Keiko Fujiie, Atsuhiko Gondai, Motoharu Kawashima, Dogen Kinowaki, Jun Nagao, Isao Nakamura, Mitsutaka Shiraishi, Toshiro Saruya, and Karen Tanaka—got one page each.

Occasionally, too, in *Ongaku no tomo* a Japanese composer is afforded the opportunity to publish an article. For example, Keiko Harada attended and wrote about the Forty-third International Asiago Festival in Italy in 2006, when Sofia Gubaidulina was featured as the "theme composer" (the article is on European music). This confluence proved to be particularly valuable for Harada, because she became acquainted with Gubaidulina and was herself invited to be the "theme composer" for the Asiago Festival in 2009.

SUMMARY

Several types of affordances for individual composers created by the connectivities among government, education, industry, and commerce were presented in this chapter. Music instruction offered by the industrial and commercial giant Yamaha was shown to provide potential composers with a path to competence outside of the government-controlled public educational infrastructure and expensive private institutions. Connected to that came the affordance of the opportunity to create new music for Japanese consumers of instruments manufactured domestically by Yamaha and

Kawai—new instructional music for beginners on piano, created by individual entrepreneurial composers and on commission from the publishing branches of the industrial giants.

The government was shown to be connected through the mechanism of nonprofit legal status for organizations that support composers—the Japan Federation of Composers, for example, whose project of new piano music for children satisfies the stipulation of volunteer and other activities freely performed by citizens to benefit society—and through copyright law, as with JASRAC, which manages copyright for composers. The government is also connected through projects of the cultural foundations of industrial and commercial companies large and small, ranging from the support of facilities such as Tokyo Opera City for cultural activities in which composers participate, to support for single events featuring new music.

Connections of the commercial activities of recording companies (particularly Camerata, Fontec, and ALM RECORDS, sometimes with support by cultural foundations) and of music publishers (particularly Zen-On and Ongaku no Tomosha) were shown to afford composers opportunities for their music to be heard and disseminated widely.

PART II

Japanese Composers in Shared Cultural Spaces of Western Music

In chapter 1 I presented the process by which musical practices of Europe and America were introduced into the educational system. While initially music was one of the many technologies introduced to help modernize Japan and create a nation-state, so widely and deeply has it been absorbed that these technologically induced practices have become a shared space for all Japanese people—a shared expressive space. Therein composers are afforded opportunities to create new music not only for the purposes of the state, but also—as addressed in chapters 1 and 2—for themselves, as actors in and contributors to the connected infrastructures of modernity that shape and cater to Japanese sensibilities and demands.

This second part of the book is devoted to the second environment in Japanese modernity that emerged as significant for the action possibilities I am interested in: the shared cultural space for all Japanese that was created by the adoption of Western music. The affording quality of the environment is that the cultural space is shared both internationally and within Japan. By adopting the music of the most influential cultures of the late nineteenth century, the government also situated Japanese culture solidly within a global, cosmopolitan musical culture. How composers in the spheres of concert music have engaged with the international aspect of that affordance is the subject of chapter 3. In chapter 4 I address the shared space internally, wherein mainstream musical culture intersects with the marginalized, discretely organized Japanese musical traditions (generally referred to as *hōgaku*). I argue that, however ironic it might seem, this shared expressive space affords composers and performer-composers possibilities for bridging the gulf that often exists in musical Japan between tradition and modernity.

CHAPTER THREE

International Participation in the Shared Space of Concert Music in the Global Cosmopolitan Culture

As soon as the Meiji leaders made the decision to adopt music from Western culture as a technology for the modernization of Japan, direct international connections were necessary. Unlike the adoption of musical instruments, repertoire, practices, and concepts from other Asian cultures, which took place over the span of about three centuries in the first millennium CE, this recent adoption was effectively in place in the short span of approximately eighty years—between the 1870s and the middle of the twentieth century. Whereas further direct musical connections with other Asian cultures through the centuries occurred sporadically and unsystematically from the eighth century on, sustained direct musical connections with Western cultures were required in order to establish what would become mainstream Japanese musical culture. Such connections are both inevitable owing to global communication systems and desired on the part of many Japanese, whether musicians, composers, concert audiences, or tourists who travel to Europe or elsewhere abroad to experience a music in its place of origin.

In this chapter I consider some ways in which composers have forged, utilized, or benefited from the international quality of the environment of shared cultural space. I begin with a very brief tracking of early possibilities for Japanese musicians that, although managed through institutions, resulted in initiatives on the part of capable and competent individuals who took full advantage of the affordance available to them and played significant roles in the formation of Japan's mainstream music culture. I then turn to individual composers' motivations for seeking experience abroad, that is, for participating in the global cosmopolitan culture outside Japan. When successful, that very participation affords composers cultural capital that is important for their success in Japan. Finally, I focus on recent ways in which individuals have facilitated international experiences for other Japanese, thereby maintaining the socially relational role of music in Japanese practice. I am not arguing that the processes and results of connections are necessarily unique to Japanese composers; rather, they are evidence of shared global cosmopolitan cultural practices.

EARLY INSTITUTIONAL CONNECTIONS ABROAD AND AT HOME

For individual Japanese musicians, direct connections with Europe (and, to a far lesser extent, the United States) first took the form of studying at institutions in France and Germany in order to acquire knowledge and develop competence. The first Japanese musicians to study in the West were sent from the ranks of the military bands:

> By 1871, the Japanese Army and Navy had become separate entities. [John William] Fenton [an English bandmaster] was placed in charge of the Navy band, while the Army band hired Gustave Charles Desire Dagron from France as its leader. However, despite a sweeping trend of fascination with Europe and the USA, the lingering xenophobic tendencies of Japanese society would not allow for foreigners to remain in such positions of power for any longer than necessary. As Obata observed, the Japanese Army band "felt the need to give the future leadership to its countrymen; therefore, in 1882, Hiromasa Furuya and Teiji Kudo were sent to the Conservatory of Paris. After 7 years both men finished their schooling and returned to Japan in 1889. A year later, Furuya was made Director of the Army Band. (Hebert 2012: 28, citing Obata 1974: 7)

As Sukehiro Hirakawa, professor emeritus at Tokyo University, reminds us: "The country's skill in using and then replacing outside foreign employees is too often forgotten" (Wakabayashi 1998: 65).

Within Japan the most significant musical developments were taking place in the new Tokyo School of Music at Ueno, to which Franz Eckert came in 1883 to teach music theory and orchestral music. One of the first talented students from the school to go abroad was Nobu Koda (1870–1946), a fine musician and composer who had a grant from the Ministry of Education that enabled her to travel from 1889 to 1895, first to Boston and then to Vienna (Galliano 2002: 40).[1] She is remembered principally as an excellent teacher. One of her students, Rentaro Taki (1879–1903), is considered the first significant Japanese composer. Taki graduated from the Tokyo School of Music in 1898 and in the spring of 1900 went to study in Leipzig for two years. In 1910 Kosaku Yamada, the first Japanese composer to gain international recognition and the first to compose a symphony, went to the Staatliche Akademische Hochschule für Musik in Berlin (Galliano 2002: 44).

Between 1870 and 1945, everything to do with Germanic musical history—the classical and romantic periods, that is—and culture was very much revered, and exchanges with Germany for serious academic musical studies predominated. In the years immediately following World War I, the number of cultural exchanges continued to grow, with an increasing flow of foreign teachers coming to Japan and of Japanese students being sent abroad to study. Up to World War II, the Japanese saw Germanic music as representing established tradition (Galliano 2002: 34). Despite the number of Japanese composers who had been going to Germany to study and who must have been aware of such composers as Arnold Schoenberg, interest in contemporary German music, with the exception of that of Paul Hindemith, came only after World War II.

French music, on the other hand, was thought of as offering new avenues to explore—perhaps, as Galliano suggests, because most contacts with French music were made through direct contact between musicians rather than through institutionalized academic channels. Kosuke Komatsu, one of the earliest of Japanese composers to study in France, worked with Vincent d'Indy between 1921 and 1924 (Galliano 2002: 76).

Kosuke Komatsu was sent to Europe perhaps because he had already proven himself to be not only an active composer, but also an energetic entrepreneur. In 1906, for instance, just before graduating from the Tokyo School of Music, he joined a graduate of the school to found the Gakuenka Association for the presentation of opera; its first production was a one-act opera composed by Komatsu himself, based on the Nō drama *Hagoromo* (*The Cloak of Feathers*) (Galliano 2002: 101). In 1907 he was appointed director of a new imperial music association, and he would later be part of the imperial theater project begun in 1911—both organizations that facilitated the newly adopted Western practice of public concerts (Galliano 2002: 92). When specialist music journals also began to emerge in the first decade of the twentieth century, Komatsu was at the forefront, as the editorial director of *Ongakukai* (*The Musical World*, 1908–23), the intention of which was to promote new music and to campaign against "all music that is weak, unworthy, reactionary, or out of date" (Galliano 2002: 96).

In 1930, his loyalty to French music still strong, Komatsu was among the founders of the Shinkō Sakkyokuka Renmei (Newly Rising Federation of Composers; see chapter 2) in "an attempt to open up new areas of pure music and as a protest against Dainihon Sakkyokuka Kyōkai (Greater Japan Composers Association), which represented the prevailing German style (Galliano 2002: 82). After a visit to Japan by two composers whose music "was colored by the French school"—Alexandre Tansman in 1933 and Alexander Tcherepnin in 1935—the group changed its name to Nihon Gendai Sakkyoka Renmei (Association of Contemporary Japanese Composers) and became the Japanese branch of the International Society for Contemporary Music.

International institutions were thus an element of the affordance of the shared musical culture. The Association of Contemporary Japanese Composers participated in the ISCM's international festivals in Paris (1937) and Warsaw (1939), receiving support for its activities from two major orchestras and a number of other performers. Between 1936 and 1940 it promoted a total of thirteen events in which seventy composers and fifty performers and critics were involved in performances of mostly instrumental works. Like all other similar groups, the French music–oriented Association of Contemporary Japanese Composers was forced to disband before the war, but it was re-formed in 1946 (Galliano 2002: 82).

It took a while for the "new avenue" of French music to be given a place alongside German classical and romantic music in the Japanese music-educational infrastructure. Only at the end of the 1930s did Tomojiro Ikenouchi (1906–1991), one of the first influential Japanese musicians to study at the Paris Conservatory, begin teaching French music in the academy (Galliano 2002: 34), with a focus on French impressionist composers. By the post–World War II period, however, the study of Ravel and Debussy was thoroughly entrenched in the Japanese academy. The composer Michio Mamiya recalled:

> At age eighteen [in 1947] I went to Tokyo, to the Academy of Music (now Geidai) in composition class; there were nine students. That was suddenly a lot; earlier there had been only two and three years before there were only four students. It was like a family. Ikenouchi was the teacher; for him the greatest composers were Ravel and Debussy. "After Ravel, no music." But the students could be free. Each had some special interest; some were crazy about Stravinsky, Berg, Schoenberg; I was fond of Prokofiev and Poulenc and Stravinsky. (Personal communication, May 14, 2006)

Beyond the academy during the period of the American occupation and somewhat after 1953, an "international experience" of a sort was afforded in Tokyo by the American Cultural Center, located first in Hibiya, then in Ginza; it moved around. The ACC was a library that, while clearly part of the American political establishment, was appreciated by some Japanese composers who were uninterested in politics but sought knowledge and competence for the purpose of participation in the global cosmopolitan culture of contemporary music. Yori-aki Matsudaira (b. 1931) spoke about the library with me.

> During the American occupation, music was very free. The American soldiers didn't think music was so important. In Germany they thought music was important, but not in Japan. The U.S. army supported the Darmstadt Festival, but in Japan there was no support explicitly for music. There *was* the American Cultural Center; it was a library, with scores, records, books about American music—Copland, Sessions, Piston, and others. (Personal communication, May 27, 2004)

Joji Yuasa recalled:

> I went there from 1950 to 1953. Takemitsu, Mamiya, and I went there to get the cutting-edge music from America. We could hear Bernstein's *Age of Anxiety*, Roy Harris, Copland, Riegger, Ives, Gershwin, McDowell, Griffes, William Schuman, Norman Dello Joio, Samuel Barber. The Center had some scores, but many recordings. I copied Copland's *Quiet City*. I was surprised when I went to the University of California, San Diego; when I talked about American composers, the students didn't know much. (Personal communication, May 12, 2006, elaborated June 1, 2011)

Michio Mamiya explained further about the library:

> Composition students went there. We could hear so much American music—Copland, Harris, Sessions, and others. Also European music, and contemporary Russian music—Shostakovich. There were "recording concerts" with explanation of the music at the Hibiya American Library. I first heard Messiaen's *Quatour pour la fin du temps* there. Lectures were given by Japanese critics and members of the Library, who spoke Japanese very well. That lasted about ten years. We called

> the library the "CIA Library." It was the biggest American support. (Personal communication, May 14, 2006)[2]

The "very tight connection" of Yuasa with Takemitsu and Ichiyanagi continued through the Cross Talk Festivals, sponsored by the American Cultural Center in 1967, 1968, and 1969 (Joji Yuasa, personal communication, June 1, 2011). The Festival was set up in 1966 by Yuasa and Akiyama Kuniharu, together with the American composer Roger Reynolds, for the purpose of presenting new developments in American and Japanese music (Galliano 2002: 205 n. 57). The Festival had a series of artistic directors, including Toshi Ichiyanagi. Since the closing of the American Cultural Center it has continued with the sponsorship of the American Embassy under the name Interlink, with Mamoru Fujieda taking a leadership role.[3]

Since World War II, many, many Japanese composers have traveled abroad for musical reasons, taking advantage of the quality of their environment that affords them, as individuals, possibilities for participating in and benefiting from international connections and achievements. Whereas in pre–World War II Japan the destination would have been Europe and the choice usually between France and Germany, after World War II the choice widened within Europe and expanded to include the United States. A very few composers have prolonged international experience in both Europe and the United States. For instance, the Tokyo-born composer Karen Tanaka (b. 1961), after studying composition with Akira Miyoshi at the Toho Gakuen School of Music, moved to Paris in 1986 to study composition with Tristan Murail and to work at IRCAM.[4] In 1990–91 she studied with Luciano Berio in Florence with funding from the Nadia Boulanger Foundation. Tanaka now resides in the United States, where she is on the composition faculty of the California Institute of the Arts. The following section I devote to individual accounts, organized first by destination and secondarily by year of birth of the composer who is cited.

INDIVIDUAL MOTIVATIONS FOR EXPERIENCE ABROAD

The initiating reasons for and means by which composers have participated in cosmopolitan musical culture abroad have been almost as numerous as the composers with whom I spoke about it. Here I will suggest that variety—a personal desire for further education or encouragement and/or assistance by a teacher or a friend or family, or some professional opportunity. In each case, the experience had an effect on the individual's future endeavors.

To the United States

Joji Yuasa

As recounted to me, Joji Yuasa's (b. 1929) interest in traveling abroad for music was spurred by a friend, the poet Shuntaro Tanikawa, who had a fellowship for six months in the United States and "introduced him" at the Japan Society of New York (personal communication, May 3, 2001). After that, Joji recalled, Rand Castile, then director of the Asian Art Museum in San Francisco, visited him in Tokyo on behalf of the Japan Society for an interview and to listen to Yuasa's music. A fellowship followed in 1968, affording Yuasa the opportunity to make a number of pertinent connections. On the fellowship, he visited professors at Columbia University and the University of Michigan (Ross Lee Finney), as well as at the electronic music studio at the University of Illinois (Ben Johnston and John Cage). While in San Francisco for one month, he went across the bay to the University of California, Berkeley, for a performance of the Merce Cunningham Dance Company. There he met David Tudor,[5] who was going next to the University of California, San Diego. Joining Tudor to see the then two-year-old program in new music, Yuasa found himself invited to present a lecture. A decade later, in 1976, supported by a grant from the Ford Foundation, Yuasa was again at UCSD, at the Center for Experimental Music, where Roger Reynolds had joined the faculty. Yuasa accepted an appointment as professor and taught there from 1981 until his retirement in 1994. At that point he returned to Japan to live, but his international connections remain very lively.

Toshi Ichiyanagi

Family circumstances combined with political forces led Toshi Ichiyanagi (b. 1933) to his first international experience. His father was a professional orchestra musician, and his mother was a pianist. Even as a young man Ichiyanagi was interested in becoming a composer, having won the Mainichi/NHK Composition Konkur in 1949 at age sixteen (during the American occupation, "when there were few composers," as he put it modestly); he also played piano well (personal communication, May 22, 2003).

> In the late 1940s many musicians had no job. Mayuzumi and others played in American "camps"—buildings in central Tokyo that had not been burned. Because my mother had gone to Oberlin, she had some

connection. For two or three years she and I played semiclassical music. In the beginning it was fun, but after a while we were not so happy. It was a hard time in Japanese life.

I was almost going to go to France as an exchange student, but only one person a year could get a scholarship to a government school. Performers and composers were competing for that space.

My mother spoke English, and while playing at "camp," we befriended Americans, including a family from Minneapolis. I was feeling strongly that it was right to go to the United States, where so many things were happening. Only businessmen—Toyota and others—were going. And Tōdai [Tokyo University] and Waseda [University] scholars. Other professors didn't have American connections. But I went to the States—first to Minneapolis to the University of Minnesota for one year, by invitation of that family. From there I went directly to New York, where John Cage was.

[When I returned to Japan] in 1961, there was an Institute of the Twentieth Century in Tokyo, directed by Hidekazu Yoshida, who became director of the Mito Geijutsukan [Mito Art Tower]. A progressive group was part of the Institute—Minao Shibata, Irino, Moroi, Mayuzumi, then Takemitsu and I. I brought back the music of Cage and Feldman from New York City. It interested architects and others, but maybe half the musicians were not so enthusiastic about it. There was also a very active Center for Contemporary Arts—the Sōgetsu Arts Center in Aoyama. I was able to interest the director, master of flower arranging Sofu Teshigahara, in inviting Cage to Japan in 1962. After that, American influence was present. (Personal communication, May 22, 2003; August 1, 2013)[6]

Keiko Abe

The performer-composer Keiko Abe (b. 1937) was already an established and respected marimba soloist by the time she traveled abroad: "People didn't like contemporary music here. I was interested in improvising and needed to find musicians. So I went to America in 1977. At Oberlin, Michael Rosen heard my LP and was surprised at the sound of the marimba. At Illinois, [I met] Thomas Siwe" (personal communication, May 11, 2001). Next she went to Europe, where Japanese pieces were gradually becoming known.

Abe's first international connection, however, had occurred much earlier and in Japan, when she went to a mission school in Yamanashi

Prefecture to which her father, a doctor with a government position, had moved. At age twelve, in the mission's junior high school, she encountered the missionary Lawrence Lacour, who "brought marimba to Japan" (Keiko Abe, personal communication, May 11, 2001). From that time she progressed in a straight line to her career as a performer and composer. She attended Tokyo Gakugei University in music education and graduated with a master of arts degree at age twenty-two, not wanting to be a teacher and still playing percussion. The composer Tomita Isao, who is associated particularly with synthesizer music, got her started as a professional performer; he needed a percussionist who could make organ sounds on a marimba. Because Lacour had played hymns on the marimba, that was no problem for her. The opportunity was a turning point in her career.

Abe is known worldwide as a result of her determination to make the marimba a solo instrument, beyond its role as just another instrument in the percussion section. To really "make it big," in the early 1960s she decided to commission pieces from the best of Japanese contemporary composers, works that she performed all over Japan.[7] Among the composers was Minoru Miki (see chapter 4), who, after hearing her play the concerto she commissioned from him, remarked to her that the American marimba she was using did not fit her musicality. She says that he told her, "You need to develop it more." So Abe went to Yamaha and asked them to help. Yamaha "gave me an engineer to work with," she said (personal communication, May 11, 2001). The result was the Yamaha YM-6000 marimba, a five-octave instrument with a resonant tone quality. With it her career has skyrocketed; she has toured North America, Europe and Asia repeatedly, recorded many CDs, and was the first woman inducted into the American Percussive Arts Society Hall of Fame. On November 1, 2001, from Grand Rapids, Michigan, Yamaha announced a Keiko Abe signature set of mallets. Wherever she has gone, she has performed not only compositions of her own (she began composing in 1985), but also compositions by Japanese composers from whom she commissioned new works. Thus, she has shared her international connections, maintaining the sociocultural role of music in Japanese society.

Haruna Miyake

As a teenager Haruna Miyake (b. 1942) spent a total of two and a half years in California when her father was visiting professor at the Scripps Institute in La Jolla, after which he went to Cal Tech in Pasadena. During that time Miyake attended American public high schools. Even before going to America, Miyake had studied composition with a teacher interested in a theory that children can compose and play simultaneously, just as we can compose and speak simultaneously. For her this was a congenial idea, because, having studied piano from age five because her parents wanted her to do so, Miyake was already improvising—playing what she wanted to play rather than what the teacher wanted her to play. She composed mainly piano pieces, simple orchestra pieces, a string quartet, and a string trio and submitted them to Juilliard. Miyake returned to America in 1961, having been admitted to Juilliard in composition. From Tokyo, to which she returned after graduating, Miyake sent to a friend in New York a tape of a piano concerto she had just written for the Yomiuri Symphony. The friend gave the tape to "someone" at Lincoln Center. The result: one of the ten to twelve commissions for new works to celebrate the opening of Alice Tully Hall in 1970 went to Miyake. She was the youngest composer to be commissioned; Darius Milhaud was the oldest. She went back and forth between New York and Tokyo for that work (*Six Voices in June*) and also to play piano for contemporary music concerts (Haruna Miyake, personal communication, March 30, 1999, unconfirmed). She has maintained her international contacts through the years and has performed as a pianist and improviser with a number of internationally known musicians.[8]

Jo Kondo

Jo Kondo (b. 1947) was interested in modern experimental music rather than earlier European composition while a student at Geidai and wondered if American composers would recognize his music as influenced by them. The opportunity for him to get to know John Cage, Morton Feldman and Steve Reich came at age twenty-nine through a 1978 residency in New York supported by the John D. Rockefeller III Fund, the predecessor of the Asian Cultural Council. He was welcomed by the composers, he said, and "being in America confirmed what I had been doing."[9] After Morton Feldman died in 1987, Kondo lost touch with the American contemporary music scene. He gravitated to Europe, and his work became particularly well-known in Germany and Great Britain (personal communication, May 13, 2003). His works have been recorded on CP2 (USA), the Hat Art (Switzerland), Deutsche Grammophon (German), and ALM (Japan), and his scores have been published by the University of York Music Press (UK) and Edition Peters. Since 2001 he has been renewing his American contacts, and in 2012 he was elected a foreign honorary member of the American Academy of Arts and Letters.

Keiko Fujiie

In 1974 eleven-year-old Keiko Fujiie (b. 1963) spent six months in Taiwan when her father, a math professor at Kyoto University, taught there as a visiting professor.

KF: My father put us [Keiko and her sister] not in Japanese school or in international school, but in a local public school so we had to study Mandarin. It was really hard.

BW: It must have been difficult at age eleven. Already that is getting a little old to learn a new language easily.

KF: And the situation in Taiwan was very different from the situation in Japan. [Taiwan was not as developed as it is now, she implied.] The textbook on history that I studied. . . . Do you know the relationship between Taiwan and China? In the history textbook, it said our . . . how do you say . . . our colleagues all sacrifice in China under the terrible government, so our aim is to save them from that terrible government. They wrote very clearly that the Chinese nation is the best nation in the world. That was a cultural shock for me. But I was not unhappy, because I [learned a valuable lesson, that] in the way of thinking, there are many, many varieties in the world. (Personal communication, March 24, 1999)

Fujiie's second international experience was in Los Angeles. After completing her master of arts in composition at Geidai in 1988, she worked in the commercial advertising business—during the "bubble," when the Japanese economy was at its postwar peak. That she would do so serves as a good example of the flexibility of most Japanese composers. Fujiie explained this working opportunity to me.

KF: At that time, many, many clients were interested in using an acoustic orchestra sound for TV advertisements. So they needed some contemporary composers. I was very lucky.

BW: So you wrote for commercials!

KF: Yes, mostly orchestra pieces. Sometimes I went to Los Angeles and players from the Los Angeles Philharmonic orchestra came to the studio to create advertising music. It was a really good exercise for me, because it is very difficult for composers to get the chance to hear the sound of their symphonic pieces. A commercial is really quick, you know. I would write for four minutes or even thirty seconds—a symphonic piece. They played it immediately! And I could correct it and they played again. . . . It was really nice for me.

BW: That's fantastic! It was like a workshop for you.

KF: Sure, sure.

BW: The Los Angeles Philharmonic players are excellent musicians, aren't they.

KF: Especially the brass!

BW: I liked the brass writing in your concerto. [The day before I had attended a rehearsal in Suntory Hall of her Guitar Concerto No. 2, written as composer-in-residence with the Kanagawa Orchestra Ensemble.]

KF: Thank you! Because of them . . . [*she laughs*] because of them maybe. I studied a lot of things.

BW: I wrote in notes that I took yesterday on your piece that I really liked the use of brass. When you put the brass with the timpani and the bass, there was a kind of a sonorous, wonderful depth to the sound. I really enjoyed it. How long did you work in L.A.?

KF: Several short trips in three years. And I got very good money.

BW: Your company sent you back and forth to L.A.?

KF: Yes.

BW: Why L.A.?

KF: First of all, because of the prestige. And they are good. In Japan we don't have many good brass players. The brass players are not very good here.[10] String players are okay. And studios—the rental fee for a studio is higher here than in United States. But the bubble economy was getting—the budget was getting smaller and smaller. I thought: if the budget is getting smaller, it means we need better ideas. If we have no money, how to use this small amount of money is very important. But the clients didn't think like that. They became very conservative. No more try-outs, no more contemporary music for the advertisements. They started to remake old advertisements, or they started to use more computers [synthesizers]. Anyway, they became very protective and conservative. I had no more interest in the field, and I quit. (Personal communication, March 24, 1999)[11]

Toshiro Saruya

Although he did not tell me so explicitly, I have the impression that Toshiro Saruya (b. 1960) chose to study music abroad because he generally likes to do things differently. While most composers of his generation went to music school for specialized study, he majored in law at Keio University. Then he took the entrance exam for Juilliard and was accepted; residence there from 1985 to 1988 resulted in a master of arts in composition. "Since you didn't go to music school, how did you prepare?" I asked him.

> I was born in Tokyo in 1960. My mother was a pianist, teaching at school. I started piano at the age of two or three, but I hated to practice. My father ran a business, teaching construction skills and materials. The teachers were not particularly encouraging. My mother trained my ear to discern complex tone clusters, adding pitches to chords. She had old records of classical music, and she started me playing the violin at about age 5. I loved the theme song for *The Untouchables*. At about age fifteen I stopped playing both piano and violin and started teaching myself to play jazz guitar. In high school and at the university, I had a group aimed at creating music that was broader than fusion music, and we called it "confusion." We played in live spots like the Pit Inn in Roppongi in the 1980s. I started composition lessons and was writing for my group, but I wanted more stimulation than jazz/rock, so I turned to contemporary music. (Personal communication, May 24, 2002)

At Juilliard Saruya studied with Vincent Persichetti (1915–1987), whom he praises as a good teacher who was flexible and let him find his own way.

Back in Japan, Saruya felt like an outsider. "People were (and are) interested in me for my background," he told me. "I'm Japanese but didn't go to Japanese music school. I'm 'different'—not good or bad—'different'; how that is treated depends on the person" (personal communication, May 24, 2002). Saruya cited an example of how he is not treated as a Japanese composer: for the Suntory Foundation, Takemitsu directed a project called the International Composer's Commission Series. Because Saruya was considered to be an "international composer," a new piece (*Fiber of the Breath*) was commissioned from him. This composition, a new piece from Hans Werner Henze, and an old piece not composed by Henze but chosen by him as one of the pieces that had most strongly influenced him were performed in a 1992 concert by the NHK Symphony Orchestra. This, Saruya's debut as a composer in Japan, appears to have made him more of a "Japanese" composer, because shortly thereafter he won three prestigious prizes in rapid succession: in 1993 he won both the Akutagawa Award for Music Composition for young Japanese composers and the Idemitsu Music

Award for young Japanese musicians, and in 1995 he took home the Otaka Prize for accomplished Japanese composers.

In 2000 Saruya started to teach at Osaka Kyoiku Daigaku (Osaka University for Education), a national university. His getting the position was in itself something that went outside of tradition: "It is unusual for a person like me to get a job like that; usually a graduate of a national music school in Japan would." He wants his students to do something different. One example: "In 2001, we had a tragic incident at an elementary school affiliated with my university. As a memorial, I am having my students work toward a benefit concert. I am getting them to make artistic paintings, scan them into the computer, make the images interact, write accompanying music for them, and compose a piece. We also made a film to show at the concert." In addition, Saruya wants his students to have a sense of international contact. When Henze and Oliver Knussen were in Japan, Saruya asked them for some messages he might give to his students about education in music for the future—that is, for the next fifty to a hundred years (personal communication, May 24, 2004).

To Europe

Sachie Murao

The most courageous composer with whom I spoke about interest in going abroad was Sachie Murao (b. 1945). In my visit to her home on June 12, 2000, she was a gracious hostess and willing to talk freely about her life—which included five short-term stays in Germany, for personal as well as musical reasons. Because her story is so exceptional, I have excerpted generously from it here.

SM: In Japan we can't make money from music. Because I have a handicap, I can't get a job. That is a big problem.

BW: How did you get to Germany? You went alone?

SM: Yes. I had no friend, no acquaintance in Germany. The first time I went to study language. In Japan I learned German from a TV program because I was blind and couldn't read the textbook. If I didn't understand a word, I just memorized it. I was very interested in the German language. I was also very interested in music in Germany. It was my dream to go. But because of my blindness, I couldn't get information at first. I couldn't read the newspaper or magazines or anything, so I decided to go to Germany anyway as a tourist. First I joined a tour for learning Germany language.

At the beginning, the travel bureau here didn't accept me as a tourist because I am blind. Even now many travel agents don't accept blind people. We have to be accompanied by someone who will help us. So I pretended to be a normal person. Made the reservation on the telephone.

I didn't have any plan in Germany. I went five or six times. Because I had to earn money for the trip [airfare], after I improved my German I worked a little bit as an interpreter there. And I worked as a sightseeing guide there, too. Once I worked as a bus guide. The driver explained and asked me to translate into Japanese for the Japanese tourists. In Germany it is very different from the Japanese situation. Even if you are blind, they will give you a job if you can work. In Japan they won't. If you apply to a Japanese company, right away they say, "You are blind," and they won't give you a job. They won't hire us.

My parents are ashamed that I am blind. They didn't want to tell people that their daughter is blind. They hid me. I was educated like that. My parents kept saying, "Don't tell people you are blind, handicapped." Now I think that because my parents educated me like that, I taught myself through my senses, and now I can even ride a bicycle. You must be surprised! But I can ride a bicycle. Of course I can't see the edge of the wall, but I can feel the movement of the air and tell that people are there. I listen to the sound of people walking, their talking, or I can sense people's emotions.

BW: So it made you independent. When did you return to Japan from Germany?

SM: I didn't stay in Germany for long, because my parents didn't want me to. I couldn't tell them that I was going to Germany because they would have objected. So I didn't tell them until about three days before I was to leave. They were very surprised, and at first they thought I was going to a German [tourist] village somewhere in Japan. Once I stayed [in Germany] for two months, once for one month.

Starting with the second time, I could buy the ticket by myself, not through a tourist agency. So from the second time on I could go by myself. In Japan I could not go to university, but I wanted to study. First I went to the University of Bonn as an auditor. At first I didn't understand much German, but I learned more at the university as an auditor, studying it a bit. Mainly I listened to concerts of music. My friends introduced me to composers and players there. I went to a very small group concert twice. Cologne and Bonn and Humboldt—each city's summer festivals—I listened to those concerts. A festival of Christianity—there are several summer festivals like that.

From the third time I started to sell origami. I stayed with a German family, and they advised me, "Why don't you sell origami to earn money?" I thought maybe, oh—that's a joke! But in Bonn and Cologne I showed them how to fold the origami and sold them on the street and made some money. I used it as a fund for my concerts in Japan.

BW: Thank you very much for telling me about your experiences. I have been talking with many women composers. They have told me about being a woman and their situations. Every one of them has some sort of support system. What is your support system?

SM: I don't have any support. But Tojo-san [a friend who was present during my interview] reads letters for me. I often make a mistake because I misread the date of the concert, or the place. One problem is that because I am blind, I can't get much information from books.

BW: Only Tojo-san helps you?

SM: I don't have any financial support. I have only a small pension. I don't have any income, so I live just on my pension.

BW: You have a lovely home here! Things seem to be OK. Are things OK?

SM: They are *not* OK! Another reason that I went to Germany is that I heard that in Germany musicians can get some financial support. And yet another reason is that they don't have a special feeling about handicapped people—prejudice [*henken*]. For instance, if in Japan I'm walking with the white cane, people stare at me or children throw stones at me. They are prejudiced. In Germany, if I'm working, they stop and ask me where I come from, and I say that I'm from Japan, and they say, "Oh . . . how did you get here?" They are very friendly. In Japan people are not friendly; they discriminate. When I buy a ticket at the station, people say I am taking too much time, I should just go away, or they hit me. . . . In that sense, I had a dream to live in Germany. But I had family problems. (Sachie Murao, personal communication, June 12, 2000)[12]

Sachie Murao studied composition with Michiharu Matsunaga and Yoshiro Irino. She has twice won the competition of the Japan Federation of Composers for publication of a new work (see chapter 5) (in 1987 for her *Kleines Stück für Klavier Nr. 6* and in 1991 for *The Four Seasons of the Ancient Capital of Nara* for a quintet including koto and shakuhachi), and her 1992 *Koto nara no shirabe V* was featured in a fiftieth-anniversary celebration concert of the JFC in 2012. Works composed for Japanese instruments are included in concerts of the Nihon Ongaku Shudan (Pro Musica Nipponia; see chapter 4). While many performances of her works have been in the Kansai area (she lives in Nara), her *Dialogue for Two Shakuhachi and Violin* was selected for the fifteenth Japan Classic Festival at Tokyo Opera City Plaza in January 2013 (Sachie Murao, personal communication, November 28, 2012).

Ichiro Nodaira

Interest in a particular music was the motivation for Ichiro Nodaira (b. 1953) to study in France (as it had been for Jo Kondo to study in the United States). It would have been logical for him to have gone to the Paris Conservatory because he had a contact in Tomojiro Ikenouchi. However, that contact with Ikenouchi was for the study of harmony, to prepare him for the admission examination for the Geidai high school (see chapter 2). After graduating from that music high school, Nodaira studied composition with Michio Mamiya at the university level of Geidai for two years. Despite the French impressionist emphasis at Geidai, Nodaira heard the music of Pierre Boulez and beyond—postserialists such as Rami Khalifé and Betsy Jolas—and loved it. That took him to the Paris Conservatory where he studied composition with Jolas (personal communication, May 28, 2007), becoming the first Japanese student at the Conservatory to achieve a first prize in musical analysis and establishing a fine reputation as a pianist (Betsy Jolas, personal communication, February 11, 2011). Nodaira remained in Paris for twelve years (until 1990), working mostly as a keyboardist on piano, synthesizer, or electric keyboard—"or anything," as he put it. His association with the Ensemble l'Itinéraire—a collective ensemble of performers and composers such as Gérard Grisey—put him squarely into the French contemporary music scene. In Japan now, he is an example of a musician who is distinguished both as a performer and as a composer.

Toshio Hosokawa

The composer who encouraged the interest of Toshio Hosokawa (b. 1955) in study abroad was the Korean composer Isang Yun (1917–1995). Around 1971 Hosokawa heard a performance in Tokyo of Yun's orchestra pieces

Réak (1966) and *Dimensionen* (1971) and reacted to them strongly: "His music left the impression that a great flow of the Asian sound universe had moved before me" (Sparrer 2001: 1). When Yun visited Tokyo later, Hosokawa was able to meet him. At the time Hosokawa had not found a teacher in Japan, and, as he put it to me, "Yun said come as soon as possible." Fortunate that his family was supportive and could afford to finance his studies abroad, in 1976 Hosokawa went to the Hochschule der Kunste Berlin, where he was able to study composition with Yun, music theory with Witold Szalonek, and piano with Rolf Kuhnert. He found it an interesting time in Germany in terms of the contemporary music scene. "The [Berlin] Wall still existed but there were many activities. Cultural events! Cheap! Berlin Philharmonic tickets were $3–4. I saw every conductor" (Toshio Hosokawa, personal communication, June 1, 2004). Hosokawa's connections with Germany remain extensive; a transnational composer, he resides there and in Japan.[13]

Atsuhiko Gondai

Catholicism took Atsuhiko Gondai to Europe. He was not raised in the Christian faith, he told me, but wanted to be a Christian and felt that Catholicism was special. Even before he was baptized, he began to play the organ at mass. Once he reached college age, he went to Sophia University for its Christian social activities, but since there is no music there, he attended and graduated from the Toho Gakuen College of Music in Tokyo. Not surprisingly, given Gondai's interest in Catholicism, he was influenced by Olivier Messiaen's writing. Nevertheless, as he put it, "every professor [in Japan] went to the Paris Conservatory if they studied abroad, so I didn't want to go to Paris" (Atsuhiko Gondai, personal communication, May 29, 2004.) Instead, he went to Freiburg because he had met Kraus Huber (b. 1924), a Swiss professor there who as a composer has "lots of Catholic mystic sense." Although Gondai found Freiburg to be too conservative a Catholic community, he spent two years there thanks to a fellowship from the German Academic Exchange Service (DAAD).

While attending the Donaueschingen Festival, Gondai met Philippe Manoury, director of the training course in computer music at IRCAM, who told him to come to Paris. This Gondai was able to do thanks to a scholarship from the Japanese Ministry of Culture—which was easy to get, he said, with a letter from Boulez. Liking Paris but needing to learn French as well as how to work with computers, he did the usually one-year course in 1992–94. Since his experience at IRCAM, according to Gondai, he has been listening to noise music and techno music, but he does not want to write computer music. What the IRCAM experience gave him was a different approach to writing music. Before, he didn't care especially about sound; writing was a creative game on a sheet. That is to say, really focusing on sound was new to him, as was the idea of starting with something small, almost microscopic (personal communication, May 29, 2004). So Gondai experienced an important shift of perspective in terms of his work as a contemporary composer. Since returning to Japan from France, however, Gondai's musical connections have been particularly good in Belgium, where his works are often performed.

The Cultural Capital of Success Abroad

One reality emerged as I continued my research in Japan: if a composer has established meaningful international connections—or, better, if he or she has achieved artistic recognition internationally, he or she will have accrued significant cultural capital, which is negotiable both abroad and at home in Japan. The same can be said for conductors and performers.

> Japanese people are very bad at finding good composers in Japan. Toru Takemitsu was not so famous in Japan; he became famous outside, then fame came back to Japan. Stravinsky found Takemitsu pieces at an NHK Library. The Nobel Prize is the same sort of thing. Kenzaburō Ōe was not so popular in Japan before he was "found" in foreign countries.
>
> So I hope it will be the same for [Japanese] children's songs. I hope children's songs will be recognized in the world. Japanese people don't appreciate these songs. If foreigners think they are good, then the Japanese people will recognize that they are good. (Mikio Itoh, personal communication, April 13, 1999)

> Music performers appear without fail in the section of the magazine that introduces internationally active people. Their success story is adorned with talk of winning competitions in the usual foreign countries, episodes showing very close relationships with well-known foreign teachers, being selected by foreign conductors and producers, and striking debuts in such renowned halls as Carnegie and Teatro alla Scala, and so on. Fussing over a person so recognized in another part of the world is nothing more than accepting another person's estimation uncritically. People who use their own discerning eye to recognize

> new talent, face the world with their own values, and have the mettle to say what they think—how many of them are there in Japan? (Fujiie 2006: 46)

After Bourdieu, I take cultural capital to be the recognition of a level of competence within Western knowledge and practice that lends the artist a kind of authenticity that, at home, can be translated into economic terms. Japanese composers who achieve that recognition have taken full advantage of the affordance of the environment of shared cultural space in Japanese musical modernity to participate fully in the global cosmopolitan culture of music. To illustrate the domestic value of international recognition, I shall take two notable examples. I begin not with a composer but with the conductor Seiji Ozawa, who has been important for Japan's international musical connections; I then move on to composer Toru Takemitsu.

It is common knowledge in Japan that Seiji Ozawa's success abroad enhanced—indeed, perhaps even permitted—recognition of him at home as a world-class conductor of note. As one individual who wished to remain anonymous put it, "Japan imported Ozawa's reputation from the United States and Europe; this is 'importation of distinction.' Japanese audiences want to see some fame in the biography on the program. When it comes to Japanese artists, we like those who have won an important international competition" (personal communication, April 15, 2005). Ozawa's path to that recognition is also well-known: in 1959, one year after graduating from the Toho Gakuen School of Music in Tokyo, he won first prize at the International Competition of Orchestra Conductors in Besançon, France. That led to an invitation from Charles Munch, music director of the Boston Symphony Orchestra, for Ozawa to attend the Berkshire Music Center (later Tanglewood); there, in 1960, Ozawa won the Koussevitzky Prize for outstanding student conductor. He then studied with Herbert von Karajan in West Berlin, where he drew the attention of Leonard Bernstein; that in turn led to his serving as assistant conductor of the New York Philharmonic for the 1961–62 season and again in the 1964–65 season.[14] In 1965, when he was appointed music director of the Toronto Symphony Orchestra, Ozawa began his long sojourn in North America: in Toronto until 1970, then music director of the San Francisco Symphony Orchestra from 1969 to 1976. His enduring international distinction was assured when he became music director of the Boston Symphony Orchestra in 1973; from 2002 to the present, he has served as its music director laureate.

Through the years, Ozawa has maintained connections with Japan, conducting the Japan Philharmonic Orchestra and founding the New Japan Philharmonic Orchestra and the Saito Kinen Orchestra.[15] He was invited to conduct at events having to do with contemporary music such as the Music Today 21 Summer Festival. (See below.)

Ozawa's successful international career has affected more than one Japanese composer. In Japan, for example, he "was a star" for the composer-to-be Atsuhiko Gondai from a young age. Gondai was born in Tokyo in 1965. Although neither of his parents was a musician, at age three or four he began to take piano from an aunt—not seriously, but with persistence. He did "solfège in general." Lots of his friends were learning notation, dictation, and sight-singing through piano instruction; that was the fashion then more than it is now, when children do more sports. Before school, Gondai also went to Toho music classes before he was even enrolled in elementary school. At the end of middle school, at the age of eleven or twelve, he encountered Messiaen's music—the *Quatuor pour la fin du temps*—on the radio. The result was sudden enlightenment. Thereafter, he said, he loved to listen to music on the radio and on TV, hearing Ozawa conducting French music, for instance. Being a conductor and composer became his goal, and he wanted very much to attend a music high school. His father needed convincing, which his mother managed to do. As for college, his father asked why he did not apply to Geidai, which is famous for the study of composition and furthermore, as a national school, is inexpensive. No, Atsuhiko wanted to go to Toho because Seiji Ozawa had graduated from there. Thus, for nine years, starting at the age of fifteen, Gondai studied music at Toho Gakuen, graduating in 1985 (personal communication, May 29, 2004).[16]

Similar to Ozawa as a conductor, Toru Takemitsu provides the single most prominent example of the process whereby for a Japanese composer international success precedes serious recognition at home. Although Stravinsky's discovery of Toru Takemitsu is among Japan's favorite musical stories, composers with whom I have spoken in Japan mark the 1967 premiere of *November Steps* by the New York Philharmonic Orchestra in New York City—conducted by Ozawa—as the turning point in Takemitsu's rise to fame. The premier was all the more dramatic a moment because the work had been commissioned by the orchestra for its 125th anniversary. Good newspaper reviews in America were translated into Japanese and picked up for publication in Japan. A performance of *November Steps* in Japan followed in 1968. From that point on, Takemitsu's career as a Japanese composer went from better to best, in terms of international recognition; he is the one best-known and most frequently performed Japanese composer—foremost in America and radiating out from there.[17]

CONNECTIVITIES WITHIN THE SHARED SPACE OF "CONCERT MUSIC"

The composer Atsuhiko Gondai, whose international experience has been in Europe, has a very practical, finance-oriented view on the importance of participating in the global cosmopolitan culture beyond Japan: "Japanese composers need to have connections with European performers and organizations because the market for contemporary music in Japan is small. For orchestra, solo, and chamber pieces, they need commissions" (personal communication, May 29, 2004). During my field research I heard a plethora of accounts of such connections—what kinds of connections are possible, how they came about, and what resulted from them. Below I offer examples of several kinds of connectivity, including musical trafficking to as well as from Japan and also the media through which contemporary Japanese music is disseminated. Opportunities for individuals are afforded by that quality of the environment of Japanese musical modernity of internationally shared musical knowledge and practices.

Through a Non-Japanese Conductor

A connection with an important non-Japanese conductor can be counted as among the most significant of connections for a composer. Minoru Miki's connection with Kurt Masur is one such instance. Masur was responsible for the Leipzig Gewandhaus Orchestra's commissioning of *Kyu-no-kyoku* (*Symphony for Two Worlds*), the third work in Miki's trilogy for Japanese instrument(s) and symphony orchestra.[18] The occasion was the bicentennial celebration of the orchestra, and the work was premiered in Leipzig in 1981 under Masur's baton.

Through a Theatrical Director or Producer

Connection with a theatrical director was another kind of connection that proved significant for Miki. His entrepreneurial advocacy of new works for Japanese instruments in the 1960s and 1970s (see chapter 4) attracted the attention of the English Music Theatre Company and ultimately led to the commissioning of Miki's opera *Ada, an Actor's Revenge*, with an English-language libretto by James Kirkup; it was premiered in London in 1979. That led to a long-term collaboration with the theater and opera director Colin Graham, which in turn led to Graham's commissioning of Miki's opera *Jōruri* for the Opera Theater of Saint Louis, where it premiered in 1985. Miki's seventh opera, *The Tale of Genji*, was also commissioned for the Opera Theater of Saint Louis; it premiered there in 2000.[19]

In somewhat similar circumstances, it was a producer who became important for Somei Satoh, who was in New York in 1983 on a grant from the Asian Cultural Council. After his return to Japan, Susan Feldman, a producer who lives in New York, heard a recording of his music produced in New York and subsequently sponsored a concert of his work in Brooklyn's well-known Arts at St. Ann (now renamed St. Ann's Warehouse) series. Subsequently she commissioned two "image operas" from Satoh, *Journey through Secret Time* (1983) and *Stabat Mater* (1987; Somei Satoh, personal communication, May 2, 2001). *Stabat Mater* was recorded on the New Albion label, as were a number of other works by Satoh.[20]

Through Non-Japanese Performers

To state that composers need connections with musicians who will perform their works might seem too obvious to need mentioning, but in fact it bears repeating, especially for composers of contemporary music. From Hitomi Kaneko I heard of an example of an important connection with a distinguished European performer. While studying at the Paris Conservatory, Kaneko became interested in writing for flute, so she went to the flute class of Pierre-Yves Artaud. In France she came into contact with many skillful players, she said, but Artaud was exceptional in promoting her. In 1997 he decided to perform her pieces *Miyabi*, for two flutes, at the Centre Pompidou and *Centrifuge*, for solo flute, in Bucharest (personal communications, May 17, 2002, and May 26, 2011).[21] Many other examples of non-Japanese musicians' promotion of Japanese works could be cited here; among them, the Arditti String Quartet stands out, with works in their repertoire by Akira Nishimura, Toshio Hosokawa, and Mamoru Fujieda, among others.

The kinds of connections I have mentioned thus far afforded composers opportunities for commissions and live performances, but those are just two among several potential opportunities. Another result of such connections is commercially available recordings.[22] As example, I have selected the somewhat complex saga of Mamoru Fujieda, whose international connections—particularly with the performer, composer, arranger, and record producer John Zorn—have been varied and fruitful for his musical career. In Tokyo in the mid-1980s Fujieda, then a young composer, was spending time engaging in free improvisation with various musicians, and Zorn became interested in his creativity. He asked whether Fujieda would be interested in releasing some of his compositions on his then-new label, Tzadik. Funding followed that totally covered recording, performance, and editing expenses for the CD *The Night Chant* (Tzadik CD TZ7003, 1995). After that, Zorn inquired about another CD, which would become *Patterns of Plants* (Tzadik CD TZ7025, 1997). "Three years ago," said Fujieda to me in February 2011, "when I met John in New York, I asked him why he released my music. He said he liked it and wanted to support a composer who continues to work in an independent and unique way."

Patterns of Plants is indeed unique. While circuitous, Fujieda's path to it compositionally exemplifies layers of international experiences and connections that can be brought together in such a fruitful way as recordings that disseminate the composer's music worldwide. Fujieda's path began when he went in 1982 to study with Joji Yuasa at the University of California, San Diego. There Fujieda learned that the composer Harry Partch had spent his last years in San Diego and that many of the instruments that he built had remained at San Diego State University; his interest in "the maverick composer" and the sounds of just intonation was piqued.[23] Meeting Lou Harrison increased Fujieda's interest in tuning, leading him to conclude that, for twentieth-century music, equal temperament was a trap. However, he wrote,

> I also found that it was not so easy to extricate myself from the constraint of equal temperament.
>
> You need a fair amount of courage and self-awareness to leave the equal temperament and try out alternative tuning systems as can be seen in the cases of Partch and Harrison. It seems to me that changing the tuning system would have a power that would affect not the exterior but the inward nature of the music. A new direction that just intonation suggests has a power to fundamentally convert the forms of music, the ways of listening to and producing sounds that modern Europe had cultivated so far. (Fujieda 2009: 141)

Returning to Japan in 1989, Fujieda determined to "start listening to actual intervals and sounds." A Macintosh computer hooked up to a Yamaha digital synthesizer was useful for training his ears to feel the intervals and sounds, but he knew that experience with real instruments was needed. Other international connections contributed to meeting that need.

> In the 1990s, I was appointed music director for the Interlink Festival sponsored by the American Embassy of Japan, and on advice from Lou Harrison, we invited Just Strings, an ensemble led by guitarist John Schneider. John submitted an idea of playing "In Just C," a just intonation version of "In C" by Terry Riley with Japanese musicians. I thought that the *koto* would be a proper instrument for the joint performance and immediately consulted with two *koto* players, Yoko Nishi and Miki Maruta. When we experimented with retuning the *koto* in just intonation, we recognized that the sound spontaneously started to resonate, vibrating the body of the instrument with its pure interval. The *koto* players were surprised more than I was. They told me that they had been using a tuner in equal temperament for playing modern or contemporary pieces for the *koto*. (Fujieda 2009: 132)

Fujieda then formed an ensemble, the Monophony Consort, of the two koto players and the *shō* (a type of ancient Japanese mouth organ) player Ko Ishikawa, for exploring possibilities of new tuning systems—just intonation on the kotos and the Pythagorean tuning on the shō.

Rather than proceeding to organize elements extracted from the tuning systems for compositional purposes, Fujieda looked for other unique possibilities. This leads us back to *Patterns of Plants*, which is featured on the two Tzadik CDs. For *Patterns of Plants*, Fujieda works with a botanist friend, Yuji Dogane, who, as he explained to me, "invented a way of recording electric vibrations from plants as the plants respond from moment to moment to the environment, gleaning data about electric currents, changes of waves—a recording like that of a brain wave from which various melodic patterns can be discerned and used creatively for music" (Mamoru Fujieda, personal communication, April 29, 2005).

> One day when I was listening to a series of sounds generated from slight changes of electric potential found in living plants, I intuitively felt that there must be beautiful melodies latent in them. . . . I patiently listened to the sonic result over and over again, which was produced from a synthesizer carefully tuned in some distinctive systems, while reproducing data of plant potentials. I found and picked out melodies

> that I liked one by one, relying on my own ears. The behavior of "finding out melodies" is similar to going into a deep forest, wondering [*sic*] there in search of beautiful flowers and rare butterflies. (Fujieda 2009: 144–45)

Between 1995 and 2008 Fujieda completed eighteen collections of *Patterns of Plants*, each consisting of four movements (Patterns A, B, C, D), and each differing in instrumentation and tuning. More *Patterns of Plants* will come, as well as other compositions that are derived from the collections. More recordings will come, too, among them, it is to be hoped, a third Tzadik CD featuring the distinguished San Francisco Bay Area pianist Sarah Cahill, who is an advocate of Fujieda's works.

Through Japanese Musicians Living Abroad

In the course of my field research I also came to understand how very important individual Japanese musicians who live abroad can be for Japanese composers. An critical aspect of this has been creating means for two-way "musical traffic," that is, for Japanese musicians to perform abroad, for Japanese musicians who are successful abroad to remain connected with Japan, and for non-Japanese performers and composers to experience music in Japan. To illustrate this, I return for a moment to Seiji Ozawa. Clearly cognizant of the value of international connections in Japanese musical modernity, Ozawa, as a transnational musician, has exerted considerable effort in Japan as well as abroad to facilitate connections for other Japanese musicians besides Takemitsu. Ozawa led the establishment in 1972 of a new professional orchestra—the New Japan Philharmonic—as a self-managed organization. In its subscription concerts the New Japan Philharmonic "has pursued a unique policy by featuring Ozawa and distinguished soloists from the world and by placing emphasis on works of the 20th century as well as vocal and theatrical music" (from the 2005 Annual Report of the Association of Japanese Symphony Orchestras). Twelve years later he founded another orchestra, this time bringing international attention to the school that gave him his musical training—Toho Gakuen, which for many decades has been considered one of Japan's finest music schools (see chapter 1).

> In September 1984, under the leadership of Seiji Ozawa and Kazuyoshi Akiyama, a unique group of more than 100 musicians from all over the world gathered together in Japan to perform a series of concerts in

> commemoration of the 10th anniversary of the death of Hideo Saito—[co-] founder of the Toho Gakuen School of Music, music educator and beloved teacher who instilled in their hearts the love of music. They were all at some point in their lives either students or teachers at the Toho School, and have since become soloists, chamber musicians and players of major orchestras in Japan, Europe and the USA. The concerts, held in Tokyo and [other locations in] Japan were world-class, the public response was overwhelming, and *the rest of the musical world could not but take notice.* Thus was the Saito Kinen Orchestra born out of a passion for music and a collective desire to perpetuate Mr. Saito's great legacy. (Oron 2002; emphasis added)

After this series of concerts, the Saito Kinen Orchestra received invitations from around the world, and as a result of these tours it was acclaimed as being of the highest caliber. Based on the reaction in Europe, the birthplace of Western classical music, a dream developed that until now had been unimaginable—"Japanese people one day transmitting western music back to its European homeland" (Ozawa, http://www.saito-kinen.com/e/about_skf/sko.shtml, accessed February 19, 2011).

The value of Ozawa's success in "transmitting western music back to its European homeland" cannot be underestimated, for it has been instrumental in making the global cosmopolitan culture a shared space for Japanese beyond as well as in Japan. That Japanese composers might share that space should by now, I think, be assumed rather than "striking," as the music critic James R. Oestreich put it in his *New York Times* commentary of December 10, 2010, on the Carnegie Hall festival of 2010—JapanNYC—for which Ozawa was the adviser: "What is striking in all of this is a strong presence, in some cases a dominance of Western composers, performers, instruments and musical styles. And that balance, or imbalance, accurately reflects modern Japanese musical culture."[24]

Beyond the obvious instance of Ozawa, any number of other examples of transnational Japanese musicians helping one another could be cited. For example, the important connection of Keiko Harada with the clarinetist Takashi Yamane developed quite unexpectedly, and the way it happened illustrates again the affordance of shared cultural knowledge and practices. Here I cite my notes from a conversation with Harada.

> Yamane-san lived many long years in Belgium, working as one of the main members of the Ictus Ensemble—one of the most important contemporary groups in the world today. He came back to Japan several

years ago to start his new life with the NHK Symphony Orchestra. He seems to be a very important person in the orchestra for the interpretation of contemporary repertoire. He is one of the most important performers for me, and one of the musicians who made it possible for me to be active in Europe.

The encounter with Yamane-san really came about by a curious coincidence. At the 1994 Akiyoshidai International Composition Seminar & Festival, my clarinet solo piece *Labyrinth IV* (1994) was to have been performed by the clarinetist of the Orchestre de la Suisse Romande, but he suddenly canceled. I heard about it while I was attending the Darmstadt Summer Course in Germany; I was twenty-six years old. The director of the Akiyoshidai seminar, [the composer] Toshio Hosokawa, was also there, and he had to search for a new clarinet player at once because the Akiyoshidai seminar was right after the Darmstadt course. He asked many people in Darmstadt and by chance met the director of the Ictus Ensemble, Lukas Pairon. He said "We have a great Japanese clarinet player, Takashi Yamane." As it happened, Yamane-san is from Yamaguchi Prefecture, where Akiyoshidai is, and he was due to be there until one day before my concert. A job with the Ictus Ensemble prevented him from staying to play my solo piece. He told me that he was "very sorry that I could not play your piece in spite of coming to Akiyoshidai, but I will soon try to play it in Brussels." And he did so, several months later. Soon afterward he contacted me, saying, "It was so good. By the way, do you have any other piece including clarinet?"

Thus our musical relationship began and members of the Ictus Ensemble heard my piece, and I really had a great time—almost eight years—with Ictus. My first portrait CD was with the Ictus Ensemble, as you may know. They are really artistic and unique musicians who love music. I have been in contact with them up to now and am still working with some of the Ictus musicians. (Personal communication, August 13. 2009)[25]

Through a Japanese Composer Who Is Well Connected Abroad

A fellow Japanese composer who is well connected abroad even if he or she is not living abroad can be of immense help in facilitating international connections for Japanese composers of contemporary music, either as individuals or as a group. This can be done in a variety of ways, as a few examples will illustrate.

The influence of Toru Takemitsu can be found in many a nook and cranny, one of which forms another important kind of connection—with music publishers. As mentioned in chapter 2, the German publisher Schott has a Japanese branch, Schott Japan, located in Tokyo. Though it is obvious from their catalog, I asked Manabu Kuretani, the president of Schott Japan, whom the company publishes. He reeled off a list of names: "Yuasa; Ichiyanagi; Takemitsu; one or two works of Takahashi Yuji; Mori [Kuroda], who assisted Takemitsu; Hosokawa; Gondai. We introduce works composed for Western instruments" (personal communication, June 7, 2004).[26] Among the composers on the list, Hosokawa and Gondai are noticeably younger, so I asked Hosokawa how he came to be published by Schott. "I met Takemitsu in Berlin in 1972, and he introduced me to Schott. That's how I got contracted" (personal communication, June 1, 2004). Schott sometimes undertakes to promote the works it publishes by sending new work to famous performers. Publication by any music publisher is hard to come by in Japan, and of all the possibilities in that sphere, publication by Schott is the surest way to become and remain connected internationally.

Toru Takemitsu was a seemingly indefatigable facilitator of major institutionalized efforts on behalf of contemporary music in Japan—and thereby on behalf of composers, including himself. Here I shall delve at some length into two different types of institutions—an urban festival and an international composition competition. The two institutions have in common what appears to me to be a very effective format: a complex of musical events that, on the one hand, provide an opportunity for international figures to experience the cosmopolitan nature of the Japanese audience for contemporary music. On the other hand, Japan can showcase the high level of expertise of Japanese musicians and composers to international figures, whose impressions will hopefully disseminate abroad abroad respect for the cosmopolitan Japanese culture. This is all based on shared musical knowledge and practices.

Through International Events Held in Japan

International music festivals like the Salzburg Festival were held in Japan for the first time after World War II, in the late 1950s. They were usually begun in celebration of the opening of a new concert hall. The inclusion of foreign culture was thought to be not only a sign of the prosperity that had come to the country with peace, but also a "tool of globalization" (Yamamoto 2004: 265), Such festivals reached a peak during the years of the economic bubble (1986–91). For instance, every summer from 1973 to 1992 a major festival for contemporary music was staged in Tokyo with the sponsorship of the Seibu Group; called Music Today, its artistic director was Toru Takemitsu.

This festival and others such as the Akiyoshidai International Contemporary Seminar and Festival (1989–99), led by Toshio Hosokawa as artistic director, were founded in the 1980s, when the Japanese government's policy of *kokusaika* (internationalization) was in play. These activities appear to be directly in line with one of the policy's statements—"becoming more modern and progressive by attaining international standards," hinting at the necessity for Japan to comply with international standards, which would lead to further Westernization. A second prong of the policy—"making Japan go international by exporting its culture," putting an end to "one-way culture"—referenced Japan's tendency to import foreign culture without exporting its own. The policy led to such moves as the establishment of the Japan Foundation, which finances foreign research on Japan in order to "diffuse knowledge of Japanese language and culture in the world" (Suter 2008: 44). The "culture" thus financed was "uniquely Japanese" (see chapter 4).

International in concept, the Music Today Festival featured music by both Japanese and non-Japanese composers and performers. Some Japanese composers candidly expressed the view that Takemitsu used the annual festival as an opportunity to invite many international contemporary music players to Japan and thereby establish relationship with foreign performers from whom he subsequently might get commissions. I often heard it said that through this festival Takemitsu also strengthened his connection with Seiji Ozawa while Ozawa was conductor of the Toronto Symphony.

The multiple events of the Festival each year are as follows.

> "Theme Composer" (a non-Japanese individual, to date)
>
> The artistic director of this portion of the Festival—in a numbered series called the Suntory Hall International Program for Music Composition—is a distinguished Japanese composer. From the twenty-third in 1999 to the thirty-fifth in 2011, the artistic director of the Festival was Joji Yuasa.

Events

- A lecture about the year's "theme composer" and his (so far all have been men) works.
- A concert of orchestral works by the theme composer (in 2010 Jonathan Harvey, for instance).
- A concert of chamber music by the theme composer
- "Music in Current": a concert of Japanese premiers of four to six 21st century chamber works by non-Japanese composers; and a concert of Japanese premiers of c. four 21st century orchestral works by non-Japanese composers
- Two concerts united by a topic: in 2004, "Master Works of the 20th Century" (by European composers); in 2005, "Vienna of the 20th Century" (orchestral and chamber music); in 2006, "A Portrait of a Patron—Paul Sacher" (works commissioned from European composers)

Unfortunately, the abundant opportunities offered by the Music Today Festival for Japanese composers and performers to make international connections have decreased considerably. A major reason has been financial, as resources have declined since the early 1990s, when the economic bubble burst. Although the international and contemporary-music nature of the Festival has remained intact in terms of programming, the number of international musicians invited to participate has declined. Now called the Music Today 21 Summer Festival, it is sponsored by the Suntory Foundation for the Arts and held annually in late August in Suntory Hall, one of Tokyo's oldest and best concert halls. Whereas international ensembles and performers were in ample supply in the Festivals before 1992, Japanese conductors, soloists, and ensembles (such as the chamber-music group Ensemble Nomad), now predominate, and local orchestras active in contemporary music are featured, such as the Tokyo Metropolitan Symphony, the Tokyo Symphony Orchestra, the Tokyo Philharmonic Orchestra, and the New Japan Philharmonic.

The percentage of international content in the total programming of the Music Today 21 Summer Festival has also decreased, albeit for a reason that was positive for Japanese composers. When the Akutagawa Prize for Composition was initiated in 1991 (see chapter 5), the prize concert, featuring the three finalists' pieces and the announcement of the winner, began to be included in the Festival. Since the competition is not an international one, its inclusion affected the amount of international content in the Festival as a whole. In 2010 the Gala Concerts Celebrating the Twentieth Anniversary of the Akutagawa Prize for Music Composition replaced the usual two topical concerts with slightly expanded offerings around the award itself for a total of four concerts featuring an impressive roster of relatively young Japanese composers.[27]

The Takemitsu Composition Award competition, on the other hand, continues to manifest Takemitsu's understanding of the importance of international connections. While the Akutagawa Prize continued the domestic focus of earlier Japanese competitions, the award established by Takemitsu only six years later is expressly *not* limited to Japanese composers.[28]

> Tokyo Opera City Concert Hall: Takemitsu Memorial, opened in September 1997, aims to stimulate creative activities in the field of music, following the principles of "prayer, hope, and peace" that the late artistic director Toru Takemitsu first set out. As a possible way of embodying these ideas with a view to their being a "Window on the Future," the international composition award named for Takemitsu continues to encourage the younger generation of composers who will shape the coming age by creating new musical works. (Guide to Three Seasons, 2005: 1)

Significantly for the purposes of making and maintaining international connections, most of the jurors to date have been non-Japanese.[29]

The marathon concert in which the finalists' pieces are judged is the climax of a noteworthy five-day event called the Composium. Its expressly international nature is stressed in the week's programs. I quote here from the program of the 1999 event.

> "Composition" plus "Symposium" equals "Composium," the contemporary music festival of Tokyo Opera City. Composium 1999 includes the final selection concert for the Toru Takemitsu Composition Award, a competition set up to encourage the creation of new musical works; an introduction to the creative world of Luciano Berio, judge for this year's Composition Award; and the appearance on our stage of several world-renowned performers on whom our Artistic Director, Toru Takemitsu (10/8/1930–2/20/1996), relied as interpreters of contemporary music. At this festival, we would like to try to break free from the image of contemporary music as something hard to understand or appreciate. We hope everyone will come and experience with us the lighthearted enjoyment of contemporary music at Tokyo Opera City.[30]

The annual "introduction to the creative world" of the judge of the year consists of three events that are paced through the five days in a format that will sound familiar from the "Theme Composer" portion of the Music Today 21 Summer Festival format: the viewing of an original biographical video about the judge, followed by remarks by him and an opportunity for the audience to ask questions; a concert of orchestral works by the judge (performed in 1999 by the Tokyo Metropolitan Symphony Orchestra, which also played the finalists' pieces in the culminating event); and a second concert featuring additional works by the judge. In 1999 this was titled "Best Album of Berio's Chamber Works" (in which the Japanese composer Ichiro Nodaira played piano). The "world-renowned performers" featured in 1999 were Paul Meyer, who offered an open master class for clarinet, and the Academia Bizantina.

The Composium also includes an event featuring a conversation with the finalist composers about their works as well as the climax of the week—the "competition concert" comprised of the finalists' pieces. The significant international professional experience that the entire Composium week provides for the five young composers from various nations who are hosted generously for a week in Tokyo is part of the Takemitsu Composition Award. This was articulated to me in tones of wonderment and gratitude at the post-prize concert reception in 2007. I had begun to congratulate but also commiserate with Andrea Protera, the young composer who had placed second, when he interrupted to exclaim at length how winning for him was secondary to the value of the experience—the opportunity to get to know Akira Nishimura, the judge, to learn from his fellow finalists, to have the opportunity to work with an orchestra on his piece—and such a fine orchestra!—and to experience the cosmopolitanism of contemporary Japan, about which he had had no idea, and so on (personal communication, May 25, 2008).

Protera's detailed remarks confirmed for me the sense I have repeatedly gotten of what I came to consider the most significant contribution of Takemitsu to his own culture other than the musical works he created: the active fostering of participation in that shared space of the global cosmopolitan culture of music that the international quality of this environment of Japanese musical modernity affords. The Takemitsu Composition Award is a major factor in keeping that vital for Japanese composers, musicians, and audiences. Through the distinguished international figures whom it brings to Japan not just to perform, but also to think about contemporary musical creativity together, it is also a means of claiming an illustrious cultural space for Japan in the global musical imaginary and reality.

All of the credit for the success of this significant venue for international connections for Japanese composers cannot be given to Takemitsu, of course. As an observer of the Composium for over a decade, I can speak to one particular remark in the 1999 program: "We hope everyone will come and experience with us the light-hearted enjoyment of contemporary music at Tokyo Opera City." I have experienced that spirit and attribute it to a number of factors. The number of events at which one might meet other audience members is one; the variety of events is another. The almost personal (but at the same time educational) tone of the presentations also contributes. To be noted particularly is the point that the Tokyo Opera City Cultural Foundation makes of setting admission charges low (by Tokyo standards) in order to attract a broad audience, made up in large part by young people, to contemporary music. The "light-hearted" enjoyment of contemporary music in the Plaza during those days was palpable. The audience at the final concert has grown each year I have attended, as more and more interest is piqued. For audience members, comparing the pieces (no matter what the nationality of the finalists) and predicting the outcome during the breaks between pieces can be just plain fun. This, it seems to me, augurs well for contemporary music in Japan, and I hope it continues.

Through an Individual Japanese Advocate

The final example of facilitation of international connections that I will mention is a unique institution of an entirely personal nature that is now creating the opportunity for Japanese composers to travel to America for the performance of new works: Music From Japan, the brainchild of Naoyuki Miura, a former cellist with the New York Philharmonic Orchestra and later vice president of Fukushima Tandaigaku (Fukushima Junior College), now retired. He is ably assisted in the United States by his wife, Mari Ono, the company's executive director and associate artistic director. Founded in 1975 as a personal project of Miura, Music From Japan is the leading presenter of Japanese music in the United States. Fine words of tribute were written in a review of CDs published by Deutsche Grammophon Japan by the composer Matthias Kriesberg:

> Ask an American who follows new music to name some contemporary Japanese composers, and you are likely to hear the name of Toru Takemitsu—and no one else. . . . [S]ince Takemitsu died in 1996, no other Japanese composer has similarly captured the attention of the new-music world in the United States.

> What little New Yorkers do know about Japanese contemporary music is largely a result of efforts by Naoyuki Miura. . . . His mission—to introduce a broad spectrum of Japanese composers and help secure a place for their work in the mainstream of American contemporary music—is paying off, he believes. (Kriesberg 2000: 30)

Music From Japan is marked by several features, one of which is a consistent format. Concerts are presented each year in New York City and elsewhere in the United States and subsequently in Japan as well where, as the composer Akira Nishimura describes it, "a sympathetic and very involved audience gathers each year" (personal communication, May 22, 2002). The two-day New York event is likely to include a lecture-demonstration by a traditional artist or a scholar that is pertinent to the program being presented that year, and also a closing forum wherein the featured composers of the year speak with American music critics and an audience. The purpose of all the events is to broaden the audience for Japanese music and encourage a dialogue between composers and musicians in Japan and the United States.

Programming, too, is consistent in that Miura presents a wide variety of both traditional Japanese and contemporary musics each on its own terms, and usually contemporary music for or including traditional instruments as well. Concerts always include world or American premieres of works by Japanese composers. The twenty-fifth-anniversary Festival 2000, for example, featured the American recital debut of the Tsugaru shamisen artist Chikuzan Takahashi II and the world premiere of Hikaru Hayashi's commissioned work *Lament*. Miura introduces each program in this manner:

> I am deeply satisfied to bring the 28th season of Music From Japan with its Festival 2003, a compelling program of 25-string koto recitals, six commissioned premieres, and much more. Keiko Nosaka's dedication to her instrument and to contemporary music resulted in the development of the 20 and then the 25-string koto, extending the range of sound of this instrument while retaining the koto's traditional tone. I look forward to sharing her artistry with audiences in New York City and across the United States.
>
> I am happy to welcome to Festival 2003 New York six young composers whose works are hot off the pen. I believe that they are part of the force which will lead Japanese music to new prominence in this century. (Miura 2003: 1)[31]

According to the 2011 program, after two decades of touring throughout North and South America, Central Asia and Japan, Music From Japan had presented nearly four hundred works, including seventy-one world premieres and fifty-nine commissions (for both Japanese and American composers). Over the course of thirty-six years, more than 130 Japanese composers have been showcased.

Naoyuki Miura assists Japanese composers in multiple ways. Perhaps most significantly, he himself commissions new works for presentation at Music From Japan; as of 2003 he had commissioned thirty-two pieces. At the thirty-fifth anniversary of Music From Japan, four of these works were heard in a subscription concert of the Tokyo Sinfonietta at the Tokyo Bunka Kaikan Small Hall. While Makoto Moroi's *Contradiction III—Landscape with Cloud* (1987) had been performed in Japan previously, three other works were Japanese premieres: Yoritsune Matsudaira's Concertino, for piano and sixteen instrumentalists (1989), Maki Ishii's *Ki-sho-ten-go*, for shakuhachi and six players (1998), and a new work, Hitomi Kaneko's *Almost Dusk*, for shō and string quartet (2009–10).

In addition, Miura and Ono manage to produce extraordinary events that position Japanese music in significant international cultural spaces. Three examples will illustrate the point. The U.S. premiere in 1995 of Toshiro Mayuzumi's opera *Kinkakuji* was co-produced with the New York City Opera as part of Music From Japan's twentieth-anniversary season. Then, in 1996, the gagaku ensemble Reigakusha was featured in conjunction with the Lincoln Center Festival '96. Reigakusha, led by Sukeyasu Shiba, a former member of the Imperial Household ensemble, performs both traditional repertoire and new works by Shiba and other composers (see chapter 4.) The twenty-fifth-anniversary season began with a commemorative tour to Central Asia in September 1999 and concluded with a celebration of Japanese orchestral music on November 9, 2000, at Carnegie Hall.[32]

Miura's efforts are supported by public funds from, among other entities, the Japan Foundation through the Performing Arts Japan program and the Agency for Cultural Affairs of Japan. The roster of foundation and private benefactors from whom he has obtained support is formidable. The consulate general of Japan in New York and the New York State Council on the Arts have also been helpful. This is a deeply international project on behalf of Japanese culture. Music From Japan as an organization received the Japanese Foreign Minister's Commendation in July 2007. Naoyuki Miura was awarded the Commissioner of the Agency of Cultural Affairs'

Award in December 2007 and the Sen Kayoko Award from the Soroptimist Japan Foundation in November 2010.

SUMMARY

In this chapter I have considered some ways in which Japanese composers have forged, utilized, and benefited from connectivities with those cultures with which they share musical knowledge and practices as a result of the systematic introduction of Western music in Japan. The Meiji-era borrowing of Western music (as it is often spoken of by non-Japanese observers) afforded composers the basis on which eventually to participate in the musical trafficking among global cosmopolitan cultures in the sphere of concert music, should a competent individual wish and manage to pursue that. Borrowing—that is, receiving something from somebody temporarily, with the expectation that it will be returned—turns out to be an apt word: what Japan borrowed it is now returning in the form of contemporary musical creativity.

The next chapter continues the discussion of the environment of shared cultural space for all Japanese, but the focus shifts from the international quality of the environment to the domestic. I will address the marginalized, separately organized Japanese musical traditions (generally referred to as *hōgaku*) within Japanese musical modernity and argue that, however ironic it might seem, the shared space in Western music affords composers and performer-composers possibilities for bridging the gulf that often exists between tradition and the modern in the sphere of music.

CHAPTER FOUR

Hōgaku in the Environment of Shared Cultural Space in Japanese Musical Modernity

SITUATING HŌGAKU IN PRESENT-DAY JAPAN

> Traditional music is in the graveyard. That was a Meiji decision. That was changed this year, but I don't expect it to make a difference. I really think that Japanese instruments are very spiritual. If students learn traditional music today, it doesn't have meaning. I think that shamisen, *biwa*, and *nōkan* are involved with religion—the sense of tradition and meaning behind it. We listen to them and hear the music, but we hear something else behind it. Koto less so. Today every student has forgotten that learning music is to learn *tao*—enlightenment. They look at technique.
>
> The biggest problem is that all are trained to the Western ear. Completely Westernized ears. If an American learns shakuhachi, koto, shamisen, it's the same. Ralph Samuelson is a good shakuhachi player, but he's American. Both Japanese and non-Japanese now stand in the same place; they share the same horizon.
>
> Can new music for traditional instruments have new meaning? I don't know, but I am trying. (Somei Satoh, personal communication, May 10, 2002)

The status quo articulated by Somei Satoh for the two musical systems of Japan can be demonstrated by contrasting two efforts to attract an audience to an event. First, Western concert music: for the opening of the fabulous new performance complex Tokyo Opera City Plaza, a small notice headlined "Seiji Ozawa to Open Hall for Takemitsu":

> In fewer than 100 days, on Sept. 10, the Tokyo Opera City Concert Hall, Takemitsu Memorial, will open with a concert of J. S. Bach's "St. Mat-

> thew's Passion BWV 244" by the Saito Kinen Orchestra, conducted by Seiji Ozawa. This was the wish expressed by the late composer, Toru Takemitsu, before he died a year ago.
>
> Ozawa will open the hall with the music that Takemitsu desired, and he will be joined by Christiane Oelze, Nathalie Stutzmann, Stanford Olsen, Piter Lika, John Mark Ainsley and Wolfgang Holzmair.
>
> The Tokyo Opera City Concert Hall is part of the large cultural complex in Hatsudai, which includes the New National Theatre. The hall is run by a private company and dedicated to classical music, while the New National Theatre is run by the national government and home to performing arts such as opera and ballet. The theater will be opened a month later. (*Asahi Evening News*, June 11, 1997)

The contrast with the great effort required to attract an audience to concerts of traditional music is striking. One April evening in 1999 I took the bite offered by an appealing flyer distributed at a concert of traditional music and headed for an event organized by Den no Kai, not really knowing what to expect. The poster read:

> The very familiar and well-known Den-no-Kai at Minami-Aoyama Mandala Live. Dining and drinking in a fancy atmosphere, enjoying exquisite shamisen performance and a lecture-demonstration of Kunitoshi and Testukuro.

The "fancy atmosphere" was a club in the upscale neighborhood of Minami-Aoyama, with seating for a hundred or fewer patrons. Below are comments on the evening from my field notes.

> A grand piano had been pushed to one side of a slightly raised stage. Clusters of chairs surrounded tiny tables on which to set a drink; as usual, the admission price to this "concert" included one drink. Attendees were mostly middle-aged, with a few young people sprinkled here and there. I was the only *gaijin* in evidence. We were all pretty dressed up, as one would be in a nice restaurant. What we were treated to was the introductory "concert" in a series of five devoted to gendai hōgaku (contemporary music for Japanese instruments) by the Den no Kai advocacy group of very talented musicians. It was an intimate lecture-demonstration, hosted by two shamisen players in fast-paced and jocular manner, following the order of the coming concerts on the flyer we had all seen. The opening piece of *nagauta shamisen* with

singing was followed by a mini-lecture, with the younger of the two shamisen players joking about the great practice required on traditional nagauta shamisen to master brief patterns, only to play them behind a lattice on the Kabuki stage. From the koto player (who would be soloist in a subsequent concert), there was explanation about the instrument, some history including mention of the old kanji character for "koto," then banter from the hosts about the koto player appearing in [a] kimono. "Best to be prepared for being photographed," she retorted as she dismissed them, to play a twentieth-century composition for koto. To prepare us for the concert of gagaku, out came a woman *hichiriki* player—dressed in a suit. We heard all about the hichiriki, then about the theme of spring for the concert to come, with a bit of playing. Next introduced by the duo was a group from Kyushu whose concert was being called *jiuta bomba—jiuta* being a shamisen-song genre for which a somewhat different shamisen is used than that introduced by the hosts. Conveniently (of course), there was a nagauta shamisen at hand so that we could see it compared it with the instrument for jiuta. The show ended with a great duet by our jokester-host-nagauta musicians. Even the least knowledgeable about traditional instruments in the audience were now ready for four more nights of music "new" to them—if the enticement worked.

Indeed, the audience for traditional music in contemporary Japan is relatively small. Those who attend are most likely to be relatives, friends or fans of the performers (even if famous), or students of the tradition.

Nevertheless, a common thread in the accounting by Japanese composers of their residence or travel abroad is that, while they might not have involved themselves with Japanese traditional music, their awareness of it—or even experience with it—as "a Japanese" is expected by non-Japanese. An example of this occurred in a closing forum that was part of the Music From Japan concert series held annually in New York City's Merkin Hall (see chapter 3). All the composers whose works had been presented sat onstage with American critics, who conducted a conversation in which persons in the audience might also participate. Recording from the audience in 2003, I came away with documentation of an exchange the likes of which I have witnessed a number of times during my research.

MICA NOZAWA: From five years ago, I started nagauta shamisen and singing because everyone asked me [about it while I was] abroad. At first,

I felt that Japanese music was irrational. Then I had to learn Japanese music; it was not natural to me. I have no desire to pursue the question of innate "Japaneseness" or spirituality. It's something you learn—Japanese music.

JULIA WOLFE: But don't you grow up hearing folk music or Japanese popular music? Isn't it in your ears?

ATSUHIKO GONDAI: Japanese folk songs . . . very rare to hear traditional music or popular or folk. If you don't look for it, you don't find it. Even though I was raised on European music, if I think of what defines me as Japanese, it's [the] Japanese language. When I compose I think in Japanese. That's my roots part.

SUNAO ISAJI: I'm the opposite. I listen to Japanese popular music [*kayokyoku*] often. Mostly I listen to samba. I almost never listen to European classical music. What drew me to Japanese music was Japanese and Chinese history. Why am I here? I'm borrowing Western music.

MISATO MOCHIZUKI: As I live in Paris, I don't hear Japanese music by coincidence. . . . If I take an idea from Japanese culture, it's not because I'm Japanese. I analyzed gagaku because someone said, "I don't find Japan in your music." But I'm not interested in it particularly. It's often said [to me], "You must have Japanese roots." But what's that? All of us are different.

TOSHIO SARUYA: Probably any composer younger than [his or her] sixties would not be telling the truth if they said they didn't hear *any* kind of [Japanese] music—it's on TV, [it's] out there. Therefore it's hard to say, "I wasn't influenced." I second what Gondai-san said. If you go to Tokyo, everything is there—the world. English in lights, Chinese words—part of city life. It is all very reflected in all of us. We are able to select, pick and choose, and build an individual voice.

ATSUHIKO GONDAI: Contrast my thinking with Isaji's "borrowing European music." I select European music.

TOSHIO SARUYA: Me too! Forget the words. It's a difference in choice, but choosing is the same.

KEIKO HARADA: I am also choosing. I have never had training in any Japanese traditional music. I'm now finding points in common between European/American and Japanese traditional music. The common characteristic of Japanese traditional music and Western music is that the players have had very strict training, practice, and discipline from childhood. Because of that, I think both Japanese and Western music players can play the same music together. Therefore I have been making a lot of music.

That there is a choice is the quality of the environment that I pursue in this chapter. Because of the persistence of the small, serious population of persons who pursue and thus preserve the various customs of traditional music, the environment of Japanese musical modernity encompasses the coexistence (however skewed the balance) of two deeply cultivated, historically grounded complexes: traditional Japanese aesthetics, forms, and instruments alongside Western aesthetics, forms, and instruments. That quality of the environment affords composers a plethora of locally grounded possibilities for creative choices. Significantly, because performer-composers—like all Japanese—partake of the shared cultural space created by Western music, they as well as composers share that condition of possibility for creative choices.

CHRONOLOGICAL TRACKING

In this chapter I begin by contextualizing that affordance of choice from the second decade of the twentieth century through the interwar years, with emphasis on individual composers and a performer-composer and the political situation in which they worked. Because so much changed in subsequent decades, I continue then only to approximate chronological tracking, organized by focusing first on performers, then on performer-composers.

The Second Decade of the Twentieth Century through the Interwar Years

By 1915 school songs reflecting Japanese traditional music had all but disappeared from the Ministry of Education songbooks. Also by that time, Japanese "composers" were composers in the Western sense of the word, not the performer-composers of the traditional music sphere. The early composers Kiyomi Fukii (1899–1944) and Kosaku Yamada (1886–1965) used Japanese folk-song melodies in otherwise Western music, and in 1918 a group of composers began to write children's songs with artistic intent (*dōyō*)—some in a superficial syncretic style—for consumption outside the school context (see chapter 6). But not until the interwar years was any but the most superficial attention paid to indigenous music.

For scholars of Japan, the interwar years begin with Japan's participation in the Paris Peace Conference in 1919; they extend either to 1929 (the beginning of the Great Depression); to 1931 (when the Japanese invaded Manchuria); or to 1937 (the beginning of the second Sino-Japanese War). Encompassed in that period was the Taisho era (1912–26) and the beginning of the Showa, witnessing on the one hand a desire on the part of some intellectuals (during the Taisho era) for greater democratization than that permitted by the Meiji era's forced modernization processes, and on the other hand the rise of radical imperialist nationalism and a strong military in an ostensibly emperor-centered system.

In the Taisho era, as the Japanese music critic Kazushi Ishida has put it, "the development of capitalism and the movement of so-called Taisho Liberalism motivated the further growth of Western music in Japan" (2002: 224). In this Kosaku Yamada played a central role, establishing what is generally recognized to have been the first professional orchestra in Japan—the Tokyo Philharmonic Society Orchestra, which lasted less than a year—and making pioneering efforts in the spheres of opera and ballet as well.[1] Nevertheless, "composers began to appear who were aware of the problem of how to express national and traditional elements of Japan" (Ishida 2002: 225).

At the beginning of the Showa era, in the 1930s, Japan was gradually moving toward World War II.

> In this context, the power bloc and those intellectuals who were disillusioned with the West [i.e., the forces of modernization] sought a distinctive Japaneseness in "indigenous" theories which could explain Japanese society. . . . A romanticized and narcissistic "Japanese essence" was systematically sought in order to contrast it overtly and covertly to the idealized West. (Iwabuchi 1999–2000: 4–5)

This was not a new idea. In the late nineteenth and early twentieth centuries, in order to cement the power structure of the Meiji era, an ideological promulgation had been invoked positing "the continued existence of national unity and morality throughout all periods of Japanese history, thereby giving birth to the concept of a historically transcendent 'national essence' (*kokutai*)" (Wakabayashi 1998: 95). Now, in the 1930s, as a reaction to the severities of the modernization process and the imposition of Westernness in Japan, a genre of literature called *nihonjinron* (discussions on being Japanese) emerged that consisted of theories of Japaneseness and specifically the purported uniqueness of the Japanese. Most works were based on the construction of binary oppositions between Japan and the West, particularly the United States. Ironically, during this interwar period, Western music performed with Japanese practices (instrumental ensembles in department stores combining movements of symphonies in a program with Argentine tangos, for example) was taking deeper and deeper root. A contradictory process was going on at the same time of appropriating from the West while at the same time challenging the cultural hegemony of Western practices.

Japan would better the West at its own game, not simply militarily but culturally as well. In cultural terms Japan had a distinct advantage, for it could place two forms and senses of Japanese culture—the traditional and the modern—into the service of its imperialistic ambitions: the traditional forms, whose authentic exoticisms were valued in the West, could help to smooth over international tensions in the comity of nations by demonstrating a common cultural bond with the East, while the modern forms, built upon the melding of Japanese content and Western techniques, could serve as models for the modern, hybrid Asian culture that was then developing under Japanese rule (Pacun 2012: 4).

In the context of the reevaluation of Western modes of thought, some composers were inclined to look inward musically. Most notably, a composers' group was formed in 1930—Shinkō Sakkyoku-ka Renmei (the Newly Rising Federation of Composers)—not for ideological reasons, but to foster creativity and increase its members' financial prospects. Guidelines encouraged all sixteen members to explore the following traits of traditional Japanese music:

1. a wide range of possibilities for melody and harmony, by using combinations of scales and modes found in traditional music, particularly the minor and pentatonic to emphasize Japanese qualities;
2. the development of Japanese tonal systems suitable for primary pentatonic and modal melodies, structured after the type of quartal harmonies derived from the vertical tone clusters of the shō in gagaku;
3. the use of linear, quasi-polyphonic textures similar to that of *sankyoku* and *jiuta* [chamber] ensemble music; and
4. a creative use of instrumental color (as cited in Herd 2004: 44–45).

Herd (2004) focuses on four of the sixteen members whose creativity and respect for traditional arts, she suggests, were particularly influential on post–World War II composers—Yasuji Kiyose, who gathered rural Japanese material; Shukichi Mitsukuri, who developed an original music theory as a possible alternative to Western tonal harmony;[2] Fumio Hayasaka, who explored gagaku and other Asian traditions in a benign pan-Asian spirit; and Akira Ifukube, who patterned his unusual style on the ethnic music and dances of the Ainu people of his native Hokkaido. Herd (1987) also devotes a great deal of attention to the works of Yoritsune Matsudaira (1907–2001), one of the founding members of the Newly Rising Federation of Composers. Well versed in European music, interested (like others of his generation in the 1930s) in Japanese folk song, and also deeply knowledgeable about gagaku, one can imagine his having taken a strong role in formulating the group's guidelines for creating music resonant with both Japanese and Western modernist musical sensibilities.

Galliano, too, points to this group's significance among Japanese composers of the period as unwitting participants in a political climate wherein culture and conquest were closely identified.

> The compositions were well constructed and showed a good knowledge of Western techniques and maturity, . . . a big advance on the music of the earlier Taishō period. More than just being generically modern the music of this group reflects each composer's search for a new compositional basis on a social as well as a musical level and the evolution of a substantial body of work that incorporated Japanese elements in a more natural manner. This repertoire was thoroughly exploited in the endless patriotic radio broadcasts of new Japanese music and was performed at public events during the darkest period of nationalist fervor, without regard for the composers' wishes in this respect or how successfully the Japanese elements were worked into the music. (Galliano 2002: 82)

Enter into this environment of the 1930s the counterpart of the composer—the performer-composer of the traditional music sphere. The most pertinent way of doing that is to understand the career of Michio Miyagi (1894–1956), who steered koto music into Japanese musical modernity. All sources with which I am familiar agree with Kiyoko Motegi's assessment: "It may . . . be said that the true beginnings of *composition for traditional instruments* commenced with the activities of Michio Miyagi and his performer-composer contemporaries of the Shin Nihon Ongaku (New Japanese Music) movement in the 1920s and succeeding years" (Motegi 1999: 28; emphasis added).

Michio Miyagi was born in the Meiji period, when the new school system and its curriculum of Western music were being widely institutionalized; but he was not educated in that system. As a boy in Kobe, a center of foreign trading companies, Miyagi grew up hearing international music. Blinded by disease as a child, it was decided that he would take up music—koto and shamisen—music being one of very few options for the blind. In 1905, when Miyagi was eleven, his father moved to Korea to work, leaving the boy to support the family left behind in Tokyo by teaching what little he had learned in three short years of traditional instruction. Within two years, however, at age thirteen, Miyagi too had to move to Korea to support the entire family; there he taught himself to play shakuhachi, presumably to get more students among the Japanese men living there. He heard Western music through friends, band concerts, and imported recordings. Residing beyond the constraints of the traditional music practices (the hierarchical iemoto system) in which he would have had to continue had he remained in Japan, the young man began to compose music, even a little nontraditionally, that is, leaning toward Western music.

At the age of twenty-one Michio Miyagi returned to Tokyo as a professional musician. In 1919 in that increasingly cosmopolitan city, he hazarded a recital that included his own compositions. Encouraged by the way his works were received by enthusiasts of Western music, he began a period of intensive study of European music theory, composition, violin, and piano. An enthusiastic, creative experimenter, he was willing to try almost anything—even plunky duple or triple meter in lieu of flowing unmetered rhythm and melody harmonized with functional chords (homophony rather than solo or heterophony), even if it meant completely forsaking music funded from the tradition in a number of new compositions. Few survived the test of time; the most successful of his fusion pieces have been *Haru no umi* (*Spring Sea*) and *Aki no shirabe* (*On Autumn*); in the latter, while the form was that of the traditional *tegotomono*, with its equal emphasis on song and instrumental sections, and the melody followed the Edo-period *Miyako bushi* scale (C–D<flat>–F–G–A<flat>–C), the vocal part seems heavily influenced by Western music. This is the first composition in which Miyagi demonstrated his familiarity with Western canon texture (Kamisango 1981).[3] Modernizing the instrument itself, in 1921 he created a larger koto with seventeen strings rather than the traditional thirteen; it was a "bass" koto meant to function with the thirteen-stringed koto as a cello would function with a violin.[4]

In 1924 the thirty-year-old artist accepted a proposal from the equally ambitious shakuhachi performer-composer Nakao Tozan (1876–1956) to ally himself with the Tozan *ryū*, which, from the time of its origin in Kansai sometime after 1896, was developing into a large nationwide organization. This alliance helps explain the rapid dissemination of Miyagi's compositions and also explains the prominence of the shakuhachi in many of them.

Perhaps most important, Miyagi was able to forge a second crucial alliance in 1930 when he was appointed to the faculty of the Tokyo School of Music, the historical seat of European musical instruction in Japan.[5] Not only did this constitute an official emplacement of traditional music in the infrastructure of music education (see chapter 1), but it brought performer-composers into the shared cultural space as creative agents in musical modernity. In response to the school's well-trained students and large ensembles (both orchestra and chorus), Miyagi composed many syncretic pieces of a startling nature from the perspective of traditional koto music—koto accompanying homophonic compositions sung in bel canto vocal style, even koto in large ensembles and with chorus. This he would be active in doing throughout the war years and beyond. Works resulting from his experimentation with the fusion of Western and Japanese musics were dubbed *shin nihon ongaku* (new Japanese music). Although a hierarchical ryū would form around Miyagi beyond the academy, his success as a creative individual was extremely important in establishing a means by which the two spheres of music might fruitfully intersect.

In her analysis of the creative output of composers in the 1930s, Herd finds significant positive developments during that turbulent period. "Reactionary politics," she writes,

> forced composers to come to terms with the relevance and consequences of their music. . . . Without it, there would have been no transformation from the identification with Other to the discovery of self. . . . Japanese composers active during the interwar years, when asked to choose between East and West, devised a dualistic format based on the accepted practices of Western art music that allowed for differences in local content based on personal interpretations of national identity. The safety of a flexible but protective coating of Western art music allowed them to freely move outside of traditional frames and expectations [now those of Western art music] to discover new forms of mutual belonging. This development heralded the first phase of what is now a time-honored tradition in the eclectic world of modern Japanese art and mu-

> sic: the continual interplay between local traditions and global ways of framing knowledge. (Herd 2004: 55–56)

Music was brought into the political space of Japanese imperial ambitions for control of all of East Asia (and beyond) in another way, as well—by the musicologist Hisao Tanabe, whose knowledge of the history of gagaku permitted him, in appearances in Korea and China, to position Japanese music as the matrix of all Asian musics. Shuhei Hosokawa encapsulates Tanabe's rationale:

> *Gagaku* is Japanese music's badge of supremacy, a distillation of Tang [Chinese] music, which was in turn an amalgam of Eurasian instruments and sound. Japanese *gagaku* thus crystallizes the "essence" of all the East-Asian cultures—just as contemporary Japanese culture, thanks to its incorporation of (rather than subordination to) the West, has become wholly universal. . . . It is Japan's cultural debt to China which legitimated her expansion to Korea, China and beyond and formed her East-Asia (*tōa*) as a political and cultural bloc. Therefore imperialism and nativism were complicit rather than contrastive.
>
> One of the forms of this imperial "interaction" was the "repatriation" of *gagaku* to China, Korea and Manchuria. By doing so, Tanabe supposed that a specifically Japanese national/imperial symbol could be converted into an East-Asian one. (Hosokawa 1998: 16–17)[6]

Given this positioning of gagaku, it is not difficult to understand the potential for tension or uncertainty with regard its being invoked by composers in the decades following World War II.

The Lead-Up to World War II and the War Years

In his accounting of composers in the first twenty years of the Showa era, that is, before and during World War II (1926–45), Ishida enumerates quite a number of groups that formed, including the Newly Rising Federation of Composers (which in 1935 changed its name to Nihon Gendai Ongaku Renmei [the Japan Society for Contemporary Music]), on which Herd (2004) focuses. All of the groups, Ishida asserts, contrasted with composers from the older generation represented by Kosaku Yamada. All—particularly Yasuji Kiyose, Akira Ifukube, and Fumio Hayasaka—showed the influences of (especially French) musical modernism and nationalism. Clearly, musical activity was accelerating. Without mentioning politics, Ishida recounts the input into Japanese musical culture of composers from Europe, the establishment of a new symphony orchestra (which would endure beyond the war) and of composers' *konkur* (competitions) on the European model, as well as NHK radio broadcasting activities.

To those who are looking for it, however, politics leap out in Ishida's account: "The apex of this compositional activity in the first half of the Showa era came in 1940, when a number of commemorative concerts were held for the Japanese year 2600" (Ishida 2002: 227). With imperialism in control at the time, the celebration of the ascent to the throne of the first Japanese emperor, Jimmu, in 660 BCE naturally invoked Japan's history, as do the titles of the compositions enumerated by Ishida. Notably, the compositions were symphonic, not for Japanese instruments: "Many [other] new orchestral pieces invoking patriotism were performed [in the same year], [and composers were] especially encouraged by the government to culturally boost national prestige" (Ishida 2002: 227). Although imperialism was directed against "the West" (and other Asian cultures) and the rhetoric of Japanese uniqueness was the order of the day, it was a Western musical modus that carried the message of the national spirit and was again working for the nation.

During World War II composers' collectives were disbanded. Some composers inevitably cooperated with the government, but others, such as Yoritsune Matsudaira (1907–2001), a charter member of Shinkō Sakkyoku-ka Renmei, stopped composing altogether. In an interview with Herd in 1984, he explained: "During that time, all of Japan was completely involved in the war, and composers weren't really musicians. They were soldiers. It was nearly impossible. I couldn't write at all because there was no love or inspiration" (Herd 1987: 148).[7]

Immediately After World War II through the 1960s

It is important to keep in mind that, during and after World War II, the rhetorical device of nihonjinron served the Allied side as well. Ironically, the American anthropologist Ruth Benedict's influential study of Japan, *The Chrysanthemum and the Sword* (published in 1946, during the U.S. occupation of Japan), persuasively endorsed Japanese otherness, which could be summed up as Japan's "unique culture." This time, the national character of Japan was being endorsed not by nationalist ideologues, but by an American intellectual who had never been to Japan. (Her study involved

Japanese prisoners of war in a U.S. detention camp.) Iwabuchi describes the interdependency of nihonjinron:

> The political nature of Nihonjinron became clearer in the 1950s when Japan was selected as an honored student of the American version of modernisation in the Cold War Era. Japan's modern history was presented as a positive model of capitalist development in opposition to the Communist bloc. . . . Japan's traditional values and structures and its modern history were for the first time positively defined and valued by the West. (Iwabuchi 1999–2000: 6)

Given the politicized situation in Japan that had obtained since the Meiji era, it is not surprising that the question of Japaneseness in music is a complex one. Performer-composers have been in much easier circumstances than have composers in that the Japaneseness of the music of the former is not in question politically. Although performer-composers have been marginalized, no one has disputed their right to draw on tradition as they wish. Decreasing that marginalization has been the challenge for them, and developments from the immediate postwar era forward have, I think, been instrumental in that cause.

After the war, instruction in hōgaku continued at the Tokyo Music School, where Miyagi Michio was on the faculty. Self-identifying as "Miyagi's last student," the respected koto player Teiko Kikuchi told me that she studied at the school (later, Geidai) because "at the time it was the only school at which one could study koto and other Japanese music" (personal communication, May 4, 2001).[8] However, the institution itself changed in 1949, merging that august institution with another—Tōkyō Bijutsu Gakkō (the Tokyo School of Fine Arts), which had also been founded in 1887. The merger created the institution that until 2008 would be known in English as the Tokyo National University of Fine Arts and Music.[9]

Miyagi's instruction at Geidai had significant results beyond the institutional emplacement of hōgaku into the shared space of Western music in the environment of musical modernity. Hōgaku students in a modern conservatory—each associated even there with the ryū of their teacher—might be inclined to push at the constrictions of the hierarchical iemoto system. Not surprisingly, some students were interested in generating new repertoire, as Miyagi had been doing. This they proceeded to do by communicating with students in the composition section (meaning Western music composition, of course) and with willing established composers such as

Yoshiro Irino (1921–1980). As my conversation with Teiko Kikuchi shows, interests led into other non-ryū directions as well, including the establishment of an independent performing ensemble, Hōgaku Yonin no Kai.

BW: Why did you form Yonin no Kai?

TK: In 1957 we [Sumiko Goto, Akiko Tsuchihashi, Kitahara Tozan and Kikuchi] went to a *konkur* together where we met folk musicians . . . a *konkur* of folklore and music.[10] We went to Russia, to Moscow for the World Contest of Folkloric Traditional Instruments. Four of us joined that contest and won a Gold Medal.

BW: Does Yonin no Kai still exist? I recently saw a CD by Yonin no Kai on the Ocora label. All classic pieces—Yaegoromo and others.

TK: The name is still used, but the people are different. I left it in 1975. Yazaki-san and I left together.

BW: Why did you leave?

TK: We had a different idea. One reason was that I wanted to study more about the seventeen-stringed koto. Before I left Yonin no Kai, the seventeen-stringed koto was not approved of as a solo instrument. Yazaki-san, who plays koto and shamisen, started creating works. We were trying to contribute to the development of modern Japanese music. (Personal communications, May 4, 2001, and August 30, 2012)

Through the years beyond her association with Yonin no Kai, Teiko Kikuchi became recognized as the musician who turned Miyagi's seventeen-stringed koto from an accompanying to a solo instrument.

In addition to widening opportunities for performers on hōgaku instruments by means of the formation of ensembles, an additional format was available in musical modernity—the solo recital. If an artist presented a solo recital on a newly solo instrument, there simply had to be new repertoire. Teiko Kikuchi involved herself in the commissioning of a number of pieces. Apparently there was a learning curve not only for herself but also for the composers.

BW: When did you start to commission new pieces?

TK: Forty years ago. I have asked many composers. At the beginning Michio Mamiya [see below] and Sumiko Hirai.

BW: Who else?

TK: Shin-ichiro Ikebe, a younger person [*Kageru* (1979, revised 1994)], Takashi Yoshimatsu [*Nabari* (1992)], Michio Kitazume, Ryohei Hirose, and Teizo Matsumura.

BW: Please tell me more about that.

TK: In the beginning, around forty years ago [while she was still with Yonin no Kai], I would explain all about the instrument to them, and we studied and learned together.

BW: Did composers come to you?

TK: Yes, they came to learn about the koto. Before that, all the composers learned only Western music, so they didn't know about Japanese instruments. But there were some composers who wanted to write for Japanese instruments. I explained [what was needed] to them. Then they made music, but some music we couldn't play because they didn't know [how to compose idiomatically for the instrument]. But eventually they learned how to make music for Japanese instruments. After that, I asked them to create pieces for me. (Personal communication, May 4, 2001)

Indeed, as Teiko Kikuchi stated, in the postwar period "there were some composers who wanted to write for Japanese instruments." Although the majority of Japanese composers welcomed the return of cultural and musical exchanges with foreigners, of the sort that had benefited composers from the Meiji through the early Showa eras (see chapter 3), composers' and audiences' interest in Japan's indigenous musics grew. The critic Hidekazu Yoshida articulated two reasons for this change:

> Owing to the changes in society after the war, the trend towards appreciation of [Japanese] culture, the emergence of music lovers, the development of the mass communication media and the growing interest among salaried workers for the appreciation and performance of art rose to a phenomenal level. There is no comparison in the prewar era. This awoke in the Japanese audience the desire for music which is closer to them [culturally].
>
> Japanese musicians realized that a European music, which until then they had believed to be the only type of music that fulfilled their needs, was actually closely linked in structure to the history and society of Europe. This gave rise to their self-reflection that a mere acquisition of technique would not enable them to really create such music on their own. (Yoshida 1959: 5, as cited in Herd 1987: 98–99)

In this cultural climate, the prewar composers who had sought a national style—but whose nationalism was not to be confused with the conservative, militaristic variety of the war years—continued to be influential and successful, albeit to a lesser extent than in the prewar era. Fumio Hayasaka, for instance, turned primarily to writing music for the burgeoning film industry. Returning to composing in the postwar period, Yoritsune Matsudaira was the first postwar Japanese composer to achieve international recognition when his Theme and Variations for Piano and Orchestra (1951) was awarded the International Society for Contemporary Music Prize (Herd 1987: 149). Connected throughout his entire professional life with developments in European music and also possessed of deep knowledge of gagaku, Matsudaira continued to experiment with the resonances between the two. The main theme of the Theme and Variations for Piano and Orchestra is taken from the canonical piece *Etenraku*, and all of the variations are related to gagaku in ways that go beyond melodic similarity.[11] Ironically, Matsudaira's works have been received better in Europe than in Japan. His publisher was the Italian firm of Survini Zerboni.

In the first fifteen years after the end of World War II, two infrastructural institutions of Japanese modernity—the Tokyo School of Music and NHK, the government-supported Japan Broadcasting Corporation—fostered new music that drew on tradition, albeit in different ways. NHK took a very direct approach with new initiatives. In 1947 a research project was undertaken in the ryū of the hōgaku sphere for the purpose of offering a series of broadcasts that provided new performance possibilities for performers from the different ryū. Then, in 1950, a competition for hōgaku music (Hōgaku konkūru) was set up with the cooperation of NHK, the Ministry of Culture, and the Tokyo newspaper *Mainichi Shimbun*. Again we see connectivities of the infrastructures of Japanese modernity affording opportunities not only for Western music–trained composers such as Makoto Moroi (b. 1930), but also, notably, for performer-composers such as Seiho Kineya (1914–1991). Every year until 1963 one prize was given for a hōgaku performance and one for a hōgaku composition. The aim was to give hōgaku performers a broader outlook on music, partly through contact with Western music (Galliano 2002: 239 and n. 54). New works in this period were given the rubric of *shin hōgaku* (new traditional music; Yamakawa 1984: 21).

That those composers involved in the project had widely varying musical backgrounds is amply illustrated by Makoto Moroi and Seiho Kineya. Moroi started composing shortly after the war and is associated with the introduction of European avant-garde music to Japan (e.g., twelve-tone technique, serialism, aleatory music, and computer music). He became interested in Japanese traditional music suddenly—while listening to a performance by the shakuhachi master, Takeyasu Sakai, with whom he then worked for many years (Galliano 2002: 238 n. 53).[12] Seiho Kineya learned shamisen from his father, who was the head of a ryū of nagauta shamisen. As expected in the family, he became a professional performer. In 1957, however, he stopped performing to devote himself to composition. He was respected for his deep knowledge of various kinds of Japanese traditional instruments, dance, and, as one would expect from his nagauta background, Kabuki.[13]

The entire country felt a sense of urgency to rebuild after the devastation of the war. The American occupation ended in April 1952, and strong conservative figures in music lost control of Japan's musical culture. With composers determined to reconnect internationally but on their own terms, creative interests went in several directions. Younger composers found themselves in an extraordinary cultural climate and circumstances—living in that shared cultural space created through the Meiji and Taisho eras and afforded a plethora of locally grounded possibilities for creative choices within the two deeply cultivated, historically grounded complexes of traditional Japanese and Western musics. In what follows I examine some of those choices and the motivations for them, sampling those who reached into both wellsprings of knowledge to engage in among the most difficult of all creative tasks—the aesthetically and formally successful synthesis of contrasting concepts and practices. Although a number of composers' groups formed as before (see Ishida 2002), individual members of newly formed groups would find their own stylistic way.

In her thesis, Herd reads as a "neo-nationalist movement" the musical efforts of those composers whose personal consciousness of Japaneseness was strong. So varied was the music that emerged, however, that the notion of a movement seems to me too cohesive for an understanding of this moment. Furthermore, the word "nationalist" is so fraught that its use can be misleading. I prefer to see this creative activity as an instance of Japanese composers availing themselves of a choice offered them by their cultural history. Some chose to cite Japanese musical materials in ensemble and solo works for Western instruments, while others incorporated Japanese concepts and practices in more conceptual ways in works for Western instruments.

Inspired by the work of Béla Bartók, in 1953 a group of three composers formed Yagi no Kai (the Goat Group). The composer Hikaru Hayashi

(b. 1931) expressed his personal motivation in an interview with Herd: "I don't intentionally add traditional elements to my music, but because I am Japanese and have been obviously influenced by Japanese music and culture—not necessarily just tradition, but popular as well. I naturally tend to use these in my music" (cited in Herd 1987: 102). Michio Mamiya (b. 1929) wrote in notes to the score of *Jū-yon no Nihon no uta* (*Fourteen Japanese Folk Songs*): "[Blending folk music with Western style composition methods] is both my own personal method of preservation of tradition and at the same time [a way] of developing a new Japanese language of music based on the musical heritage of our common people. The clarity and tenderness of spirit are the most important in the music. I have constantly endeavored to re-create within myself this spiritual clarity" (cited in Herd 1987: 116).[14] Ishida described the efforts of Yagi no Kai as "advancing the national independence and the connection of music with society" (2002: 229).

Another group that formed around the same time—Sannin no Kai (Group of Three Men, 1953), made up of Yasushi Akutagawa (1925–1989), Ikuma Dan (1924–2001), and Toshiro Mayuzumi (1929–1997)—was considerably more controversial, for several reasons. One was their modus operandi. According to Herd, "these three enterprising men openly promoted their own music and hired full orchestras and choruses to perform in large concert halls at their own expense. At the time, a discussion arose in the music world as to whether it was wise for younger composers to be entrepreneurial and aggressive when promoting their music. Classical musicians in Japan, historically, had always had to self-promote. However, in the past, they were more subtle and anonymous amid larger numbers of their peers who were members of the same contemporary music groups" (1987: 131).

Another reason for controversy had to do with the ways in which two members articulated their interest in Japaneseness, that is, in terms of prewar political stances. Ikuma Dan did not subscribe to the combined identity and dichotomy of "Japan" and "the West"; rather, he associated Japan with "oriental" and "Asian," a way of thinking that for some invoked the "Eastern/pan-Asian" discourse that had been so strong in the imperialist war years, when Japan intended to control all of Asia. Dan wrote as much forthrightly:

> The problem, as I see it, is profound and complex. It is not enough to write Japanese-sounding compositions using Western forms and harmonies. . . . The purpose of the composer, first of all, must be to write good music, and this we are not likely to have through mere re-

> arrangement of traditional music for Western instruments. Something new, but at the same time fundamentally Japanese, must be created.
>
> Musicians in Japan today are doing two things. On the one hand, they are striving for a very high level of mastery of Western music theory, without which there can be no successful modification or development of it. On the other hand, some of them already are making significant efforts to create a new basis for musical form along oriental lines. Western musical forms are based on Western ideals of logic and symmetry. These are not necessarily Eastern ideals. The East has its own ideals, and it is in relation to them that truly oriental musical forms must be evolved. In such forms will the Japanese Western style of the future be cast. (Dan 1961: 216–17, as cited in Herd 1987:146)

Another member of Sannin no Kai, Toshiro Mayuzumi, partook enthusiastically of the European modernist practice of drawing on musics of others, working with Balinese gamelan, Indian *rāga*, popular music, and jazz (in this, notably modernist, but not high modernist). He spent six months in Paris learning the techniques of Boulez and Messiaen (finding them conservative), mastered most of the avant-garde styles ranging from aleatory music and prepared piano to strict serialism. Mayuzumi would become one of the best-known Japanese composers internationally.[15]

Mayuzumi's political stance and the way it can be heard to be expressed in his compositions fascinates the music theorist Steven Nuss. This is not rhetorical Japaneseness (i.e., easy to identify as Japanese), but it is nevertheless "deliberate Japaneseness" that Nuss finds upon close analysis of Mayuzumi's *Essay for String Orchestra* (1963):

> A deep-level adaptation and transformation of traditional Noh vocal and instrumental textures, contours, and forms. . . . For Mayuzumi's deliberate Japaneseness . . . was a shrewd, tough, yet subtle political statement; eschewing, for the most part, any reliance on the use of traditional Japanese instruments or Japanese titles, his consistent use of the instruments, form-suggestive titles, and conventional ensemble groupings of Western art music was a clear attempt to take what he saw as the West's insidious (musical) colonialism and flip it on its head. (Nuss 2004: 86–87)

The drama that Mayuzumi adapts and transforms for *Essay for String Orchestra* is *Tsurukame*, a play unlike any other in the Nō repertory, without any plot and largely devoted to praise of the Japanese emperor:

> While the various structural proportional, and textural similarities to *Tsurukame* that I have discussed illustrate the *mechanics of Tsurukame*'s manifestation in *Essay*'s recompositional plan, it was this emperor-centered subject matter, this text that glorifies the figure most dear to the Japanese right wing, that drew Mayuzumi to this specific play. *Essay* as recomposed *Tsurukame* is heard then not just as an exoticizing piece of deliberate Japaneseness but as a subtle, yet powerful call for emperor worship: a specific political statement meant to call Japan back from the brink of what Mayuzumi and others saw as the abyss of psychological and cultural westernization. (Nuss 2004: 117; emphasis in original)

The phrase "and others" in that last sentence refers to Japan's most celebrated novelist and playwright, Yukio Mishima, who, denouncing contemporary society, made a "desperate call to revive imperial sovereignty before Japan lost all cultural mastery" (Miyoshi and Harootunian 1989: viii). His devoted circle of intellectual contemporaries included Mayuzumi, and the two collaborated artistically several times.

A third group of the same 1950s decade—the internationally connected Jikken Kōbō (Experimental Workshop,; formed in 1951)—is routinely cited to characterize the postwar avant-garde movement in Japan. Two of its member composers, Toru Takemitsu and Joji Yuasa, took full advantage of the affordance of the cultural environment. Trained not in any of Japan's schools of music but with prewar composers noted for their interest in traditional music—Yasuji Kiyose, Fumio Hayasaka, and Yoritsune Matsudaira—Takemitsu and Yuasa experimented with whatever musical practices interested them. In the works of both, certain musical procedures, and the aesthetic principles of Japanese art that lie behind them, are deeply integrated with Western music.[16]

Takemitsu and Yuasa were dealing musically with Japaneseness at a conceptual level and as sound, and their works resonated easily with international contemporary music practices.[17] By the time Jikken Kōbō was formed, Takemitsu had already explored the meaningful juxtaposition of sound and silence in his *Futatsu no rento* (*Lento in Two Movements*) for solo piano, which he presented in 1950 at Mainichi Shimbun Hall in Tokyo. He would become known as the composer who articulated to Western audiences the *ma* concept of "pregnant nothingness" (roughly translated), taken from traditional Japanese arts, and continued to apply it aesthetically in his works.[18] Yuasa's subtle use of elements of the Nō drama—including aesthetic structure, vocal and instrument sounds, and sense of time—was a long-standing one. After the disbanding of the Jikken Kōbō, Yuasa's interest in musique concrète continued; one example is *Aoi no ue* (*My Blue Sky*, 1961), based on the Nō play of that name, which draws on the sounds of *kakegoe* (drummer's vocables), the deconstructed sounds of *tsuzumi* (waisted-shape drums), and *utai* (singing) of the Nō.

Independently of composers' groups, other composers were taking advantage of the bimusical heritage that their culture's history offered them. In 1959 a rubric, *gendai hōgaku* (contemporary music for Japanese instruments), was coined for NHK programming and taken up over the next decade as a dynamic movement (Yamakawa 1984).

> The movement as a whole was greatly encouraged by the radio program *Gendai no Nihon ongaku* (*Japanese Music of the Present*) of NHK. Its weekly programs introduced new works in contemporary artistic mediums based on traditional cultural aesthetics. These works explored the possibilities of musical expression on individual instruments and broadened the principles of traditional ensemble performance. (Nagahiro 2002: 191)[19]

Ryohei Hirose (1930–2008), a Geidai graduate, was among the most successful of composers of gendai hōgaku. A 1963 work, *Torso*, for five instruments, combined the traditional instruments of the sankyoku ensemble (koto, shamisen, and shakuhachi) complemented by the seventeen-stringed koto (as in the Yonin no Kai ensemble) and, notably, cello.[20] Thanks to the work's clear texture, the traditional sounds of the instruments can be heard clearly, particularly in some of the material of the first movement. Starting with koto, single tones are embellished with *ato-oshide* (an upward-slur ornament created by pressing the string after plucking), scraping, glissandi, and octaves up to 1:07 when the shamisen part begins with its distinctive plectral plucking sound. Shamisen and koto are played off melodically. But at 1:42 it changes to steady *kinuta* (strumming) on koto (with periodic vertical intervals, however) while the shamisen carries the melody. At 3:14 there is a lovely imitative *kakeai*-like exchange between the two kotos. A trio movement follows, scored for cello, then cello with shakuhachi with vertical consonances, then with the shamisen joining in; the four instruments repeat melodic material that is not rhetorically Japanese. The movement ends with cello alone. Only the third movement involves much of the heterophonic texture of traditional music—koto paired with shamisen and shakuhachi paired with cello in traditional kinds of dissonance, ending with sankyoku heterophony. Comfortable working across traditions, in future work Hirose would ask cellists to produce melodies very like those of traditional shakuhachi music. His 1976 Concerto for Shakuhachi and Orchestra won the Otaka Prize for that year.

In the 1960s Japan's recovery from the war began to be obvious in many ways, in particular economically. The 1964 Tokyo Olympics were in effect an announcement that the nation was ready to return to an international position, and on very different terms than ever before. That year two composers—Minoru Miki (1930–2011, a graduate of Geidai) and Katsutoshi Nagasawa (1923–2008, a graduate of Nihon University)—cofounded an ensemble, Nihon Ongaku Shudan, that would offer performances of their and other composers' contemporary works specifically for Japanese instruments only (i.e., gendai hōgaku) both in Japan and abroad. Minoru Miki would serve as the group's artistic director for a number of years.

Although it has been accused of having little to do with traditional music beyond the use of Japanese instruments, the Nihon Ongaku Shudan was without doubt a cultural force in a very gradual process of bringing traditional music into the mainstream of Japanese musical modernity. A primary principle of the group was that the constraints of traditional sociomusical practices would be avoided. Ryū affiliation of the performers was not an issue; willingness to experiment was. Any combination of instruments would be acceptable for new works. Known abroad as Ensemble Nipponia in the 1970s (touring under the auspices of the Asia Society of New York when I first heard them) and subsequently as Pro Musica Nipponia, the ensemble consisted at first of fourteen musicians. According to Takuo Tamura, conductor of the ensemble, there are approximately seventy now, some of whom have performed with the ensemble for a number of years and some for only a short while. Tamura estimated that about a thousand musicians have been part of the group at some point (personal communication, May 8, 2001). One becomes a member by recommendation or, in the case of young musicians, by means of an annual audition. Although some hōgaku musicians have doubts about the aesthetic viability of works performed by Nihon Ongaku Shudan, its members have included, among many others, such illustrious artists as Keiko Nosaka (b. 1938), and Kifu Mitsuhashi (b. 1950), Katsuya Yokoyama (1934–2010), who played Takemitsu's *November Steps* in 1967.[21]

Still going strong, Nihon Ongaku Shudan does about a hundred presentations of several kinds per year. When touring abroad, their primary aim is to take to as many people as possible for the first time contemporary Japanese music for traditional instruments. Their extensive international concertizing in North and South America, Europe, and Asia is tracked on their website (searched as Pro Musica Nipponia, under "Our History") from the first tour in 1972 to 2010. Within Japan, introducing hōgaku instruments in schools is a major priority of the group; when they travel around Japan, they might do three concerts a day in primary, middle, and high schools. (In schools, Takuo Tamura said, "they" don't know Japanese instruments, so the Shudan musicians introduce the traditional instruments and the modernized koto). The ensemble continues to commission new works and to perform pieces composed for them in the past, as well as pieces composed by non-Japanese composers for Japanese instruments. Since 1981, according to Kifu Mitsuhashi, he has periodically produced a concert for Nihon Ongaku Shudan to feature new pieces by non-Japanese composers; in 1990 the featured composer was Tan Dun. Others have been Neil McKay (United States), H. J. Kohleuter (Germany), Ensho Oh (China), John Neptune (United States), and Jack Body (New Zealand) (personal communication, May 5, 2001).

A significant spin-off from Nihon Ongaku Shudan/Pro Musica Nipponia was the encouragement given by the composer Minoru Miki to the kotoist Keiko Nosaka to create a koto more suited for contemporary music than either the thirteen-stringed or the seventeen-stringed instrument. In 1964, having graduated from Geidai's postgraduate program in hōgaku, Nosaka joined the ensemble; that year she also gave her first solo recital. Just as her kotoist mother, Soju Nosaka, iemoto of the Matsu no Mi kai subgroup of the Ikuta ryū, had undertaken to learn the *shin nihon ongaku* repertoire with Michio Miyagi to keep abreast of contemporary trends, Nosaka wished to explore means by which possibilities for contemporary koto music might be expanded. The result was the creation, by the time of Nosaka's second solo recital in 1969, of a twenty-stringed koto (which quickly evolved into a twenty-one-stringed instrument and, by 1991, a twenty-five-stringed one) that offered a greater range of pitches, more flexible tuning possibilities, and a broader range of both dynamics and volume. For the premiere performance of the twenty-stringed koto Nosaka played *Tennyō*, by Minoru Miki.[22] For future recitals, just as Teiko Kikuchi had had to do for the seventeen-stringed koto, Nosaka has commissioned new works from several composers, including Yuji Takahashi, Teizo Matsumura, Akira Ifukube, and Joji Yuasa. Furthermore, thanks to her study of composition with Akira Ifukube, Nosaka herself has become a performer-composer.

In 1966, two years after the Tokyo Olympics, government support for domestic culture was renewed in a dramatic manner: a significant new institution was created that was to have a considerable positive effect on the reception of hōgaku and, through composers, on its place in the nation's shared cultural space. Shigeo Kishibe explained the move: "We realized that a great deal had been lost and that something had to be done about it" (personal communication, April 22, 1999). An observation by the anthropologist Marilyn Ivy seems pertinent here:

> In Japan, as elsewhere . . . , the residues of modernity [here, traditional arts—Nō and gagaku in particular] are efficiently taken up by culture institutions and circulated as citations of difference. When the marginal is temporally inscribed within the nostalgic register as the vanishing, it then functions as a special, and fetishized, guarantor of social status. Fetishized in the sense that the vanishing is never allowed actually to disappear, but is kept hovering, with anxiety and dread, on the edge of absence. (Ivy 1995: 242)

Founded as a special legal entity in accordance to the National Theatre Law, the National Theatre of Japan had two purposes: to foster the preservation of Japan's traditional musics and to renew the relevance of traditional music for contemporary Japanese. That year the National Theatre opened in Tokyo (Chiyoda-ku), with large and small concert spaces that remain a hub of presentations of traditional music, dance, and theater.[23] That second purpose—to renew the relevance of traditional music for contemporary Japanese—would be significant for the next two decades and a half, specifically with regard to the involvement of composers.

THE 1970S AND BEYOND

Like the NHK gendai hōgaku initiative in the 1960s, among the primary means the National Theatre chose to renew the relevance of traditional music for contemporary Japanese was to fund a program of commissioning new works for traditional instruments. This, I think, had enduring positive effects for Japanese musical modernity.

> The first works were produced in the context of *gagaku* (court music) concerts, and later in connection with the reconstruction of ancient instruments, while others came into being in association with concerts of *shoomyoo* (Buddhist chant). In addition, a substantial number of new works for the *koto*, *shakuhachi* and *shamisen*, for drums, and for

the vocal genres of *jooruri*, *noo*, and *kyoogen* were also commissioned. (Motegi 1999: 28)

The rubric under which the new works for traditional instruments fell was *gendai nihon ongaku* (contemporary Japanese music; Yamakawa 1984).

New works for gagaku instruments received the bulk of the commissions. One can think of multiple reasons for that. It is the only large-ensemble practice in Japanese traditional music, and, with the prominence of the orchestra among Western musics in Japan (chapter 5), a large ensemble would potentially be of interest to composers and audiences alike. Also, the variety of instruments in the ensemble presents a corresponding variety of creative possibilities. And because the National Theatre is a governmental institution, inclusion of particular attention to the imperial ensemble would not be unexpected.

However, according to the National Theatre's director, Toshiro Kido, the program of commissioning new works for gagaku instruments was initiated by a crisis for the National Theatre: the audience for concerts featuring traditional pieces declined to 18 percent of seating capacity in 1969, the third year of the theater's existence. As a result the director started to commission new music for the venerable ensemble of imperial court culture, hoping to attract bigger audiences.

The first two composers selected for the series of new works for gagaku ensemble had established international reputations. Toshiro Mayuzumi's orchestra piece *Bugaku* (1962) had been commissioned by the New York City Ballet for a George Balanchine work that premiered in New York in 1963. (Bugaku is the dance component of gagaku.) His *Shōwa tenpyōraku ichigu* (1970), for the National Theatre, is a piece of "contemporary gagaku" that "aimed at the continuance of the tradition." While Mayuzumi "respected the forms of gagaku as much as possible," he attempted "a method of broadening those forms by means of experimenting outside of them" (as quoted in Motegi 1999: 28). "Broadening" meant calling for instruments whose use in gagaku practice had been abandoned long ago. And the commission given to Toru Takemitsu resulted in *Gagaku: Shūteigwa—In an Autumn Garden* (1973), which has been recorded several times and given analytical attention.[24] For *Autumn Garden*, Takemitsu expanded the size of the ensemble he used for *November Steps*, which in 1967 had sparked his international reputation, and worked with the instrumental sections both spatially onstage and musically.

However, it was the autumn 1977 premiere of Karlheinz Stockhausen's *Licht—Hikari—Light* that was to have the strongest repercussions in the field of new compositions for gagaku ensemble. In its final form the work certainly embraced ideas that were fundamental to gagaku as a musical form, but at first it seems completely different from present-day gagaku and provoked puzzled responses from its performers (Motegi 1999: 29). Of the "puzzled responses," Galliano wrote: "The Japanese found Stockhausen's use of traditional instruments uninteresting and almost blasphemous, so after this it was decided that commissions would be given only to Japanese composers" (2002: 253).[25] I spoke with Toshiro Kido, who offered the commission to Stockhausen.

TK: In contemporary music you have total serialism. Stockhausen . . . after World War II, in Darmstadt, he started this idea of all these elements when you compose—not only sound, tone color—all these elements included in serialism. Stockhausen analyzed the abilities of gagaku instruments. It was his idea—Stockhausen's. He put them in order in his own way—all these elements included in gagaku pieces and gagaku instruments.

BW: How did you know Stockhausen?

TK: The Exposition in 1970 in Osaka. I met him there and asked him, "Why don't you compose gagaku?" That was the ten-year anniversary of the National Theatre, so I commissioned for the commemoration. (Personal communication, May 27, 2000)

The historian of gagaku Steven Nelson also commented on Stockhausen's piece, but from the point of view of the performers required:

> Stockhausen's piece "Licht" was a big step forward. It was difficult for the Imperial court musicians—written in Western notation, using new techniques. There was also the Tokyo Gakuso ensemble that often played at the Kokuritsu Gekijo [National Theatre]. The central players were Imperial Household musicians but there were also young people, including women for flute, shō and percussion. Koto players were often of the Ikuta ryū. (Personal communication, June 3, 2000)

The distinguished shō player Mayumi Miyata, who began to play gagaku later (see below), recalled hearing about the musicians' reactions to the Stockhausen piece: "In the beginning most of the court musicians had wanted to play [the new pieces]. But they did not like Stockhausen's music; it was torture for them. Some of them did not want to continue" (personal communication, June 5, 2000).

Perhaps most notably, because Stockhausen's *Licht—Hikari—Light* was so non-Japanese musically, it permitted public awareness of gagaku as a performance genre rather than a repertoire of ceremonial music inextricably linked to the imperial household (Motegi 1999: 29). That was congenial to Kido's differentiation between "gagaku" and "gagaku instruments"—the former local, the latter having international characteristics (Kido 1984: 42–44).

BW: Was there any idea about gagaku being a kind of national music for the National Theatre?

TK: No, I dealt with gagaku as ordinary music, not special national music.

BW: But it seems to me . . . gagaku is not just old music. It is associated with the imperial household. It has a meaning. . . .

TK: In Japan, ordinary Japanese academics [*gakusha*] were conservative people. They considered gagaku as connected with the imperial court, but I opposed that idea. Gagaku that you hear now is only since Meiji. . . .[26] I also commission because I want composers to use "the hidden parts of the instrument" rather than the ordinary usual gagaku sound.

BW: So you are interested in the instrumental sound.

TK: So, so, so, so.

BW: And you want them to compose using the instruments in new and different ways?

TK: That's it. (Personal communication, May 27, 2000)

Kido revealed to me yet another criterion for some of his further choices of composers: it was heavily weighted, he said, by his desire to attract some who had not previously involved themselves with traditional music (personal communication, May 27, 2000). Several of the composers have confirmed that it worked on them. Most notably, Keiko Fujiie, the last individual (and the only woman) commissioned to write for gagaku ensemble, went to considerable lengths to study gagaku from historians and historical sources, and that knowledge has been informing new works since.[27]

Composers were afforded further opportunities by a second project of Kido's. The National Theatre's project of reconstructing ancient instruments began in 1975, with the idea of reconstructing (not restoring) a bamboo panpipe, a shakuhachi, and a transverse flute, all from the collection of the Shōsō-in, the imperial storehouse associated with the Nara Buddhist temple, Tōdai-ji.[28]

> This led to a series of concerts in which other ancient instruments were reconstructed and played, eventually forming a major project which came to be known as *reigaku*, with a view to distinguishing it from the performance of *gagaku* in its contemporary form. It developed into a creative attempt to uncover the original forms of Japanese music by examining the structure of the ancient instruments themselves. . . . The composer Yuji Takahashi collaborated in the reconstruction of many of the instruments from fragmentary remains, and produced a series of works for the instruments, including *Zanshi no Kyoku* (1988), *Ten o Yumemu* (1989), and *Unebiyama* (1993). These works focused individual attention on instruments that had until then largely been considered as part of a group, and in the process developed possibilities for solo expression that had remained unexplored until that time. (Motegi 1999: 29–30)[29]

The composers Yoshihiro Kanno and Toshi Ichiyanagi (see below) also received commissions for new works in the reigaku project.

As of 1999, a total of thirty-seven composers had had works commissioned by the National Theatre, including the three non-Japanese. The list of Japanese composers represented a cross-section of well-known composers from a wide range of age groups, three women, and performer-composers from the traditional genres as well as composers of contemporary music. Several composers received multiple commissions. That year also saw the beginning of a major effort to publish an invaluable source: the scores and CD recordings of commissioned works, in an elegant edition, along with bilingual commentary on the composer and the work. Published in each volume is a list of all the works that were commissioned from each composer, along with an article by the musicologist Kiyoko Motegi (Motegi 1999), who participated in the projects.[30] Because scores of new works involving traditional instruments are so hard to find, this publishing venture is invaluable.

When I interviewed Toshiro Kido in 2000, he had retired; much to the disappointment of several composers with whom I spoke, with his retirement the commissioning project ended. Composers' comments to me couched the end of the project as the loss of a potential financial opportunity and also the loss of government support for contemporary music.[31]

This National Theatre effort on behalf of traditional music had effects beyond a set of new compositions and performances. "After Takemitsu's *In an Autumn Garden*, the floodgates burst," commented the shakuhachi player Christopher Yohmei Blasdel. "In 1978 Sukeyasu Shiba began teaching [gagaku] at Geidai as a part-time member of the faculty. In 1977 *shakuhachi* was added to the main [hōgaku] curriculum at Geidai. Goro Yamaguchi [Kinko ryū] and Hozan Yamamoto [Tozan ryū] were the first teachers" (personal communication, May 22, 2002). Instruction in gagaku and other traditional music at community centers burgeoned and continues to thrive to this day. Here again we see a significant nexus of performer-composers and composers with performers.

PUTTING PERFORMERS INTO THE PICTURE

Motegi wrote of the performers who came together to participate in the National Theatre concerts:

> It is their cooperation that has made possible the realization of the ideas of both the producers and the composers involved. It is possible to divide these performers into three groups. The first group comprises specialist performers on the traditional instruments, the instruments of *gagaku* and *noo*, the *koto*, *shakuhachi* and *shamisen*, the percussion instruments of *kabuki*, and the like. The second group is made up of performers, like the Buddhist priests, who rarely appeared on stage before their contact with the National Theatre, and who come from a world quite distinct from that of the professional musicians. The third group is that of performers on Western instruments, who in many cases had never been required to perform on traditional Japanese instruments. . . . It was extremely rare for performers from such different fields to come together in creative efforts. . . . The positive sense of tension that resulted from this new state of affairs attracted a great variety of responses to the creative efforts of the National Theatre, and served as a strong stimulus to the creation of new music for traditional ensembles. (Motegi 1999: 32)

Among the performers, Sukeyasu Shiba became a singularly significant individual. Born in 1935 into the Shiba family, a branch of the Koma clan of more than four hundred musicians associated with the temple-shrine complex of Kofukuji–Kasuga Taisha in Nara through hundreds of years, Shiba was one of the musicians of the imperial household gagaku ensemble. In great demand and deeply involved with musical activities beyond the Imperial Music Bureau, however, he retired in 1984 to devote himself to teaching, performing, and, most significant here, composing. In 1985 he founded and is still (as of 2013) music director of the most prominent of several non-court gagaku ensembles, Reigakusha, which is in demand throughout Japan and internationally for concerts consisting of pieces from the surviving court repertoire, Shiba's reconstructions of ancient pieces, and new works (including some commissioned by or for Reigakusha)—and some by Shiba himself (see below).

It bears repeating that for composers who want to draw on both of the grounded traditions in Japanese musical modernity by writing for a traditional instrument, the availability of capable and involved performers is an absolute prerequisite. From the beginning of my research on this project in 1999, three such specialist performers of traditional instruments, beyond those already mentioned, have been consistently put forward as individuals who are especially enthusiastic about and skilled at playing contemporary music. I consider their contribution to their culture to be important: by attracting composers who want to write for them and working with them as they do so; by commissioning composers to provide them with new repertoire; by teaching contemporary music and thereby fostering it in the environment of shared cultural space; and in other ways. Those three are Nanae Yoshimura, Mayumi Miyata, and Kifu Mitsuhashi.

The koto player who is the most avid commissioner of new works for twenty-stringed koto is Nanae Yoshimura (usually referred to simply as Nanae). Her study of thirteen-stringed koto began in childhood with her mother, Soho Yoshimura. She went on to study with Soju Nosaka, iemoto of the Ikuta ryū subgroup Matsu no Mi kai, and then with Keiko Nosaka. By age sixteen she had completed the requirements for her teaching license in the traditional system. Nanae's interest in contemporary music was heightened by her experience with Keiko Nosaka, creator of the twenty-stringed koto, and she took the instrument up in 1971. (Nosaka later enlarged the instrument to twenty-five strings, but Nanae specializes in the twenty-stringed version.) In the 1970s the repertoire for twenty-stringed koto was still very small, and only time would tell if the instrument would "take" among koto players. It did, and the need for repertoire grew. Nanae's entrepreneurship, in the form of commissioning new works for her recitals, began in 1988 and has become her creative signature. The roster of leading composers from whom Nanae has commissioned works is very long, as each of her annual recitals is made up mostly if not entirely of new works.[32] She is building a repertoire that permits her to show off both a strong, dynamic musical sensibility and her considerable virtuosity. An entrepreneur also in seeking opportunities to perform abroad, Nanae has showcased Japanese works in international contemporary music festivals, and she participated in the centenary celebrations of New York's Carnegie Hall.

Short biographical sketches of two other performers illustrate how some performers on traditional instruments, like composers, engage—despite the lack of a family background in such instruments—with the possibilities offered by the coexistence of two deeply cultivated, historically grounded musics in modern Japan. Mayumi Miyata is recognized by "everyone" as the performer who is at the center of the shō being used "everywhere." When I first met with her, I asked why a student of piano at Kunitachi College of Music would have begun playing such an unusual instrument as the shō. Her explanation resonated with the way I had heard composers speak of the instrument—that is, it was based on the instrument's sound:

> In music college it was not satisfying to practice only eighteenth- and nineteenth-century piano music every day for so many hours. I wanted something else. Then I took a course in music aesthetics with Kuniyasu sensei about Greece and the Greek line of thought that music is a medium between humans and the universe. I didn't know about gagaku then, but I wanted to find something. I continued to study music aesthetics, reading ancient philosophy with Tadashi Isoyama. While preparing for the M.A. course, my imagination was affected by a book on music aesthetics in the ancient world—India, China, and Greece—and also imagination from the landscape.
>
> Since I was a child, I have loved nature, stars, air, the galaxy. I have wondered what the universe is. Light from the sun in the late afternoon. Sunbeams coming from clouds. So beautiful. Looking at these, some sounds came to me. I didn't know what they were. I had a recording and had been to a concert of gagaku in which, at the time, I had only slight interest. But when I saw the light, I remembered the sound of the shō. I just wanted to listen to the shō. I remembered the shō in the Kunitachi museum and wondered, if I blow the shō, will the sound be different from what I am imagining?
>
> Then I heard about the Sennichidani Gagakukai, in which Sukeyasu Shiba sensei, Hiroshi Togi sensei, and Tadamaro Ohno sensei were teaching. I went and started to study shō with Tadamaro Ohno sensei. Some women were playing then, any instrument. It was a community course. Then there was a movement in the National Theatre. They had just started to commission new pieces for gagaku—that started in

> 1971–72. In '78, '79, and '80 they started to do it annually, even two or three times a year. . . . . Shiba-sensei, Ohno-sensei, and Toshiro Kido-sensei were working together on the National Theatre concerts. (Personal communications, December 13, 2012, and June 5, 2000)

Tadamaro Ohno facilitated Mayumi Miyata's involvement with the National Theater, and at the first performance of Takemitsu's *In an Autumn Garden*, she participated as one of the two dancers in the piece. When the work was recorded, she joined the ensemble as a performing member of Tokyo Gakusho, and her career as a player of shō was launched. Miyata was a founding member of Reigakusha (personal communication, December 13, 2012).

Toshiro Kido pushed her to give recitals. "So what do you play?" she asked me rhetorically. "There are only six pieces for shō in traditional music. Few are played as solo pieces—they are the six *chōshi* [long preludes to establish the musical mode of a piece]—and the audience doesn't distinguish between them. So I started to commission—first, a solo piece from Ichiyanagi." Why him, I asked? "Ichiyanagi sensei had just written some new gagaku music for the National Theatre" (personal communication, June 5, 2000). That would certainly change. Other Japanese composers from whom she has commissioned works include Toshio Hosokawa, Maki Ishii, Somei Satoh, and Joji Yuasa.

Miyata is in demand overseas for contemporary performances of shō and, unusually for a player of a traditional instrument, she commissions pieces from European (Italian, French, German, eastern European) as well as Japanese composers, so she is building quite a varied contemporary repertoire. She is known to be good at showing composers how to write for shō and has even written instructional manuals. Miyata teaches shō at a number of music colleges, including Kunitachi in Tokyo. Her student at Ginza Gagakudo, Ko Ishikawa, has become a skilled and successful performer-composer of music for shō in his own right.[33]

The early education and musical experience of the shakuhachi player Kifu Mitsuhashi (b. 1950) was typical of a child growing up in the Showa era. His mother was a graduate of one of Japan's best music schools, Kunitachi University, a singer who became a teacher in Kanagawa Prefecture; his father was a journalist (personal communication, May 5, 2001). In high school he loved only jazz. The school's big band—the New Heard Armonics—played the repertoire of Glenn Miller, Stan Kenton, Buddy Rich, and others. He also played in the high school orchestra, which, as in other schools, was a club. Across the hall in the clubhouse was the

Koto-Shakuhachi Kenkyu Kai (Koto-Shakuhachi Research Society). At age eighteen—late for someone who would become a professional—he first tried shakuhachi on a whim, simply because it was at hand; nothing in particular inspired him to do it, he said. Because the orchestra and shakuhachi group lessons were held at the same time on Saturdays, his orchestra teacher told him he had to make a choice. He chose shakuhachi. In 1968 he pursued shakuhachi training with Sofu Sasaki of the Kinko ryū, and during college he attended the NHK Hōgaku Training Academy. In 1972 he completed that program and also graduated from Aoyama Gakuin with a major in economics.

The biography of Kifu Mitsuhashi on the website of the International Shakuhachi Society names his two teachers: Sofu Sasaki and Chikugai Okamoto of the Meian *sōryūkai* tradition [http://www.komuso.com/people/Mitsuhashi_Kifu.html]. To me he stressed that he studied with two teachers with different musical traditions—unusual in the traditional system (personal communication, May 5, 2001).

Immediately upon graduating from college, Mitsuhashi auditioned for Nihon Ongaku Shudan and began working with the group as a *kenkyūsei* (a kind of assistant/student/intern). After two years he became a performing member. He presented his first solo shakuhachi recital in 1980 at age thirty and now travels widely, including internationally, to perform.

Mitsuhashi's first recital in 1980 was the occasion of his first commission, he told me. He had studied composition with Minao Shibata but found composing to be "too heavy" for him, so he asked his teacher for a new piece.[34] He commissions "with the Chinese idea of *onkochishin*: *on*—warming up/learning/knowing; *ko*—old, as in theory; *chi*—knowledge; *shin*—new" (personal communication, May 5, 2001). He wants, he said, to create new pieces that will become classics.

When choosing a composer from whom to commission a work, Mitsuhashi researches the candidate's music, ideas, techniques, whether or not the composer's music has a good connection with an instrument, and the feeling of the music. When he works with a composer, he gives him or her a demonstration performance, lends the composer recordings, and shows him or her a sample of notation that other composers have used. Most important, he says, he needs to get prospective composers to understand the world of shakuhachi music because "they must develop a new world for it." This has led him to commission works from such Japanese composers as Masanori Fujita, Ryohei Hirose, Toshi Ichiyanagi, Makoto Moroi, Katsutoshi Nagasawa, Akira Nishimura, Somei Satoh, and Takashi Yoshimatsu.

At the time I met with him, Mitsuhashi was teaching in five locations in Japan, including Yokohama and Shizuoka, in a compressed ten-day-a-month schedule. He will teach students contemporary pieces if they want to learn them, but his students must first learn basic classical pieces. It is possible for students to learn both contemporary and classical repertoire at the same time, he says, because traditional techniques are used in contemporary pieces (personal communication, May 5, 2001).

Putting Performer-Composers Back into the Picture

It is significant that, for the first time in a very long time, new works for the venerable gagaku ensemble and for the instruments outside of their ensemble context are being created by an individual performer-composer from that tradition, namely Sukeyasu Shiba. While his works for the ensemble are well funded "by the tradition," that he is an open-minded creative artist is evidenced by his *Tsubura-e*, for shō and shamisen (1994)—two instruments that inhabit unrelated cultural spheres in Japanese tradition. The shamisen player Kazuko Takada, who chose the instruments, found a way to connect them meaningfully through songs performed in the ceremony of the enthronement of the emperor "even in our time," and Shiba was a willing collaborator.[35]

The shamisen is among the most difficult of Japanese instruments for which to write contemporary music, and only a few composers have done so. Among the most successful is Yuji Takahashi (b. 1938) who enjoyed a close musical collaboration with an extraordinary shamisen player, the late Kazuko Takada (d. 2007).[36] Raised in a thoroughly musical family—his father was a music critic and editor and his mother a serious pianist—early signs of creative talent led Takahashi to composition lessons with Ikuma Dan while Takahashi was still in primary school. At fourteen he started studying harmony and counterpoint with the Toho Gakuen instructor Minao Shibata, an energetic musical entrepreneur and fine composer. As a young musician, then, Yuji Takahashi was in the thick of an exhilarating experimental music scene in Tokyo, and only just a bit younger than the generation of composers who established themselves in the immediate postwar years. Toru Takemitsu and Toshi Ichiyanagi, among others, were bringing many illustrious American and European composers to Japan. In 1961 Takahashi was introduced to Iannis Xenakis, who came to Tokyo for a conference and was very impressed by Takahashi's talent as a pianist; Takahashi was including works by avant-garde composers in his many concerts. As a result of his international contacts and interests, he left Japan in 1963 for what would be a period of ten years. He went first to Berlin, where he studied with Xenakis, then in 1966 to the United States for experience with computer music. His personal account to me of this time was short and sweet, minimizing mentions of grants and academic appointments: "I went first to Boston, where I lived for three months in a basement room of Sarah Caldwell's [director of the Boston Opera], working as a rehearsal pianist for the Boston Opera's production of *Moses and Aaron*. Then I got the grant to be at the Bell Lab. I visited SUNY-Buffalo at the invitation of Lukas Foss and Bloomington, where they were beginning a computer lab" (personal communication, April 28, 1999). He returned to Japan in 1972 and since has been by everyone's estimation one of Japan's most independent and original composers.

Yuji Takahashi is equally accomplished as a concert pianist and composer; in an interview in 2000, he revealed that he thinks of himself as a performer, and composes from that perspective (personal communication, April 28, 1999). (Thus, I have put this into the subsection on performer-composers.) That has taken him in multiple directions, one of which has been to learn to play other instruments that particularly interest him for one composerly reason or another. The shamisen is one of them. Takahashi explained to me that because the instrument has no frets, playing shamisen is about tactility and kinetic energy; through the learning experience, he became sensitive to the performer's perception of music not as pitches, but as positions on the instrument. In addition, shamisen music is about sonority; the instrument is distinguished by a detail of construction that produces *sawari*, a buzzing tonal quality. Furthermore, different timbres and effects are achieved by placing the finger on a string not just in a certain place, but also in a certain way. That is, desired sonorities are achieved not only by the inherent properties and construction of the instrument, but also in ways that are produced physically by the player. To compose sensitively for an instrument such as the shamisen without experiencing it physically is extremely challenging.

Another consideration for a composer is that, traditionally, most shamisen music has been vocal music with shamisen accompaniment. A composer might write purely instrumental music, but in a modern recital, the variety offered by a mixture of purely instrumental and shamisen-with-voice works in a program is a likely desideratum. Yuji Takahashi has written both. But the vocal quality demands a choice; while contemporary audiences expect Western vocal production, the shamisen is intricately linked with traditional Japanese vocal qualities.

For his 1994 composition *Kagehime no michiyuki*, for two nagauta shamisen and voices, Takahashi solved the problem of vocal quality by exploiting and dramatizing the traditional voice. As for the shamisen parts, he wrote:

> "Two shamisens are tuned a semitone apart. The same pitch resonant on one instrument sounds assonant on the other. Within the traditional intervals and playing methods, the result is highly unstable." Using that instability, the composition is a weeping song, referring to an episode in old Japanese literature: Kagehime's fiancé was murdered out of jealousy by the Crown Prince at the time, and his funeral cortege is in process. The name "Kagehime" means "the girl in the shadows." It must be a name that hides her identity.[37]

In the first four minutes of the piece we hear slow walking, each pitch articulated, but with uneven pacing and expressively ornamented so that uncertainty and distress are suggested. Into the second minute, the pace picks up a bit, and distress begins to be expressed by dissonances between the two shamisen parts as well. The wavery, intense weeping that begins in the third minute is reminiscent of a traditional style of both vocal and shakuhachi music, here invoked and intensified to express extreme emotion. Pain is expressed through the utterance of *are*, a wordless outcry. As the piece proceeds, the sung text names the places where the funeral is passing, the offerings the girl carries, and the girl's name reiterated as if in soulful sympathy at the end. The alternating, punctuating, responding nature of the shamisen parts in relation to the vocal parts is reminiscent of traditional music. The walking motive returns as the funeral cortege continues, and the piece comes to an end without any suggestion of having arrived at a destination.

In my accounting of the decade of the 1930s earlier in this chapter, I presented the kotoist performer-composer Michio Miyagi. Here it is important to follow up with performer-composers who continued the challenge taken up by Michio Miyagi to write contemporary works from a firm base in the hōgaku sphere of music making in modern Japan. From the mid-twentieth century to the present, for instance, Shin'ichi Yuize of the Seiha ryū-ha (Ikuta koto) has been particularly prominent. Yuize, for whom the American composer Henry Cowell wrote his Concerto no. 2 for Koto (1965), was a full participant in the gendai hōgaku movement. Although Yuize had already composed numerous Western music–engaged pieces for koto before, he undertook the study of composition with Cowell in the mid-1950s (Sheppard 2008: 529) and himself composed for Western ensemble, as in his Concerto no. 3 for Koto, Shakuhachi, and Orchestra (1959).[38]

Another prominent performer-composer was Tadao Sawai (1937–1997), whom I highlight here because of the energetic, sustained effort that he made to connect contemporary music for koto with Japanese musical culture beyond the sphere of hōgaku. Sawai studied koto from the age of ten, was a student of Michio Miyagi, and graduated from the Tokyo National University of Fine Arts and Music in 1959. He was intent on following in the footsteps of Miyagi, continuing the modernizing of music for his instrument, but he did so in a variety of ways. As one CD liner note encapsulated it forty years later: "His performances have shed a new light on koto music by incorporating everything from Bach to jazz. He has changed the koto from being a traditional Japanese instrument to an instrument of universal expressiveness" (Kojima 1997: 6). He not only concertized widely throughout Japan, a number of European countries, and the United States; he also took on the role of composer. Writing for solo thirteen-stringed koto, solo seventeen-stringed koto, duets, and small and large ensembles, Tadao Sawai expanded the repertoire with new works written for his students and also for his wife, Kazue Sawai, who is considered one of Japan's finest artists. Because the degree of difference in the music introduced by Tadao Sawai as a performer-composer was large and because a socially relational context fostered it, a new group formed around him—the Sawai ryū, whose emphasis is on contemporary music. The socially relational contexts that permitted the formation of the new ryū comprised both the pedigree offered him as a student of Miyagi and the death of his teacher early in Sawai's musical career. Also significant was his authenticating association with Geidai, the most prestigious of Japanese music institutions. Not only did a koto group form around Tadao Sawai, but, in very modern fashion, he founded a degree-granting formal school, the Sawai Koto Academy of Music, and served as its president.

As is said of composers, Tadao Sawai found his "own musical voice," one that allows traditional and contemporary to intermingle in musically sensitive ways. *Gosechi no mai,* a composition for koto ensemble, references history—a dance of heavenly maidens at a legendary event of the seventh century—but the music is not intended to be programmatic. The piece begins with relatively explosive energy on two seventeen-stringed kotos, from which the classically phrased thirteen-stringed koto part is born quietly. "The sound of this koto part," as the recording's CD booklet says, "entices the sounds of the seventeen-string, developing gradually into an ardent dance."[39] The interplay of traditional and contemporary musical content and of the sounds of the two sizes of instrument is beautifully done; an acceleration toward the end is a traditional feature. Not heard in this piece but found in other ensemble pieces are gestures I associate with the Sawai compositional voice: multiple instruments on a part and multiple parts weaving in and out among each other, as well as juxtaposition of a soloistic seventeen-string part with ensemble—the player standing, exerting great energy for the wide range of dynamics and virtuosic demands—sectional repeats, motivic repetition, contrasts between lyricism and driving, pulsating rhythms, calls for extended playing techniques such as hitting the strings with a stick, and great ensemble climaxes.

Significantly, Tadao Sawai (and, after his death, Kazue Sawai) connected with fellow Japanese musicians by commissioning works from composers with other competencies but shared sensibilities. For the celebratory concert on the occasion of the tenth anniversary of the Academy, a composition was commissioned from Yuji Takahashi. With his deep interest in traditional Japanese music and broad education in European music, Takahashi was the perfect composer from whom to commission a work that would be performed by Tadao Sawai, showcasing the koto as "an instrument of universal expressiveness," though the work could not have been written by the kotoist Sawai: *Thread Cog Wheels,* for koto and orchestra (1990). It is striking to me that while Sawai asked for a piece that put the koto in company with the orchestra—the pinnacle of European musical civilization, in the opinion of most Japanese—Takahashi found a way to treat the orchestra as individual instruments and smaller groups, the forces not only for which Takahashi much prefers to think creatively, but also that are consonant with traditional koto practice.

Thread Cog Wheels is not a concerto; the koto is a member of the orchestra. The piece begins with a sparse texture that might remind the knowledgeable of the aesthetic of traditional koto ensemble music, except that gong and brass complement it—a very unlikely combination but, to my ear, entirely consonant. Just over two minutes in, we hear the koto solo a bit; then a motive of plucking on the koto, paired with the string bass, pulls together the plucking playing technique these two instruments have in common. Through this piece, motives are picked up among the instruments; at 3:40 on the Fontec CD, for instance the clarinet picks up a motive from the koto, which drops out. Takahashi explained that "there is no score. The orchestra musicians are given several patterns and a cue sheet. The conductor gives the cue for the entrances and exits of the instruments."[40] The timbral juxtapositions continue to be interesting, and, to me, deliciously unexpected. From 4:00 in, the percussion section is featured, joined by the koto. To my ear, all these juxtapositions work, in different ways.

At the end of *Thread Cog Wheels*, Takahashi engages in the intertextual process so vital in Japanese arts by incorporating "an oblique reading" of the koto classic *Rokudan*. It seems to me that in so doing, he is reminding all listeners of the deep tradition from which the Sawai ryū emerged. Through its "oblique, referential reading," however, the composer is engaging with the performer-composer by means of a creative bridge of just the sort that Sawai devoted his career to creating. Takahashi's response to my interpretation was a grin. "That's a beautiful interpretation, but it is yours, not mine. I create a relationship with players who ask me to write—something the person is used to. You start from there and go on from there. Some kind of connection they can make" (personal communication, May 30, 2011). Apparently, it was where Tadao Sawai wanted to go as well. With such a work, the two were making a new, more balanced shared space in Japanese musical modernity.

SUMMARY AND ADDITIONAL REMARKS

This chapter has explored from an internal perspective the environment of the shared cultural space that was created by the systematic introduction of Western music in Japan. Emphasis has been placed on the condition of possibility within that environment whereby composers might engage with Japanese tradition and vice versa—performer-composers might engage with Western music either by creating new music themselves or by commissioning works by composers. Japanese composers' and performer-composers' motivations for engaging with both the musical systems available to them, including engagement as performers, and the musical results are surely among the most significant aspects of Japanese musical modernity.

If a performer-composer or composer chooses seriously to engage creatively across spheres of expertise, he or she must pursue multiple musical competencies. Here and there in the chapter I have addressed the necessity of gaining musical competence—for example, Michio Miyagi's studying Western music while on the faculty at Geidai, Teiko Kikuchi's teaching composers about the seventeen-stringed koto, Yuji Takahashi's undertaking to learn to play shamisen, and Mayumi Miyata's and Kifu Mitsuhashi's teaching composers about shō and shakuachi, respectively.

Deliberations on the Japaneseness of this and that music continue—mostly on the part of Western observers. Gordon Mathews has written:

"When a particular musical group or genre emerges that can convince a broad range of people in Japan and throughout the world that it is 'Japanese,' this will be the new Japaneseness" (2004: 347). Whereas Mathews does not appear to conclude that that has ever happened, I argue that it has. Surely creative output in Japanese musical modernity that benefits from the affordance of drawing on two grounded musical systems has done that.

In another instance, Anthony Palmer takes Minoru Miki to task for his integration of Western orchestra and gagaku ensemble: "It is my contention that Takemitsu remains Japanese . . . while Miki is striking out upon the murky waters of hybridization, always of questionable fruitfulness" (1991: 425). Palmer's remark suggests that he has espoused the proposition of Japanese uniqueness—that the Japanese possess an essence that must be left alone, unchanged and therefore enduring. That is not the spirit we find in the recent musical creativity of most Japanese composers and indeed performer-composers as well.

I give the last word here to the composer Toshio Hosokawa, a number of whose works have engaged with traditional music and the articulation of which resonates, I think, with the feelings of a number of composers at present: "As a Japanese living in the latter half of the 20th century, I am engaged in a search for a new music which is an adventure not in the spirit of assimilation. I am searching for a new form of spiritual culture and music of the Japanese people, which is at the same time true to my self and to my origins."[41] True as well to the quality of Japanese musical modernity, Hosokawa embraces musical inclusivity:

> I believe that we Japanese should not limit ourselves to Japanese . . . music, but should continue to study all kinds of new and excellent music. . . . We must study the West once again in greater depth in order to view ourselves objectively, in order to really come to know ourselves. . . . Through such studies, I hope to create a new music and a new voice that has not yet been heard from Japan. (1994: 78)

PART III

The Presence in Japan of European Spheres of Musical Participation

In the course of adopting Western music in the nineteenth century, it was perhaps inevitable that music making in Japan would come to be organized very much along the lines it was organized in Europe at the time. In Europe there had been a long history of choral singing, opera, chamber music practice and wind bands, and with the Industrial Revolution and modernity had come orchestral instrumental practice. Finally, ensembles formed specifically to perform contemporary music were formed in the twentieth century. The presence in Japan of those European spheres of musical participation is the third environment of Japanese musical modernity to be taken up in this book.

There was no inevitability in what the Japanese would make of those practices, however, and the quality of the environment for composers in each sphere of participation must be considered in turn. Chapter Five is devoted to the reception in Japan of instrumental ensembles and the degree to which the reception of each type affords composers opportunities for creating new music; similarly, Chapter Six is devoted to the sphere of choral singing. A major factor that emerges in considering affordances for composers is Japanese reception to the repertory with which each type of ensemble was introduced in Japan.

In this part I present further evidence that, with the exception of a very few individuals, Japanese composers in the sphere of "concert music" remain connected with "the people," doing social as well as musical work for their culture.

CHAPTER FIVE

Composing for European Instrumental Ensembles

In Japanese musical modernity, European repertoire and types of instrumental ensembles are pervasive. The quality of the environment considered in this chapter is the particular Japanese reception of each type in the sphere of concert music and the affordance it offers (or fails to offer) individual Japanese composers for providing new repertoire. I begin by situating each type—orchestras, chamber groups, and contemporary music groups, as well as wind bands—for both professional and amateur musicians. Unlike the environment discussed in other chapters, where the evidence weighs in on the positive side of affordance—that is, what the quality of the environment offers composers—this is not consistently the case with instrumental ensembles. Finally, the evaluation of competence for instrumental ensemble writing is discussed as a factor of considerable significance, as are the rewards of being judged highly competent.

SITUATING TYPES OF EUROPEAN ENSEMBLES IN JAPAN

Orchestras

Among European ensemble types in Japan, the orchestra is clearly at the top of the pecking order in terms of cultural status and economic commitment. To gain a sense of the prominence of the orchestra in Japanese musical culture, I analyzed the events in one of Tokyo's main halls that is a likely site for orchestra concerts. Suntory Hall, fruit of the economic boom of the 1980s, opened in 1986 to join the venerable Tokyo Bunka Kaikan (built in 1961), which had served as the premier institutional center for classical and avant-garde music performances. Suntory Hall offers some programs of its own (such as a monthly organ recital) but is also available for rent. In 2009, 233 events were booked in the main hall, some for multiple days. Of those, 145 were orchestra concerts: 115 by Tokyo orchestras, both professional and amateur, and 5 by orchestras from elsewhere in Japan, as well as no fewer than 25 by visiting orchestras, the appearance of which suggests an enormous outlay of resources.[1]

"The orchestra'" in Japan is no single musical institution. Naomoto Okayama, former chief executive officer (and present senior adviser) of the Association of Japanese Symphony Orchestras laid it out for me in 2006 with respect to professional groups:

> There are (1) sinfoniettas, (2) small orchestras, and (3) big orchestras. In Japan, when the word "orchestra" is used, it always implies a big orchestra. The small orchestra has a smaller budget, but it still performs almost the same activities and brings enjoyment to the people. They play Mozart, etc. Sometimes two small orchestras together present a big piece. For example: Orchestra Ensemble Kanazawa is a small orchestra, and they sometimes invite another orchestra. They can tour easily. A small orchestra has to be good, especially for the Tokyo audience, which has *so* many orchestras. The ear of the audience is consequently good. From the orchestra side, they must maintain high standards, the same as those met by Western orchestras. Otherwise . . . (Personal communication, May 10, 2006)

The sinfonietta, or chamber orchestra, is a relatively recent development in Japan. The two most prominent ones are the Tokyo Sinfonietta, which is associated with Kioi Hall, and the Izumi Sinfonietta Osaka, which is associated with Izumi Hall there. Their smaller financial scale makes the ensemble easier to manage. Most pertinent here, sinfoniettas often play contemporary music (Naomoto Okayama, personal communication, May 10, 2006). This is illustrated by excerpts from the website of the Tokyo Sinfonietta:

> Tokyo Sinfonietta was founded in 1994 for the purpose of performing postwar music and of being actively involved in the creation of contemporary works. . . . This is an ensemble specially formed to meet the demanding requirements made by contemporary composers, and its feature is the deep understanding of music created and performed today. The [twenty-seven] members are select soloists also who are blessed with outstanding skills and insight. They give Tokyo Sinfonietta the kind of versatility needed to cover a wide range of music from the works writ-

ten for a small ensemble to a larger chamber orchestra. (http://orchestra.musicinfo.co.jp/~ts/index_e.html, accessed April 8, 2011)

Among the nine composers listed on the website whose works have received world premieres through the Sinfonietta are three Japanese composers—Jo Kondo, Misato Mochizuki, and Ichiro Nodaira.

Although the Izumi Sinfonietta Osaka does not put itself forward as an organization "actively involved in the creation of contemporary works," it was established through a proposal by the composer Akira Nishimura (himself from the Kansai region), who has programmed and supervised a series of concerts titled "New Journey toward the Future of Music" to promote contemporary music at Izumi Hall.[2] Chamber music–sized concert halls sometimes co-commission a new work. In 1998, for example, three halls (Kioi, Izumi, and Shirakawa in Nagoya) commissioned Hitomi Kaneko to write a new piece for sinfonietta (CD booklet, p. 15, Fontec CD FOCD 2557); because her teacher, Gérard Grisey, had died the day she received the commission, she called the piece *Le tombeau de Gérard Grisey* (2000).

The ensemble that Naomoto Okayama used as his example of a small orchestra is also named to indicate its size: the Orchestra Ensemble Kanazawa, founded in 1988 by the eminent conductor Hiroyuki Iwaki (1932–2006), a former conductor of the NHK Symphony Orchestra. As described in the 2005 Annual Report of the Association of Japanese Symphony Orchestras, "The initiative was taken by conductor Hiroyuki Iwaki to create the country's first multinational chamber orchestra, consisting of forty musicians from all over the world" (n.p.).[3] The ensemble is generously supported by the city of Kanazawa and Ishikawa prefecture, and its home is Ishikawa Concert Hall, owned by the Ishikawa-ken Foundation.

The Orchestra Ensemble Kanazawa has been very important for Japanese composers. Under Iwaki, who is legendary in Japan for his interest in contemporary music, "although program building is based on classical repertoire, great emphasis is put on interpretation of contemporary music. The endeavor to commission, explore, and perform new music has led to more than 50 world premieres, mostly of pieces written by composers in residence" (Annual Report of the Association of Japanese Symphony Orchestras 2008: 81). Needless to say, the opportunity to be appointed composer-in-residence is a highly coveted one among Japanese composers.

The total number of orchestras of various sizes in Japan is formidable. As of this writing, there are twenty-five full-time professional orchestras in the country, all of which belong to the Nihon Orchestra Renmei (Association of Japanese Symphony Orchestras). But there are many more professional orchestras (such as Seiji Ozawa's Saito Kinen Orchestra) that do not offer a full schedule of concerts. In terms of location, the huge metropolitan area of Tokyo is clearly a hub for orchestras.[4] I shall return later in the chapter to what this means for composers.

Amateur orchestras are legion in Japan. At the time of our first conversation, Naomoto Okayama told me that it was impossible to know the precise number of such ensembles. He made some inquiries and then reported back to me: "There are 150 amateur orchestras, according to the Federation of Japan Amateur Orchestras Corp. If one includes college (not middle or high school), however, perhaps there are even around 1,000. The amateur orchestra association is doing well, but so many don't want to belong" (personal communication, May 12, 2006).

When I began to realize how significant amateur music making is in Japanese musical modernity, I assumed that an ensemble that was referred to as an "amateur" group was an independent, adult group. When I began to inquire systematically into "amateur music making," however, it became obvious that school groups of all ages are automatically included in the category of "amateur ensembles," in recognition of a kind of flow of experience through the years that extends from the school experience into post-school life. Thus, I was not surprised when Okayama's count included school ensembles.

One reason for the interest in playing in an amateur orchestra is the opportunity it offers to continue playing violin for the large number of Japanese who, as children, took violin lessons. They begin very early—sometimes as young as age three or four. Orchestra experience starts in middle school, continues into high school, and might very well continue in college or university.[5] Except in music schools, the ensembles are always clubs, not classes, with two or three rehearsals a week in late afternoon, in the evening, or on a weekend—whenever it works for the participants, who pursue music "with much passion" (Ken Takaseki, personal communication, May 18, 2006). Each university and college is likely to have more than one.

The conductors of school orchestras are sometimes nonspecialist schoolteachers or some other amateur conductor, although a professional conductor might be invited to conduct a concert. For example, the eminent professional conductor Ken Takaseki told me that he would conduct the Tokyo University student orchestra for their regular concert in January 2009. The Waseda University orchestras are especially well-known;

the largest one, Waseda Kangengakudan Gakuseikaikan (Waseda Orchestra Student Association) was guided by Takasaki for a number of years.

Amateur orchestras have been an important part of the practice of music in Japan for a very long time. In the first decades of the twentieth century, the instructional model established at the pioneering Tokyo School of Music was followed by the private universities attended by children of the modern elite. As the musicologist Tokiko Inoue has shown, the "young intelligentsia" who played in the school orchestras brought within reach the possibility of playing the European orchestral repertoire being discussed in music journals and, starting around 1926–27, heard on domestically produced recordings. They were largely responsible for the establishment of the canon of certain European works that is still in place to the present (Inoue 2009).[6] This occurred before the NHK Symphony became the dominant influence on orchestral music in the Showa era.[7]

In Japan at present there are many amateur orchestras beyond the schools. Many cities have an amateur orchestra, and each of Tokyo's twenty-three districts (ku) has one—the Kita-ku Orchestra, for instance, and the Bunkyo-ku Orchestra. The local government does not necessarily support them beyond perhaps discounting rental fees or offering free space for rehearsal in a civic building, or lending the name of the governmental unit to enhance the group's prestige. Customarily, orchestra members pay a fee to cover such expenses as the cost of score rental and hiring the conductor (Kimiko Shimbo, personal communication, May 1, 2001). Companies have orchestras—the big banks, and Sony for example; it appears to be considered commonplace, if not expected.

One amateur adult orchestra in Tokyo trumps all others in reputation: Shin Kokyo Gakudan (the New Symphony Orchestra), with about 120 players—so many and such good players that they can play Mahler, Strauss, and contemporary music. Founded by the composer Yasushi Akutagawa (for whom the prize is named; see below), the New Symphony Orchestra is comprised of business- and professional persons and presents four concerts per year, inviting professional conductors to conduct concerts (Ken Takaseki, personal communication, May 26, 2008).

It bears repeating that the adjective "amateur" does not necessarily indicate musical groups of a lower level of musical competence: Toshio Hosokawa, whose *Hiroshima Requiem* (1989) was commissioned by the New Symphony Orchestra, declared the performance of it conducted by Chikara Imamura to be "stunning, superb" (personal communication, June 1, 2004). About this extremely serious and expressive work, Hosokawa wrote: "I composed this requiem with the grieving soul of a Japanese born in post-war Hiroshima; this music is my personal prayer" (CD booklet, p. 6, FOCD 9118). The further history of the *Hiroshima Requiem* is evidence that Hosokawa did not hesitate to juxtapose writing for amateur groups in Tokyo and writing for professionals in Europe. He later incorporated the two movements of *Hiroshima Requiem* almost unchanged into *Voiceless Voice in Hiroshima* (1989/2001), to complete which he added three new movements. About these Hosokawa commented:

> I wrote this piece for the Musica Viva, a contemporary music festival in Munich sponsored by Bavarian Radio. In commemoration of the millennium, the Music Viva Prize of ARD and BMW AG commissioned three composers of differing nationalities to write a work on the theme of a question: Is it possible for the traditional musical forms like oratorio which use chorus, vocal soloist and orchestra to survive into the new century? . . . Of all the works I have composed (with the exception of my opera *Vision of Lear*) *Voiceless Voice in Hiroshima* is the longest, and all my musical ideas have been intensified within it. (CD booklet, pp. 5, 6, FOCD 3491)

Small Ensembles for Chamber and Contemporary Music

From the many works for small ensemble—accompanied song, duets, a small selection of instruments—that one sees in publishers' catalogs and on CD recordings, it is clear that chamber music is ubiquitous in the artistic production of Japanese composers. Many chamber music works scored for a great variety of combinations of Western instruments can be found recorded on Fontec's portrait CDs of Japanese composers. Chamber works can also be found on the Camerata label's portrait CDs as well. The Fine Duo, consisting of the violinist Sonoko Numata and the pianist Akemi Tadenuma, for instance, has presented recitals widely in Japan since 1985, and Camerata has issued three CDs of them playing works by Japanese composers (the most recent being a recording of the music of Toru Takemitsu).

Mysteriously, however, specifically chamber music concerts were not a category of performance event that I found frequently announced among the hundreds of flyers distributed at concerts I attended. Moreover, I had to ask pointedly about contemporary chamber music before anyone brought it up. Strikingly, the number of enduring Japanese professional chamber ensembles is very small. References to two—the Tokyo String Quartet and the New Arts String Quartet—come easily, but the Tokyo String Quartet is transnational: it has been an ensemble-in-residence for more than three decades at the Yale School of Music and has performed outside Japan as much as or more than in it.[8]

The New Arts String Quartet, whose performing history has focused more on Japan,

> was founded in October 1974 aiming to bring a breath of fresh air to the world of music in the footsteps of the Ars Nova movement of the 14th century. NASQ has wide-ranging repertory from classicists to contemporary composers. Especially in contemporary music, NASQ has been giving a large number of Japanese premieres to works by foreign composers and also has been quick to present the work of internationally active Japanese composers such as Toshi Ichiyanagi, Maki Ishii, Toru Takemitsu, Akira Nishimura, Toshio Hosokawa, and Joji Yuasa. NASQ has regularly taken part in various contemporary music festivals in Japan including "Music Today" under direction of Toru Takemitsu and "Summer Festival" presented by Suntory Music Foundation. In 1994 celebrating its 20th anniversary, NASQ held two commemorative concerts which were highly successful and also commissioned new works [from] Toshi Ichiyanagi, Joji Yuasa, Toshiro Saruya as well as Karen Tanaka and gave them the world premier in 1996. (CD booklet, pp. 6–7, Camerata CD 30CM-557)[9]

Ichiyanagi wrote about his String Quartet no. 3, *Inner-Landscape* (1994), for the twentieth anniversary of the New Arts String Quartet: "It is out of respect for their sincere activities concentrated on contemporary music for twenty years, under difficult circumstances, to continue the activities of string quartet in Japan [that I give them this quartet]" (CD booklet, p. 6, Camerata CD 30CM-557). The New Arts String Quartet no longer concertizes, however, since its key members have retired. Ichiyanagi remarked to me on May 31, 2011: "There is no base for chamber music here."

The composer Tokuhide Niimi confirmed that "there are many temporary string quartets, but permanent ones, maybe two"—one of which is the Quatro Piacelli, which had premiered his commissioned String Quartet no. 2 the day before our most recent conversation on June 2, 2011.[10] The Quartet Excelsior is the most active string quartet and one of the only touring permanent string quartets in Japan. "It takes a lot of time to make a good quartet," Niimi remarked, "and members receive no salary." The group must rent a hall, and the appropriate halls are so small that ticket sales cannot cover costs and pay performers at a professional level as well. Small ensembles are more likely to be formed from among the regular members of an orchestra or sinfonietta—when they want to play a piece for flute and violin or oboe and piano, for instance.

In the sphere of performance, I gained the impression that chamber music plays a much smaller role in amateur music making in Japan than does music for larger ensembles, and I began to seek explanations for this phenomenon. One of them, from the composer Keiko Fujiie, who does not hesitate to say what she thinks, confirmed my impression:

> Chamber music in Japan in general? There's not much of it, not even string quartet. Why? There is no trainer—no conductor or teacher. In an orchestra, the conductor says what to do. In chorus, conductor says what to do. In private solo instruction, the teacher says what to do and the student follows the example. Players want a model; they don't have to/don't know how to listen to each other. Also, the skill level has to be higher in chamber music, with individual parts. (Personal communication, April 21, 2005)

Another composer, Keiko Harada, was equally forthcoming:

> Concert producers and halls like big things. And in Japan, the tendency is for people to like wind ensembles, choirs, orchestras. There are many amateur groups. In chamber music performers relate directly to each other. But the way of communication of Japanese people is different. Japanese people are not open with each other. Japanese people feel safe in orchestra and chorus, although wind players always feel pressure. It is different for string players. (Personal communication, May 25, 2007)

The composer Yayoi Kitazume, who prefers writing for chamber groups to writing for larger groups, saw the "safety zone" for players in another light, namely as a constraint imposed on orchestra players. Kitazume, whose music was described by her peer Haruna Miyake as "quiet, sparse, and spatial" (personal communication, March 30, 1999), explained:

> I don't want big success as a composer [which requires writing for orchestra]. I enjoy small groups. I prefer *not* to compose for orchestra because the conductor is in charge; the individual players can't move, do the natural thing. I always take space and movement into consideration—breath and body. Not only singers, but instrumentalists can

> sing by their body movement and breath. Also I believe that other important factors are to listen to silence and to improvise without a score. (Personal communication, May 20, 2007)

The situation for contemporary music ensembles is similar to that in the sphere of chamber music. Mentioned by several composers, including Joji Yuasa and Keiko Harada, was the contemporary music group Ensemble Nomad, created in 1999 as the resident ensemble for the new Tokyo Opera City Plaza. As Harada, who worked as its first artistic coordinator, tells it, Toru Takemitsu asked the guitarist Norio Sato: "Please use the funding of this Foundation because there is no paid regular ensemble for contemporary music in Japan" (Keiko Harada, personal communication, May 25, 2011). While Ensemble Nomad still functions as a resident ensemble, its members "have soloistic activity, and some belong to an orchestra or the Tokyo Sinfonietta" (Joji Yuasa, personal communication, June 1, 2011).

Wind Bands

The third category of instrumental ensemble that Japan adopted from Europe is the wind band, a mostly amateur activity. The figures for wind bands, kept by the All-Japan Band Association (AJBA), which mounts annual competitions, encompass the categories of primary school, middle school, high school, college/university, company, and community. The enormous popularity of this musical activity can be glimpsed by the grand total of 13,595 ensembles that participated in the AJBA competition in 2000, comprising approximately 500,000 contestants. By 2007 the number of registered wind bands in Japan exceeded 14,000, and with an average band size of at least fifty members, the total exceeded 700,000 contestants in a single year (Hebert 2012: 127). The quality of the competing bands is apparently quite stunning, drawing American band directors every year to witness for themselves what they have heard about.

Prominent among the professional organizations are the Tokyo Kosei Wind Orchestra, founded in 1960. It has produced hundreds of recorded albums over several decades, including the annual recording of the competition pieces for the year, which serves as the model toward which the amateur bands strive. Other prominent professional groups are the Osaka Municipal Symphonic Band and the various bands affiliated with Japan's self-defense forces.

European instrumental ensemble types, then, make up a prominent environment in Japanese musical modernity. As for the quality of the environment—the particular Japanese reception of those types—it is clear that the large ensembles are the best-supported ones, with small ensembles for chamber and contemporary music being of more interest to composers than to audiences or even performers. Wind bands are received well particularly as school clubs and as a site for participation in competitions.

AFFORDANCES FOR COMPOSERS OF WORKS FOR INSTRUMENTAL ENSEMBLES

Having established the differing receptions accorded by Japanese people to the various types of European instrumental ensembles, the question now arises of the extent to which each of them affords Japanese composers the possibility of creating new repertoire, should they be capable of doing so. How supportive of its own composers is this environment of Japanese musical modernity when it comes to instrumental music? To address this question, I have organized the following discussion by type of ensemble and consider reasons why an instrumental ensemble might foster Japanese composers and their works, along with reasons why they might hesitate to do so.

Music for Orchestra

When it comes to orchestras, affordances for composers must be seen both as potential opportunities for creating new works and as possibilities to have existing works performed ("in the repertoire"). Statistics on the performance of works by Japanese composers by orchestras suggest a lack of support. Junko Kitagawa's interest in twenty-first-century repertoire performed by Japanese orchestras led her to compile a list of concert programs from the regularly scheduled concerts in 2006 and 2007. The source of her information was the home pages of thirteen professional orchestras: five based in Tokyo, three in Osaka, and five in areas outside of those two cities.

> The aggregate result was that 103 composers' works were taken up. Those performed by all orchestras were Mozart and Beethoven. Other than those, composers taken up by many orchestras were Tchaikovsky, Mahler, Shostakovich, Dvořák, Ravel (more than 9), Elgar (8), Richard Georg Strauss, Mendelssohn (7). . . . Conversely, there were 51 composers, other than Knussen, who were taken up by only one orchestra.

> Of that 80% (41 people) are "new" composers, who are active in the twenty-first century from the twentieth century, and in addition, less than 20% (7 people) were Japanese composers. (Kitagawa 2008: 61)

As the material presented below illustrates, some orchestras make a point of presenting works by Japanese composers in special events, so the impression drawn from programming in regularly scheduled concerts does not provide a complete picture. Nevertheless, a recent statement by the composer Tokuhide Niimi presents a similar view: "Orchestras don't do much of my music. One conductor said, 'It's difficult for the usual audience to understand. If you have a piece—not so long, like a maximum of ten minutes and if it's easy for listening—I can take it into my program.' But longer—it's almost impossible. A piece like *Fujin raijin* works for them, because Japanese drum is easy to understand" (personal communication, June 2, 2011).[11]

To gain a sense of how full-time professional orchestras position themselves vis-à-vis the performance of works by Japanese composers, I turned to their brief profiles in the 2005 Annual Report of the Association of Japanese Symphony Orchestras. I have excerpted details on some orchestras' projects here. They appear in chronological order based on the founding of the orchestra—all after World War II—to lend a sense of the pace of that cultural activity in Japan. Regrettably, such statements have disappeared from the profiles published in more recent annual reports.

- The Tokyo Symphony Orchestra (TSO), originally founded in 1946 as the Toho Symphony Orchestra, with a name change in 1951, has been "energetically giving premiere performances of Japanese composers as well other major contemporary works—premiering well over 200 compositions" (Association of Japanese Symphony Orchestras 2005: [n.p.]). Contradictory to the oft-expressed opinion that audiences do not want to hear contemporary music, the TSO attracted the second-largest total number of people to their performances in 2004 (approximately 230,000), compared to the attendees at performances of other professional orchestras.
- The Kyoto Symphony Orchestra was founded in 1956 under the management of the Kyoto City Government "to create a new culture in the city" (Association of Japanese Symphony Orchestras 2005: [n.p.]), which is renowned for its traditional culture: "Every year since 1973, the orchestra has been performing Japanese works with a theme of Kyoto that were commissioned by the city" (As-

sociation of Japanese Symphony Orchestras 2005: [n.p.]). The composer Toshio Hosokawa wrote of *Ferne-Landschaft I* (1987), for orchestra, which the city commissioned from him: "The city required that the work be inspired by the image of Kyoto, so I set to work, keeping in mind a variety of [landscape paintings] I had seen at Zen temples in Kyoto" (1997a: 6).[12]

- The Japan Philharmonic Orchestra (JPO) was founded in 1956. "The 'Japan Philharmonic Series' (the project of commissioned works by Japanese composers) continues from the orchestra's foundation; there are 40 works in the series and each of them has a reputation as 'a masterpiece of contemporary music'" (Association of Japanese Symphony Orchestras 2008: 61). Ichiro Nodaira, who received a commission in the fortieth year of the orchestra's existence, has also been invited to conduct the orchestra three or four times a year, especially in concerts of contemporary music (personal communication, May 28, 2007).
- The Sapporo Symphony Orchestra was inaugurated in 1961 as the Sapporo Citizen Symphony Orchestra but took its present name the following year. It is the only professional orchestra on the island of Hokkaido, and "in 1985 the orchestra caused quite a sensation with its recording of Toru Takemitsu's soundtrack for Akira Kurosawa's film *Ran* and international attention again in 2001 for a CD of works by Japanese composers on the UK Chandos label [CHAN 9876]" (Association of Japanese Symphony Orchestras 2005: [n.p.]).
- Yomiuri Nippon Symphony Orchestra was founded in 1962 by three members of the Yomiuri Group—the *Yomiuri Shimbun* newspaper conglomerate, the Nippon Television broadcasting network, and the Yomiuri Telecasting Corporation—to promote orchestral music throughout Japan: "Since 2001 it has had an annual plan to commission works by young Japanese composers, but previously had commissioned pieces composed by Akira Miyoshi (*En-soi lointain*), Toru Takemitsu (*Twill by Twilight*), and Akira Nishimura (*Hoshi-mandala*)" (Association of Japanese Symphony Orchestras 2005: [n.p.]).
- The Tokyo Metropolitan Symphony Orchestra, established by the Tokyo Metropolitan Government in 1965 on the heels of the 1964 Tokyo Olympics, is frequently credited by aficionados as one of the few Japanese professional orchestras that foster contemporary compositions. This is not mentioned in its self-description in either

the 2005 Annual Report or the 2008 Yearbook of the Association of Japanese Orchestras. In 2004 their modus operandi was to program European composers for the subscription concerts. Japanese composers were featured only in a "Discover the Music of Japan" concert; however, the works in the October program of that year were composed between 1948 and 1965.

- The Sendai Philharmonic Orchestra was founded in 1972 as the Miyagi Philharmonic Orchestra, a citizen's (i.e., amateur) orchestra, "as a result of the enthusiasm of musicians and music lovers in Sendai" (Association of Japanese Symphony Orchestras 2005: [n.p.]). It was incorporated as a professional orchestra in 1978. "The Sendai Philharmonic Orchestra did the world premiere of *The Far Sail*, an opera composed by Akira Miyoshi in 1999" (Association of Japanese Symphony Orchestras 2005: [n.p.]).
- The Hiroshima Symphony Orchestra, founded in 1972, is the only professional orchestra in the Chugoku and Shikoku regions of Japan. According to the CD booklet of a Fontec recording, *Ferne-Landschaft III: Seascapes of Fukuyama* (1996) was commissioned from Toshio Hosokawa by the Fukuyama Art and Culture Promotion Foundation in the 1996 commemoration of the eightieth anniversary of the founding of the city of Fukuyama, on the Seto Inland Sea, close to Hiroshima. It is dedicated to the conductor Naohiro Totsuka and to the Hiroshima Symphony Orchestra. Because Hosokawa's birthplace is a village close to Hiroshima, *Ferne-Landschaft III* invokes personal experience as well as the memory of the world for the "black rain" that fell in the area (Hosokawa 1997c: 10).
- The Orchestra Ensemble Kanazawa, founded in 1988, placed great emphasis on the interpretation of contemporary music under the leadership of the late conductor Hiroyuki Iwaki (see p. 141). One hopes that the residency invitations to composers will continue to be offered. The last mentioned on the ensemble's website is Misato Mochizuki, listed as Composer of the Year, for 2011–12 (www.oek.jp). Recordings of Japanese contemporary works commissioned and/or performed by the Orchestra Ensemble Kanazawa are also displayed on the website.[13]

Unless an orchestra has made a particular commitment to programming music by Japanese composers, the reasons to avoid it are weighty. The primary reason I heard has to do with financial risk—a reason not peculiar to the Japanese situation in that the music would be "contemporary." The financial risk is created by several perceived and real factors. Chief among them is the conservative taste of the audiences. As summarized by Naomoto Okayama, chief executive officer of the Association of Japanese Symphony Orchestras at the time of our first conversation, "Japanese audiences for orchestra are still big, due to the program of subscription concerts. But it is hard to get an audience for new music" (personal communication, May 10, 2006). "Contemporary" or "new" music includes Japanese composers as well as non-Japanese.

Michio Takemori, an administrator for the NHK Symphony for six years, quipped: "The subscription concert audience was *most conservative.* One contemporary piece would be programmed with, for instance, Tchaikovsky. They would wait in the lobby until the contemporary music finished. The conductor Charles Dutoit said, 'We need contemporary music.' 'What kind?' I asked. 'Penderecki,' was the response. NOT contemporary!" (personal communication, June 2, 2008). Finding conservatism to be a factor on the part of both audiences and the orchestra, Takemori suggested that Tan Dun, Lowell Lieberman, and such be programmed—more contemporary music and in different styles. He managed to start a series where in one concert six or seven different contemporary pieces could be heard. He commissioned a number of new works between 1994 and 2000—a four- or five-year "adventure." Takemori felt that it created a different atmosphere for the subscribing audience. When Akira Nishimura's work was performed, for instance, his students came to the concert. The programs were held each Saturday, and people's reception to the music changed gradually. It takes time. "But orchestras don't think long-term," he said ruefully. "Three months, half a year, because good new works are so few—only one or two." When Takemori left the NHK Symphony Orchestra, these concerts were discontinued (personal communication, June 2, 2008). The involvement of the NHK Symphony Orchestra with the Otaka Memorial Prize (see below) is the most prominent example of that orchestra's involvement explicitly with contemporary music.

There are other reasons that programming contemporary works creates financial risks. While programming works that are no longer under copyright protection eliminates the necessity for payment of rights, royalties must be paid for copyrighted works, and that could influence concert planning. When a living or recently deceased composer's work is programmed, JASRAC's effective tariff rate per live concert is 4 percent of the box-office receipts. In cases where a comprehensive agreement is concluded with a concert organizer who organizes concerts frequently, the rate is reduced to 2.5 percent of the box-office receipts. JASRAC negotiated for many years with the representatives of concert promoters and agreed to the current rate, which JASRAC considers to be on a par with international standards (Satoshi Watanabe, personal communication, August 9, 2012). In addition, the cost of renting the score for a new work or a work that might not remain in repertoire must be factored in, adding to the enormous cost of mounting one evening's performance of a professional orchestra in Tokyo; in 2005 it was between 3.5 million and 4 million yen ($35,000–40,000; Naomoto Okayama, personal communication, May 10, 2005).

Finally, there is the high cost of commissioning a new work for orchestra—a crucial matter for composers. A foundation (such as the Suntory Foundation) or an individual is more likely to commission a new work than is an orchestra. Here the practicality of the commissioning aspect of two of the major composition competitions comes into view, discussed in the section titled "Competitions for Evaluating Competence" below.

The potentially lower quality of an organization's performance is another deterrent to programming a new work, specifically with respect to the amount of time required to learn a new piece relative to the time that can be allotted for rehearsal. According to the composer Keiko Harada, a total of only three rehearsals of fifty minutes to an hour each will normally be allotted for each new piece, so the musicians may not know the music by the time of the concert. Except for contemporary music players who have lots of experience, many players have to face new music and play it in concerts without really understanding it. Therefore, after the concert they forget the music. If Harada has an invitation to write for orchestra, she starts going to rehearsals to learn about the players and talk with them. But still no time is given to her because orchestra members, who are unionized, may say that they do not want to work more hours. "The whole system is bad for new music," she asserts. A respected, self-confident young composer, Harada says that she refuses to let an orchestra piece be presented if she is not given more rehearsal time. She sympathizes with other young composers who are trapped in a catch-22: they are afraid they will never get a performance again if they refuse to write without more time, but she knows the effect that a bad performance can have on the public's opinion of an aspiring composer's music (personal communication, May 25, 2007).

The factor of rehearsal time for a new work was brought up to me also by the composer Akira Nishimura, through whom I shall introduce another possibility for commissions for new works: from those amateur orchestras which function without the constraints of professionalization but whose musical production can be extremely fine. Nishimura singled out the Utsunomiya Girls' High School for its excellence as well as the Waseda University Orchestra. But he also mentioned Shin Kokyo Gakudan (the New Symphony Orchestra), whose players are businessmen and dentists, for instance. Such ensembles spend a longer time in rehearsal: "The composer sits in the conductor's chair and really works with the musicians on details. A very friendly relationship" (personal communication, May 17, 2006). Nishimura pronounced the experience of working with the New Symphony Orchestra on a new piece "very fine," attributing it as well to the quality of their playing of contemporary music.[14]

Of course, not all amateur orchestras are equally excellent, and, it must be stressed, not all are willing to play (not to mention commission) contemporary music. The composer Yoshihiro Kanno addressed reasons that might prevent amateur orchestras from programming contemporary works, including two that resonate with the JASRAC response about professional orchestras.

> Composers write music for too many instruments. Most amateur orchestras are smallish; the new music is too much for them to play. It is also difficult to get music—to rent it from a publisher. That requires time and money.
>
> In addition, Japanese contemporary orchestra pieces are too difficult, technically. They require special sounds from the strings, complex fingerings for the winds, too much percussion. Musicians are not familiar with how to play these effects. [15]
>
> There's lots of repertoire from the romantic period and classical periods. An orchestra has so much repertoire to play—European repertoire—and orchestra players are interested in playing that music. Beautiful music. Comfortable. It has to be melodic, tonal mostly. (Personal communication, May 24, 2007)

Indeed, the word "amateur," when coupled with "orchestra," is most likely to imply a preference for historical repertoire over contemporary music. The conductor Ken Takasaki's explained why: "Violin is especially difficult, and they learn on classical repertoire—Vivaldi and Bach, for instance. When they grow up, they want to play romantic pieces and they have no opportunity to play contemporary music" (personal communication, May 26, 2008). On another practical note, the composer Keiko Fujiie commented about amateur orchestras with whom she has interacted,

"They do not commission because they need to hear a recording of a piece to learn it" (personal communication, April 21, 2005).

Chamber Music

> Orchestra commissions are few, chamber music commissions even fewer. (Toshio Hosokawa, personal communication, July 1, 2004)

> If chamber groups are amateur, they play classical repertoire. The reason is not financial. They are mostly conservative, wanting to play music they know—their pleasure is limited to classical music. They don't have eyes to look beyond the boundaries [of their experience]. (Joji Yuasa, personal communication, April 17, 2005)

After a late-afternoon performance in May 2006 of Joji Yuasa's chamber work *Cosmos Haptic IV* at Oji Hall in the Ginza, Yuasa and I wound up going to dinner with the cellist, Saeko Tominaga, and the pianist, Kyoko Sasaki. I took the opportunity to ask these chamber-music specialists about contemporary chamber music in Japan. Tominaga and her friends are interested in performing contemporary pieces, she said, but scores are hard to get. She had called up Yuasa to get hold of *Cosmos Haptic IV*. Appreciation was expressed for the scores published by the Japan Federation of Composers, which runs a competition that is germane to the matter of new chamber music in Japan.

The annual competition of the Nihon Sakkyokka Kyogikai (otherwise known as the Japan Federation of Composers [JFC]; see chapter 2) is open to members only. The award is the publication of a new work, with preference given to first-time winners, so the opportunity is a good one for many members. From among the approximately three hundred new pieces that are likely to be submitted, an internal committee chooses between fifteen and twenty for publication.[16] A primary function of the series is making Japanese composers' music available to performers who are competing in konkur, and who, in the first and second stage of the competition, must include Japanese compositions or post-1980 pieces. In choosing the pieces to publish, the JFC jury considers both cost and purpose; the works tend to be for solo instrument or some small ensemble. Performers know about the publication series, research the pieces in the cumulative catalog published annually by the JFC,[17] and obtain scores at the cost of printing (Akira Nishimura, personal communications, May 22, 2002, and

August 27, 2012). Furthermore, each year a compilation CD is made of a small selection of the published works. Because in Japan a great deal of the new music that is composed is not published, the publication series is arguably the most important service provided by the JFC to its members.

The significance of the JFC publications was brought home to me by Setsuko Miyahara, president of the Japan League of Women Composers. We were discussing her piece *Ningen no daichi* (2005), for two flutes, piano, and narrator, which had been released on a CD published by Kokusai Geijutsu Renmei (the Japan International League of Artists [JILA]).[18] How did the recording come about, I asked? That she didn't know; but it was her second contact with JILA, which had chosen another of her pieces for a concert previously, one they had discovered because it was published by the JFC. She confirmed that the JFC publication competition was excellent because the series had been very helpful in her career not only as a composer but also as a pianist (Setsuko Miyahara, personal communication, May 26, 2009).

For chamber music particularly, it seems, consortiums formed by composers themselves or by performers are important for the circulation of new works through concerts, printing of scores, and production of recordings. JILA is a prime example of such a consortium. In the CD booklet for *The Third Japan Contemporary Music Festival* (JILA-1002, 1997), the producer Kazuhiko Hattori explains that the CD features six pieces recorded live at the organization's third Japan Contemporary Music Festival, held over a period of two days in August 1997: "The 'Japan Contemporary Music Festival' began the year before last to remedy a question of meaning of contemporary music and impart its interest [for] a new era. Because of the result of the composers' and the players' support, finally at the third try we are able to create a CD to publish how the music festival progressed. In parallel with publishing sheet music, we are planning to try to enlarge this festival little by little as a series every year" (Hattori [1997]: 1).[19]

Another important organization for organizing concerts of chamber works is Nihon Gendai Ongaku Kyōkai (the Japan Society for Contemporary Music), usually referred to as Gen On.[20] As told to me by Yori-Aki Matsudaira, who at the time we spoke was the head of Gen On, a composer group had been founded in 1930 (his father, Yoritsune Matsudaira, was among the founding members) for the purpose of producing concerts. Currently, usually two a year are held, in autumn and spring, and composers join the organization as a way of getting their works heard. Frequently the pieces performed have been commissioned by one or more performers, but the composer contributes to the cost of the concert, so the commission is recycled. Responsibility for producing each concert is taken by one member, who searches among the members for new pieces, selects the program, and recommends it to a committee who will "work out the details" (Yori-Aki Matsudaira, personal communication, May 27, 2004). Although Gen-On members pay an annual membership fee that goes toward maintaining the office, printing membership lists, and the like, it is the responsibility of the producer of the concert to help with raising funds for the event from such sources as the Ministry of Culture, JASRAC, businesses, arts foundations, and SARAH. Here the affordances from the infrastructures of modernity come into play (see chapter 2). For the spring concert, government money is more likely, from funds left at the end of March—the end of the fiscal year. For the fall concert, the responsibility for fundraising falls more on the composers and producer of the event.[21]

As the Japanese Section of the International Society for Contemporary Music, Gen On plays a significant role in keeping Japanese composers connected internationally and participating in that environment of shared cultural space in Japanese musical modernity (see chapter 3). In 2001, under the leadership of its president, Yori-Aki Matsudaira, Gen On organized the ISCM Festival, World Music Days 2001, in Yokohama.

Music for Wind Band

Composers for band are afforded opportunities to compose new repertoire by a huge nationwide competition held since 1939 by the All-Japan Band Association (AJBA), which in turn is supported by both the education sector of the government and the music industry as a whole—both instrument manufacturing (Yamaha, Roland, Kawai, Korg, Ibanez, Tama, Casio, etc.) and the recording industry, from production (Hitachi, Maxell, TDK, Nakamichi, Boss, etc.) to marketing and distribution (Sony, JVC, Columbia, Epic, Toshiba-EMI, etc.). The foremost researcher of Japanese wind bands, David Hebert, notes that "an effective system of cooperative relationships between composers, publishers and consumers has produced the body of repertoire commonly performed by Japanese bands."[22] I have articulated this in more theoretical terms, that is, as opportunities for composers afforded by connectivities among the infrastructures of modernity.

For the AJBA national competition, each band is required to perform two pieces. One, the "required piece" (about five minutes long), is chosen from a selection of new band works commissioned each year by AJBA specifically for the event. In recent years the Association has selected four of them from four different composers for use as a required piece. This practice of annual commissions has fostered the development of a large body of original Japanese band works and encouraged many young Japanese composers to create music for wind band. The other composition performed for the contest, a "free piece" that must (in accordance with the competition's guidelines) be no more than five and a half to six and a half minutes long, is selected by each ensemble. Japanese band directors view such free pieces in terms of three categories: band arrangements of famous orchestral classics, original band works by Western composers, and original Japanese band works. According to Hebert, the proportion of bands choosing to perform an original Japanese band piece has increased from around one-sixth to nearly one-fourth of the total.

While approximately two-thirds of the bands that make it to the national level of the tiered competition choose to perform arrangements of European orchestral works, composers are still circuitously afforded creative and economic opportunities. Composers' connections with commerce reemerges here as well:

> It is important to note that despite the international appearance of these selections, most pieces listed as compositions by famous European composers actually consist of band transcriptions by Japanese arrangers that are published on Japanese presses. Upon careful examination of the pieces played by middle school bands at the 50th AJBA national competition, one finds that 19 of the "free pieces" were either composed or arranged by Japanese composers. Therefore, if one views the 29 bands—performing 2 pieces each—as 58 distinct performances (which is the legal position in terms of intellectual property), one finds that 49 of the 58 pieces performed (85%) were either composed or arranged by Japanese musicians and made available exclusively through Japanese presses and distributors. In other words, all profits remain in Japan associated with the sales and performance of such pieces (as well as recorded models) to the thousands of bands participating in the AJBA competition. (Hebert 2012: 160–61)

While some composers with whom I spoke were not interested in writing music within the very constraining boundaries of the competition context for which the music is needed, others are actively involved. Among those Hebert mentions are Michio Kitazume; Toshi Ichiyanagi; Isao Matsushita (b. 1951), a professor of music composition at Geidai; Hiroshi Hoshina (b. 1936), professor of music at Hyogo University of Education; Yasuhide Ito (b. 1960), who teaches at several schools in the Tokyo area (see chapter 2); and Toshio Mashima (b. 1949) and Masamichi Amano (b. 1957), who have managed to establish strong careers as professional composers entirely outside of academia (see Hebert 2012: 162).

An explicit example of the connectivities among the sectors of industry, commerce, and education that affords composers the opportunity to create new music is the Band Restoration project sponsored by the Hamamatsu Cultural Foundation in Hamamatsu City, home of two major instrument manufacturers, Yamaha and Kawai. "Band Restoration" is the title of an annual event in which wind ensembles of the city's middle and high schools (also possibly a Tokyo band) perform pieces newly produced by Japanese composers well-known in a variety of fields including concert music, jazz, popular music, computer music, music for broadcasting, and so on. Each comments on his or her work in a lecture the day before the concert.

One existing piece is selected for the performance each year by a jury of four composers, and others are commissioned under the leadership particularly of Michio Kitazume (b. 1948). Kitazume had a work performed in each of the 2008 and 2009 programs. Most of the names will be familiar from previous mention, and I repeat them here to drive home the point that most Japanese composers exercise artistic flexibility in their creative endeavors: in 2008, Katsuhisa Hattori, Toshi Ichiyanagi, Makiko Kinoshita, Reijiro Kuroku, Kazunori Maruyama, Akira Nishimura, and Shigeaki Saegusa; in 2009, Toshiharu Kataoka, Norio Maeda, Tokuhide Niimi, Naomi Niu, Ichiro Nodaira, Yuzo Toyama, and Toshiyuki Watanabe.

Michio Kitazume himself offers a fine example of the artistic flexibility of Japanese composers.[23] He is among the few holding a professorship (at Kunitachi College of Music) who manages to maintain an active career as a composer and achieve distinction both in Japan and internationally. He has twice won the Otaka Prize (1994 and 2001), and was awarded the Nakajima Kenzo Music Prize (2004) for his achievement in composition. A "good citizen" among composers, Kitazume is a director of Gen On.

Since he is the son of a clarinet player, the Band Restoration project was not the initial motivation for Kitazume's interest in the possibilities that wind instruments present. Having already composed a number of works for wind band, he understood the potential for connecting diverse musical spheres and making their music accessible to more people by commissioning composers in a variety of musical fields for the project:

> Almost every middle school in Japan has its own wind band, and many of these bands seem very eager to play music, attending a competition

> held nationwide every summer. Unfortunately, however, the percentage of the students who continue to play the instruments they have played in the bands is very low. Nobody knows exactly why this is so. Of course, there could be many reasons, but one may be that the field of the wind band in Japan is sometimes very closed, so to speak. Some of them mainly focus on ceremonies at school or on the competition in the summer, and their repertoire is limited to marching or to the pieces they need to learn for the competition. This prevents the students and others concerned with wind ensembles from widening their view through many contacts with other fields of music, and it may lead the students to quit playing their instruments after their graduation. So the basic idea of Band Restoration is to present a variety of music for wind band, enabling students (some of whom start their musical experience with their wind band activity) to experience the variety through playing instruments themselves; this would be better for the musicians. (Personal communication, September 1, 2012)

In 2008 a Band Restoration CD series was begun by Brain-Music.Asia to introduce those composers' new works to the world; each portrait features works for wind band by one of the commissioned composers.[24] Scores for the works for a given year are published by Hustle Copy, a company that since 1973 has created scores and printed music for many kinds of music, from television programs to orchestra concerts.[25]

In this Japanese environment of European instrumental ensemble types, the matter of a composer's competence (or, as stated in Gibson's definition of affordance theory, "capabilities") comes to the fore. In chapter 1 I addressed the means by which one might gain musical competence to become a composer and, as a teacher, assist others to gain competence. In chapter 3, gaining further competence was shown to be a motivation for international experience. In chapter 4, different competencies were shown to be meaningful for performer-composers and composers. In the next section, I consider the perspective of means by which a composer's competence is evaluated.

COMPETITIONS FOR EVALUATING COMPETENCE

In Japan competitions are the most prominent site of evaluation of a composer's competence for writing new works for instrumental ensembles. Because prizes can be crucial for the careers of Japanese composers—and for the infrastructural institutions that support them—I investigated them fairly closely. After illustrating with one graphic example the weight given to composition prizes in general, I shall look closely at the most prestigious—those that position composing for orchestra at the pinnacle of achievement for a composer in Japan, with composing for chamber ensemble in second place despite the situation for the performance of small ensembles that I detailed above.

While it is not surprising to find a litany of prizes won by a composer featured on a CD recording in a CD booklet, or in the program note about the composer whose work is being played in a concert, what seems a significant amount of detailed information for a concert flyer appeared, for instance, on the poster for the Music Tomorrow concert of July 8, 2007, by the NHK Symphony Orchestra. Featured in that event was Tokuhide Niimi, who had received the Otaka Prize that year for his orchestra composition *Élan vital* (see below). Relative to other types of biographical information on the eight-and-a-half- by eleven-inch glossy flyer, the amount of space devoted to the prizes that Niimi had won is notable. The complete profile reads:

> Born 1949 in Nagoya. After graduating from Tōdai [University of Tokyo], Industrial Department, he went into music. He graduated from the Composition Department of a Geidai [Tokyo University of Arts]. In 1974 he won the NET-TV Composition Competition. In 1997 he won the Grand Prix in the Geneva Competition for Ballet Music. In 1982 he was awarded a Bunkachō [Agency for Cultural Affairs] Special Prize for Butai Geijutsu Sōsaku [Stage Arts] and also the IMC International Music Hyōgikai. In 2004 he won the Grand Prix for the CD *Fujin raijin* in the Bunkachō Arts Festival. In 2005 his opera *White Bird* was given its world premiere in Aiichi prefecture at the Aiichi Arts Theater. He was awarded the Sagawa Yoshio Music Prize. In 2006 he was the composer-in-residence for the Orchestra Ensemble Kanazawa. This piece is a world premiere.
>
> Niimi is now a professor at Toho Gakuen Daigakuin. He also teaches at Toho Tankidaigaku (temporary). He is a lecturer (not permanent faculty) at Tokyo Ongaku Daigaku and is on the board of directors of the JFC. (Translated by Fukiko Shinohara)

For the sponsors of Music Tomorrow, this information served as a marketing tool for a potential audience that would understand that prizes are meaningful. For Niimi, it presented an accumulation of cultural capital, testifying to his competence and to his success in his chosen profession.

In the CD booklets for the series of portrait CDs of the works of Toshio Hosokawa that have been issued by the Japanese company Fontec,[26] the litany of prizes is likely to begin: "Since 1980 (Darmstadt) Hosokawa has presented his works in Europe and Japan, gaining an international reputation and winning numerous awards and prizes, including. . . ." A leading transnational composer who has for most of his career made his home in both Germany and Japan, Hosokawa received most of his prizes in European competitions, and Fontec as well as his publisher, Schott Japan, knows that Japanese purchasers of the CD will be impressed by that international recognition of his competence. While those details are visible only after one has purchased the CD and are thus not the immediate marketing tool that a profile on a concert flyer is, the purchaser of the CD is assured of the distinction of the composer and "hears" the music with that in mind. For Hosokawa's career beyond 2001, as traced in the CD booklet, residencies get serious attention, along with commissions for and performances of works in music festivals. It would appear that prizes were an important means for establishing his reputation, and part of his reward for participating in competitions was being invited to participate at some other point in prestigious musical events.

From conversations with composers I came to understand the importance to them of prizes. For example, Hitomi Kaneko concurred with my casual observation (at that point I had done no systematic research on the matter) that prizes seem to be more important for Japanese composers in Japan than for composers elsewhere, and she offered a personal anecdote. She won the 1990 NHK/Mainichi first prize, she told me, and for her, in Japan, that was like a small license to enter the professional music world. It greatly encouraged her to keep writing. Later, while she was studying in France, she had told Grisey about it and tried to explain to him how important it had been to her. She was deeply disappointed with his reaction: "He didn't understand, and it was so anticlimactic" (personal communication, May 17, 2002).

The greatest test of a Japanese composer's competence is writing for orchestra. That is clear from the fact that all of the most prestigious awards are for new works for orchestra. This is not surprising on a number of counts. Members of the elite—students in the top universities, for instance—were well aware of the high status of the orchestra in German music at the time that European music was being systematically introduced into Japan—mostly by Germans. Furthermore, respected foreign musicians established prizes there. Alexander Tcherepnin, a Russian composer who took up residence in Shanghai in 1935 and visited Japan, provided awards that supported orchestral compositions by Japanese composers who had not had any academic training. One early winner of the Tcherepnin Award, an international composition competition, was Akira Ifukube, for his first orchestral work, *Japanese Rhapsody* (1935). In 1937, during a successful tour, Felix Weingartner (1863–1942), conductor of the Vienna Philharmonic Orchestra, also started a competition, first prize in which included a performance in Europe of the winning composition. "Many compositions were submitted and more than eighty were chosen for consideration—a sign of how highly active Japanese composers were. The prize was won by Shukuchi Mitsukuri, Fumio Hayasaka and Masao Oki" (Galliano 2002: 93). The Japanese musicologist Midori Kobayashi suggests that the implied values in the high regard for the orchestra are big space, big sound, and epic length (Kobayashi 1999). How very different those are from the aesthetic ideals of Japanese traditional music!

The most prestigious prizes for composition given in Japan are the Otaka Prize, the Akutagawa Memorial Prize, and the Takemitsu Composition Award. A fourth, the oldest and most venerable competition—the *Mainichi Shimbun*/NHK Japan Music Competition (composition section)—is awarded for an orchestral work and a chamber work in alternating years, as is the fifth, the Irino Prize.

The Otaka Prize

The Otaka Prize honors the memory of Hisatada Otaka (1911–1951), a composer of the German tradition—the prevailing influence in the Japanese system at the time—who died at age forty. The prize has been awarded annually since 1952 for a work by a Japanese composer that was performed by any orchestra between January and December of the previous year. That the prize is awarded for an orchestra piece is not surprising when its very existence is linked with the second-oldest professional orchestra in Japan—an orchestra founded in 1926 but fully supported financially by the Nippon Hōsō Kyokai (Japan Broadcasting Corporation) from 1951—hence the ensemble's name change to the NHK Symphony Orchestra.

Nominations for the Otaka Prize emerge from an invitation issued to thirty-nine music "associations," including music universities and colleges. In 2004, for example, twenty-three pieces from ten associations were nominated. A composer is eligible to win the Otaka Prize multiple times. Toshi Ichiyanagi has won it four times, Joji Yuasa four times, Shinichiro Ikebe twice; the first woman recipient, Keiko Fujiie, has also won it twice.

As for the cultural position of the Otaka Prize: "The Otaka Prize is the most prestigious because the top orchestra (NHK) selects a piece" (Kimiko Shimbo, personal communication, April 15, 2005). Indeed, this prize is unusual in that it is managed by an orchestra. The jury consists of eight musicians and nonmusicians: three conductors, three individuals (by position) in the NHK Symphony, and two individuals in certain positions in the NHK. For a number of years the three conductors were consistently Hiroyuki Iwaki (1932–2006; for a time conductor of the NHK Symphony Orchestra), Yuzo Toyama (b. 1931; currently conductor of the NHK Symphony Orchestra), and Akira Wakamatsu (d. 2010; also a pianist and professor at the Tokyo College of Music). Of those three, only Toyama is a composer as well. At present Tadaaki Otaka, son of the man for whom the prize is named and also a permanent conductor of the NHK Symphony Orchestra, is on the jury.

The Akutagawa Memorial Prize

The Akutagawa Memorial Prize honors the composer Yasushi Akutagawa (1925–1989). Organized and sponsored by the Suntory Foundation, the competition has been offered annually since 1991 for a completed composition by a "young" Japanese composer (although no age limit is stipulated). A call goes out for recordings and scores. Each year there is a three-person jury, one of whom since 2004 should be a former winner; in 2006, for example, Tetsuji Emura, who won the fourth competition, would have been a juror, along with Joji Yuasa and Toshio Hosokawa, had he not died. (Notably, he was replaced that year by Keiko Harada.) Some jurors serve for several years.

Three pieces are selected for performance at a special Akutagawa Memorial Prize concert. For equity, the orchestra that performs the concert changes each year; for a number of years, however, Kazuhiko Komatsu has conducted the orchestra because of his specialization in contemporary music. After that performance of three finalist pieces, the jury discusses each of them onstage, in front of the audience, coming to their decision in a very transparent manner. The winner then makes a speech onstage.

The Takemitsu Composition Award

The first competition for the Takemitsu Composition Award, named for the composer Toru Takemitsu, was held in 1997; it turned out to be a memorial to Takemitsu. This is an international competition for aspiring composers 35 years or younger at the time of application; it is announced very widely throughout the world. The entire project is sponsored by Nippon Life Insurance Company, NTT Urban Development Co., and Odakyu Electric Railway Co., Ltd.. Since the competition is international and sponsored by the industrial and commercial sectors, and the award is specifically for a new work for a European ensemble type, the Takemitsu Composition Award sits comfortably within all three of the environments under discussion in this book.

As Takemitsu set up the competition procedure, each year only one judge is solely responsible and that judge will be a composer. With the exception of Joji Yuasa (2002), Akira Nishimura (2009), and Toshio Hosokawa (2012), up to 2012, the judges have been non-Japanese. The judges are selected in three-year cycles. Takemitsu himself chose the first three; after he died, the first three judges selected the next three. For the third three-year cycle (2003–5) the system was changed: selection of the judges would be made by ballots from previous judges and an advisory committee. The judge gives a blind reading to scores of pieces that are stipulated to be for large orchestra—except when Steve Reich stipulated a minimum of six players rather than large ensemble (and, further, that the piece not be a concerto), and when Helmut Lachenmann stipulated a soloist with the orchestra. The judge is to select a "certain number" of works to be performed in a competition concert, which he will hear on a Sunday afternoon in late May, sitting alone in the spacious balcony of the large hall at Tokyo Opera City Plaza with the audience and the finalist composers on the main floor (see chapter 3). The competition being an international one, there is no guarantee that there will be a Japanese finalist (though the audience is always hopeful, and usually—but not always—there is at least one). After a short break following the concert, the judge appears onstage with contest officials to announce his decisions and explain the reasoning behind them.

The Mainichi Nihon Ongaku Konkur (Music Competition of Japan)

The Mainichi Nihon Ongaku Konkur (Music Competition of Japan) is a competition for aspiring young composers who are invited to submit their own new works for orchestra. Often referred to as the Mainichi/NHK Prize, it is managed by the Cultural Projects Division of the *Mainichi Shimbun* newspaper and NHK. Whereas in the beginning, in 1932, there were two separate competitions, the two organizations have long cooperated in sponsoring a single competition, thereby manifesting another connectivity between commerce and government in the field of music. Composition is one of several divisions. The newspaper announces the contest all over Japan; because everyone with whom I spoke about the prize thinks of it as solely Japanese, I was surprised to see the website announcement stipulating that non-Japanese musicians and composers based either in Japan or abroad are eligible.[27] A large roster of jurors—eleven in 2009, including former prizewinners—considers the scores submitted and selects three finalists, from whom a winning piece is chosen. Keiko Harada told me that she realized the importance of this prize for the career of a young composer only after she had won it (personal communication, September 5, 2012).

The Irino Prize

The competition is sponsored by the Irino Prize Foundation, the president of which is Reiko Irino, widow of esteemed composer Yoshiro Irino (1921–1980). Yoshiro Irino is remembered both as one of the first to introduce serialism in Japan and as an unusually fostering teacher (Judith Herd, personal communication, March 2, 1999). The Irino Prize started in 1981 with two categories: the first Irino Prize (orchestral) and the second (chamber). Beginning in the competition's second year, the prize was offered in alternate years for orchestra (1982) and chamber music (1983). Between 1982 and 1988, the prize in the orchestra category was in the form of a commission for a new work. Since then, thanks to the influence of composer Satoshi Tanaka, the prize recognizes an already-completed piece. As in the 2008 competition, "orchestra" might mean chamber orchestra (sinfonietta). Eight jurors (consistent from year to year) select the winners, although it is possible that a guest juror may be invited if there is a special reason for it.

Other Prizes for Orchestral Works

Perhaps in recognition of the fact that chamber orchestras are more willing and able than large orchestras to perform contemporary music, in 2001 the Japan Federation of Composers started a competition for Japanese composers younger than thirty-five who are writing for chamber orchestra. The JFC Awards Competition Concert is held every other year.

One other type of prize for new works remains to be discussed: those offered by foundations that exist expressly for the purpose of promoting a particular kind of music. An example pertinent here is the Nihon Kōkyogaku Shinko Zaidan (Japan Foundation for Promotion of New Works for Orchestra), the office of which is located in Tokyo's Kanda business district. Curiously, no one mentioned this prize to me; I learned about the competition from a flyer for an upcoming concert that was distributed with the many others that potentially interested concertgoers receive upon entering one of Tokyo's performance spaces. The often bulky packet of flyers, stuffed into a thin plastic bag and handed out to all attendees as they present their admission tickets, are a major means of marketing performances in competitive and sprawling metropolitan Tokyo. At an orchestra concert one receives flyers for imminent orchestra concerts; at a concert of traditional music, flyers announcing other traditional music concerts; at a livehouse (a relatively informal venue for live performances), announcements of other performances of the featured group in other spots or of coming features at that livehouse, and the like. The flyer from which I learned of this prize announced concerts of prizewinning works in the Foundation's competition for new pieces for orchestra.

Criteria for Evaluation

As I was inquiring about the prize systems in Japan, I kept hearing certain names repeatedly mentioned as serving on this and that jury, and it began to seem to me that some individuals might predominate in the evaluations that were being made. In 2004 I mentioned my impression to Atsuhiko Gondai. No, he insisted: "In Japan there is less a network of teachers controlling konkur than in Europe. Less. It's very open, free still, even though the same three sit on all juries—Yuasa, Ichiyanagi, Ikebe. Almost no connections matter. In performance there is terrible competition, but not in composition" (personal communication, May 29, 2004).

A "network of teachers": that is the crucial part of Gondai's analysis. Of the three he mentioned (there are a few more now), Yuasa is the only one for whom teaching of composers has been a priority professional activity, but his teaching career has been mostly in the United States, at the University of California, San Diego. Unless I have missed some undercurrent, Gondai's sense of a lack of control over competitions on the part of teachers rings true. In fact, when the student of a judge was selected for first prize in a recent competition in Japan, I heard expressions of considerable concern about the appearance of impropriety.

Whereas I could not find a clear articulation of the criteria by which works are evaluated for the prestigious Otaka Prize, several people articulated the criterion of playability; this may reflect the perspectives of the jury members or perhaps the relative lack of experience with contemporary music on the part of players in the NHK Symphony Orchestra, which programs all its performances of such music by Japanese or foreign composers in a single annual event. That playability might not be a primary criterion, however, was confirmed in a statement by the conductor and jury member Hiroyuki Iwaki in 2006: "I imagine that the awarded piece *Cloud Nine* elicited many complaints from people involved in the premiere performance—performers, namely the members of NHK symphony—for the difficulty with performing the piece" (from the Fifty-third [2005] Otaka Award Selection Statement, extracted from a full statement cited in the subsection on gender below).

The transparency of the decision process for determining the winners in the Akutagawa and Takemitsu Memorial Prize competitions gives some idea of criteria for evaluation. Since there is only one judge for the Takemitsu Prize, the criteria will be personal ones for that particular year. This can be illustrated by notes I took while attending the prize concert in 1999.

> The announcement of the winner took place thirty minutes after the concert ended. A woman officiant called the session to order and called Luciano Berio onto the stage. Two men accompanied him—one a translator and the other, the head of the Tokyo Opera City Foundation. Berio was asked to make remarks; he seemed surprised to be asked to speak so suddenly but did so in good English. He applauded the project and the activity of Toru Takemitsu in initiating it on behalf of young composers. Then he straightaway announced the winners, who came from the hall onto the stage: first prize Katsuji Maeda, second prize Ken Ito, and third prize Toshiya Watanabe. Then Berio, who was clearly expected to explain his selection, said: "I believe that creativity is synonymous to research. Creativity without research has no place for us. The works of Maeda and Ito are full of research. These are very precious works of Japanese composition because both composers are looking to work with roots in their own origin [translated by the onstage interpreter into Japanese as "Nihon no dento no rootsu"], while also looking to the future. The third prize to Watanabe goes to his young age. He is VERY young."
>
> Then the foundation head handed each man the awards—a plaque (or so it seems from a distance), and a large envelope [which I later learned contained cash].

Among the criteria for selecting the winners of competitions, gender has been raised as an issue. The Fifty-third Otaka Award Selection Statement (2005), penned by conductor-juror Hiroyuki Iwaki and distributed with the application materials for the next award, went beyond praise for the winner, Misato Mochizuki, to comment on the standing of women composers in Japan at the present time.

> I think Misato Mochizuki is the most prolific composer today. She is not only prolific but also always inventing fresh, daring, and shocking grammars one after another, and she is interesting. Since she was a complete rookie, she has been dealt with throughout Europe as if she didn't care much for Japan, and it seems that she simply ended up becoming a composer. She also has a publishing contract with Breitkopf. . . .
>
> She is the second female composer in the history of fifty-three Otaka awards. Fujiie Keiko san has been awarded twice, so this piece becomes the third piece by a female composer to be awarded. In the past several years, female composers have been remarkably active. Karen Tanaka, Hitomi Kaneko, Kyoko Yamaguchi, Naoko Hishinuma, Minako Tokuyama, et al.—the salience of female composers resembles the Mongolian sumo wrestlers forging ahead in the realm of *ozumo*. At present, the world of male composers is not collapsing, but it might perhaps face a scary future. Furthermore, if you list the names of Japanese piano or string performers who are successful internationally, there are hardly any men. The word *joryū* [woman] has become obsolete, and perhaps we should use *danryū* [man] instead from now on. I hope that a good balance is kept in the composition world. (Translated by Marié Abe)

Iwaki's reference to the Mongolian wrestlers in ozumo (the respectful form of reference to sumo wrestling) is meaningful. Sumo carries huge cultural weight as an indigenous traditional ritualized sport, and the recent success of Mongolian (i.e., non-Japanese) wrestlers in getting to the top in the sport was of huge concern to a number of Japanese people. This reference is the closest that Iwaki came to suggesting "outsider" status for female composers. The term *ryū,* as in *joryū* and *danryū,* is not a gendered word. Rather, in the sphere of music, it implies a similarity of style in musical production, as in a statement that would suggest that all women (or all men) wrote piano music in a similar style—in the style of Ravel, for example. *Joryū* is a word I have seen in reference to music by women composers, implying that they have not—in modernist terms—"found their own musical voice." Iwaki, who was known to be extremely supportive of composers of both genders, was complimenting the women while throwing a challenge to men composers.

In 2006, when Tomiko Kohjiba became the sixteenth winner of the Akutagawa Memorial Prize, the fact that a woman composer was among the major prizewinners was the cause of explicit public commentary. The composer Shin-ichiro Ikebe, along with Iwaki one of the best-known of Japanese public intellectuals, published a response in the newspaper *Yomiyuri Shimbun*; his title referenced the remarks that Kohjiba made to the audience upon receipt of the prize. As you read, be cognizant that the Akutagawa Memorial Prize is awarded to "a young composer" but that the age is not stipulated; at the time she won, Kohjiba was not particularly young (she was born in 1952), but it was her first recognition in the form of a major prize. The subheadline of the story read: "First prize after raising her son; Mother and composition: She thinks of them as equal."[28]

"Mimi no Nagisa: Kohjiba Tomiko san no Kotoba"
By Shin-ichiro Ikebe

Kohjiba was winner of the sixteenth [Akutagawa Prize]. I understand that she won, but here I won't write criticism about the piece. I was very interested in her speech onstage.

"I am old," she said, but I don't think so. I think she said that because this prize is for new composers. Kohjiba said, "A few years ago when my son became an adult, I said to him, 'You are now twenty years old. I want to take some time for myself, so I wrote this piece.'" I think this was a wonderful speech. Already she was well-known for her *Hiroshima Requiem* and a few other works, but beyond that, she had made many hidden efforts [raising her son]. Then I thought: for example, the Akutagawa Prize in the last fifteen konkur—there were four women composers involved, Naoko Hishinuma, Miyako Mochizuki, Keiko Harada, and Yumi Saiki. There were a number of other women composers. In the last article I wrote about Hitomi Kaneko, Keiko Fujiie, Karen Tanaka, Haruye Kunieda, Noriko Hisada, Makiko Kinoshita, Midori Takashima, Kyoko Hagi, and others. These are the younger generation of women composers. Of course there are many women composers in the older generation. There is an organization called Nihon Josei Sakkyokka Renmei. They have connections with international composers and are working very hard.

> In the Meiji era, perhaps the first woman composer was Nobu Koda, sister of the famous novelist Rohan Koda. She was the first Japanese composer to write a violin sonata. Since then, women composers have been basically very strong. . . . It reminds me of Mendelssohn's sister, Fanny; Schumann's wife, Clara; and Mahler's wife, Alma. These women were hidden behind the great composer but have now come to forefront.
>
> But now I'm not discussing a matter of gender. As Kohjiba-san says, "It is very difficult to balance my talent and motherhood." That difficulty is beyond men's imagination. But I dare to say, let's cooperate with these women. We men want to assist them. It may be very hard to find the balance between talent and a mother's hard work. We hope they can find the balance. You may think I'm saying something peculiar today, but it is not. For human beings, one of the dangers is that the [Japanese] population is getting smaller [a reference to the fact that women are having fewer children]. We should be concerned about that. (Translated by Fukiko Shinohara)

As I read the end of that statement, Ikebe was praising Kohjiba for having put motherhood ahead of her creative work, although it delayed recognition of her talent as a composer. That certainly makes gender an issue for Japanese composers.

Another woman composer who had to make composing a lower priority than family obligation (in her case, caring for an elderly family member) for many years is Setsuko Miyahara, president of the Nihon Josei Sakkyokka Renmei (Federation of Women Composers in Japan) to which Ikebe referred. The FWCJ, as Miyahara called it, is an association formed in the early 1980s by Nagako Konishi for the purpose of putting on performances of members' music. The FWCJ has four branches—in Kyoto, Osaka/Kobe, Nagoya, and Tokyo—with a total of forty members (Setsuko Miyahara, personal communication, May 26, 2009). Every month members pay a membership fee that helps with the printing of concert programs and other such expenses, although ticket sales and, hopefully, sponsors help with the costs, particularly that of renting a hall. Each year there is a meeting in one of the four locations to plan concerts and go over the budget. Each branch presents one or two concerts a year, but a member of one branch can send a piece to another branch. Young women cannot afford to join the association and pay performers for their pieces, Miyahara said, and the purpose of the organization is not to foster younger women composers. Miyahara did not mention any purposeful international activity of the association; since, as president, she is "keeper of the seal" and thus responsible for imprinting the association's seal on each official communication such as a news release or an appeal to a sponsor, she is fully aware of association activities (Setsuko Miyahara, personal communication, May 26, 2009).

What Winning Affords

For composers, the potential opportunity to hear a work performed is an important part of each of the five most prestigious competitions. In three instances the performance is part of a discrete special event. Since 1988 the Otaka Award-winning work has been performed by the NHK Symphony Orchestra at a summer special event in Tokyo called Music Tomorrow; it is broadcast over FM radio networks and worldwide through NHK World, the network's international news service, with obvious benefits for the composer. Similarly, the Akutagawa Memorial Prize–winning piece is performed at a concert held every summer during the Music Today 21 (the Suntory Music Foundation Summer Festival) for contemporary music. The concert at which all the finalists' pieces are played distinguishes the Takemitsu Composition Award. For the other two competitions, a piece is premiered in an ensemble's regular concert. The prizewinning piece in the *Mainichi Shimbun*/NHK Music Competition is performed (usually in August) in a regular general concert of the Tokyo Symphony Orchestra. In the case of the Irino Prize, the performing organization changes as the piece requires; in 2008, for example, the world premiere of the winning composition took place in a subscription concert of the Tokyo Sinfonietta.[29]

A commission for a new piece for orchestra is a coveted part of the reward in two of the competitions—the Otaka Prize and the Akutagawa Memorial Prize. In each case, the new piece is premiered in the special prize concert two years after the competition.

Even when not part of an award itself, of inestimable value for a composer is the possibility that recognition, in the form of a prize, of the composer's success in writing for orchestra will result in a commission for another orchestra piece. Makiko Kinoshita put the matter succinctly: "Without a big prize, no commission from an orchestra. No prize, no commission" (personal communication, June 2, 2004).

While no one brought it up to me, prize money is of course a welcome part of an award. The winner of the Otaka Prize receives 300,000 yen, the figure established when the prize was initiated; the amount is considered small compared to other prizes, but the meager purse is offset by other aspects of the award. The commission fee in the Akutagawa Memorial Prize is 1 million yen, offered by the Suntory Foundation. The Irino Prize was raised from an initial 200,000 yen to 500,000 yen; the Irino Prize award for the chamber-music competition is 200,000 yen. Three levels of award are given by *Mainichi Shimbun*/NHK for the Music Competition of Japan: 600,000 yen for first prize, 300,000 yen for second prize, and 150,000 yen for third prize.[30]

The single judge of the Takemitsu Composition Award has the right to select as many winners from the four or five finalists as he or she wishes. When he was a judge, György Ligeti decided not to award the prize to any of the finalists. (The shock of that lives on and was expressed to me in numerous conversations, but no one would go into detail.) Whereas Luciano Berio awarded three prizes, George Benjamin decided to give all five finalists an award. The judge may also distribute a total of 3 million yen to the winners in any way he wishes. In 2008 Akira Nishimura awarded very large amounts to the first- and second-place winners, and a much smaller amount to each of the other three contestants.

More personal effects of winning an award for a Japanese composer were expressed to me in several conversations. Toshi Ichiyanagi told me: "I graduated from high school after World War II. In my time there was no music high school. In 1949, when I was sixteen years old, I entered a composition contest—the *Mainichi*/NHK Composition Konkur. There were few composers at the time, and I won; it awakened me to the idea of becoming a composer" (personal communication, May 22, 2003). "After [winning] a prize," commented Kimiko Shimbo, assistant to the secretary general of the Japan Federation of Composers, "a young person will be taken seriously [by others] as a composer" (personal communication, May 31, 2008). This was confirmed by Keiko Harada: "I think that the Japanese contemporary music world recognized me for the first time because I won first prize in the *Mainichi*/NHK Composition Konkur. Winning a prize does not guarantee your future, but it does encourage and maybe give you a chance or energy for a new piece" (personal communications, May 17, 2002, and September 5, 2012).

From her experience with the Irino Prize, Reiko Irino can see affordances of an international nature from winning. "Japanese winners of the Irino Prize are invited to some contemporary Music Festivals in the United States, Europe, and elsewhere. And there are many chances for performances of their compositions in various countries, especially outside of Japan" (personal communication, November 27, 2012).

In an entirely different vein, Reiko Irino stated her opinion emphatically of one advantage that prizewinning does *not* bring: "Winning a prize doesn't help you get a job. Which university you graduate from helps. If one goes to a private school, it's hard to get a job at public institution" (personal communication, May 30, 2008).

SUMMARY

In this chapter the environment under discussion is the presence in Japan of European spheres of musical participation, and specifically European instrumental ensembles types—orchestras, small ensembles for chamber and contemporary music, and wind bands. The affording quality of the environment is the particular reception by Japanese audiences to the different types and thus the opportunities (or lack of them) for composers either to create new works (for either professional or amateur musicians) or to have existing works performed. Competence on the part of a composer is a factor of considerable significance in this environment.

The reception of European instrumental ensemble types in Japanese musical modernity has differed according to the needs and desires of musicians both professional and amateur and of the audiences and institutions that support them, each for their own reasons. Orchestras flourish, while chamber-music groups exist more as temporary cooperative efforts than as permanent organizations. Permanent ensembles organized specifically for the performance of contemporary music are few. Wind bands—the first European instrumental ensemble introduced to Japan—flourish as military organizations (not discussed here) and among amateur musicians, largely as after-school clubs for students at the pre-university level.

Affordances for composers for commissions for new works for European instrumental music ensembles in Japan vary with the type of ensemble. With the exception of some projects undertaken by a few professional orchestras, for a variety of reasons neither professional nor amateur orchestras afford Japanese composers many opportunities to create new works or even to hear with any frequency works they have already written. For this and other reasons, competitions/*konkur* for new orchestral and chamber music works are very significant, providing opportunities for the performance of works, for a commission for another new work, and certainly for establishing or maintaining one's reputation as a competent composer in the most challenging of media.

Because the number of enduring professional chamber groups is small, and because amateur chamber musicians generally prefer the familiar European repertoire, opportunities for commissions from those sources are scarce. It seems that composers write new chamber works because they want to, often because they would like to collaborate with musicians whom they respect. For performers who would like to present recently composed works, scores can be hard to get, so the Japan Federation of Composers in particular is helpful both to its members and to performers in affording the publication of scores.

To increase opportunities for their new works (or even already-premiered works) to be performed, composers participate in organizations made up of composers (such as the Japan Federation of Composers and Gen-On) or of performers (such as JILA) that organize and present concerts. To do so, they must draw on the affordances offered by such sources as commercial enterprises, banks, and cultural organizations on a concert-by-concert basis. The motivation to draw on that affording environment of shared cultural space and seek opportunities for commissions and performances through international connections becomes all the more logical.

In the sphere of wind bands, competitions mounted by the All-Japan Band Association—with the affording support of the education, industry, and commerce sectors—offer composers opportunities for writing new works on commission, as do such special projects as the Hamamatsu Band Restoration project. In fact, it appears that that project is affording composers who have not previously been involved in writing for wind band an opportunity and a reason to do so; in this, the project is strikingly reminiscent of the commissioning program of the National Theatre for new works for traditional instruments (chapter 4).

That some composing for orchestra and almost all for wind band is done for amateur musicians brings me back to my argument that most Japanese composers have continued to maintain the social role of music in various ways. Rather than composing music as an autonomous art, most composers have been and are grounded in the social—they "remain connected to the people." If a composer wishes to earn a living even in part by composing, the prevailing attitude of artistic flexibility can be seen to be a very useful—and, under the conditions of Japanese musical modernity, natural—stance. In the final chapter of this book, I turn to another type of ensemble practice introduced to Japan from Europe—choral singing—in which a huge number of Japanese have engaged especially since the 1950s, and which contributes meaningfully to keeping Japanese composers "connected to the people."

CHAPTER SIX

Composing for Chorus

In post–World War II Japan, just as orchestras and wind bands were forming in considerable numbers, the practice of choral singing became an extremely popular musical activity. So positive has been the reception to choral singing, so widespread have choruses become for citizens of all ages, that they offer a significant affordance for composers. The conditions of possibility for that to happen, I suggest, were put in place from the very beginning of the modernization process—both institutionally and, for composers, attitudinally. While some individuals specialize in writing choral music, composing for chorus became just part of what many composers do. Because, as in Europe and the United States, most (but not all) composers put writing for chorus lower on the musical evaluative pecking order than writing for instruments, I explore in this chapter why they take advantage of the affordance as they do.

One clarification is in order. By "choral music" I mean for the most part sung multi-part music, whether heterophonic, polyphonic, or homophonic.[1] However, when it comes to Japanese choral music it is crucial to recognize that the monophonic texture of unison is frequently utilized by composers and performers as a textural option. My idea about why this is so has to do with the close relationship between performance of song and choral music, and between song for children and that for adults, which I address below.

I will first situate the practice of choral singing—that is, the chorus as a type of performance ensemble—in the environment of European spheres of musical participation in Japan. This I will do chronologically, tracing the emergence of the practice and its positive reception as it was invoked in response to needs that emerged from sociopolitical imperatives of the processes of modernization (see the frontispiece). Again, connectivities among the major infrastructures of modernization—education, government, industry, and commerce—for the propagation of choral music are in evidence.

In this chapter another process of modernization—that is, urbanization—comes into play, and the agency of individuals is again shown to be significant: responses of individual composers and conductors to both the needs of the nation and the desires of Japanese modernity can be seen to have resulted in individual initiatives of considerable force. Finally, I consider some composers' artistic motivations for involving themselves in the choral sphere, and some musical results. This chapter offers perhaps the most telling evidence of the socially relational nature of composers and composing in Japan today.

SITUATING CHORAL SINGING IN JAPAN

> Japan is one of the countries in which choruses are extremely popular. Including all the choruses in elementary schools, junior and senior high schools, colleges, companies, women's groups, and private groups of ordinary individuals, there are said to be between twenty and thirty thousand choruses in Japan today. All the people who belong to these choruses are becoming more familiar with music while enjoying themselves in chorus activities, which is certainly transforming Japan into a stage on which its singers are greatly improving the musical culture of the land. (http://www.jcanet.or.jp/inter/JCA_guide.html, accessed August 8, 2010)

This statement from the website of the Japan Choral Association (JCA), the largest of Japan's choral organizations, attests to the popularity of choruses, and their careful membership data backs their statement up. In 2005, according to the JCA's records, the actual total membership in all categories from middle school to adult was 5,091 choruses, totaling 150,000 persons. In addition, there are many choruses that do not choose to affiliate with that association, as the website also acknowledges.

The JCA website statement reveals a continuum of musical activity from school days on—the same sort of continuum I noted for amateur orchestras. Unison group singing is a basic part of the musical experience of children in primary schools; beyond that, choral clubs in the schools constitute a sociocultural formation that persists into adulthood.[2] Other societal factors in modern Japanese history have contributed to the popularity of choral singing, and I shall proceed to tracing that briefly, in chronological order.

THE FIRST DECADES OF THE MODERN ERA

The roots of choral music in modern Japan lie in a succession of events in the early Meiji period that will be familiar from histories traced earlier in this book but that I quickly recap here in order to provide a chronological perspective. Influenced by the military bands attached to the embassies of the Western nations pushing into Japan for trade in the 1850s and 1860s, the powerful Satsuma clan formed Japan's first brass band in 1869 for both pomp and military discipline (Eppstein 1994). In 1872 an imperial decree established universal education as a tool of modernization. Following the model of the military in its decision to include Western music in its new primary school curriculum, in 1879 a circular from the Ministry of Education ratified a Music Investigation Committee, with Shuji Izawa at the head. The committee was charged with preparing to facilitate the decision. Musicians had to be trained, and the need was pressing for new didactic materials, including a repertoire of pedagogically suitable music. Before the domestic manufacture of European musical instruments made them widely available, singing was the most affordable musical activity in schools and beyond. In 1889 a national conference on education agreed to introduce music education in secondary schools as well (Galliano 2002: 91), though that would take some time.

Although the first books of school songs comprised largely Western materials, the creation of new songs became work for Japanese musicians who would become composers in the Western sense.[3] Traditional Japanese sensibility would remain in some songs in some ways, but through their new songs as well as Western ones, children learned to read staff notation, to feel comfortable with harmonized tunes, and to sing together. The example in Galliano's book (Fig. 1.2, p. 31, undated) is the beginning of *Haha* (*Mother*) by the composer Kosuke Komatsu (1884–1966), with lyrics by Takehira Yumeji. In the key of A-flat, in 6/8 time, the melody sits comfortably within the harmony clearly stated in the piano accompaniment. Without melodic repetition or consistent phrase lengths in the fifteen measures reproduced by Galliano, however, to me there is a kind of melodic flow that is reminiscent of traditional chamber music. The priority given to the text through its syllabic setting—a strong trait of choral and much vocal music to the present—is to be particularly noted. Comprehensibility of the text is paramount.

Choral singing was brought into higher education as well, but by foreign missionaries. After the prohibition against Christianity was lifted in 1873, American Protestant missionaries quickly arrived, bringing with them the practice of singing hymns. When in 1889 the Methodists founded Kwansei Gakuin University in Nishinomiya City, in Hyogo prefecture, the wife of a pastor taught the students hymns for the services. In 1899 the school president's sister-in-law started teaching not only English hymns, but also Japanese hymns and some other songs, and in 1900 the choir was officially named the Glee Club by the president.

The first musical group consisting of non-music-major students, a glee club called the Wagner Society, was founded at Keio University—not a mission school—in Tokyo in 1901. The establishment of glee clubs in universities has played an important part in propagating the practice of choral singing.[4]

The further propagation of choral singing in Japan since the beginning of the twentieth century has owed much to the combination of determined creative individuals and the institutions they fostered. Kosuke Komatsu serves as an early exemplar of that;[5] again, infrastructures of Japanese modernity—government and industry (here, publishing)—offered affordances:

> [Komatsu] was sent by Japan's Ministry of Education and the Department of Interior to Germany, France, Italy, and the United States to research social music in these countries from 1920 to 1923. Komatsu was impressed with the competitions for chorus and brass band supported by citizen organizations in these countries. He realized that not only schools and churches but also the public supported the development of social music in Western countries. . . . Komatsu was confident of the importance of popularizing music among the public and having choral competitions to develop the level of musical performance. Immediately after he returned to Japan, Komatsu started writing articles in newspapers and journals and lecturing about the value of musical competition. Although his views met with a negative reaction from some musicians who believed competition would desecrate music, Komatsu nevertheless founded the National Music Association in 1927. The purpose of the organization, which derived its name from French music organization *Société National de Musique* founded by Saint-Saëns in 1871, was to promote social music. (Tsutsumi 2007: 9)[6]

Komatsu stated as its goals: "First of all, we would like to socialize music, then cultivate Japanese composition, introduce fresh musicians, and hold exhibitions, concerts, and lectures. Thereupon, as our first project we have organized a choral music festival, which immediately join[s] people, to promote and develop music" (Komatsu 1957:27–28). The most active and effective of choral organizations in existence today—the Japan Choral Association—continues to pursue Komatsu's goals.

Strikingly, it was in terms of need that Komatsu explained his effort to foster choral music. Writing in 1927 in the program for the first choral competition organized by the National Music Association, Komatsu expressed concern about the condition of his country and what choral music could do to help: "In our country, the social conditions are bloody, our thoughts are ominous, and our lives are insipid. In a time such as this, it is very important to harmonize public spirit and to smooth our lives" (cited in Tsutsumi 2007: 10) by promoting social music (Tsutsumi 2007: 9).

> The explicit stance of the influential early twentieth-century composer, Kosuke Komatsu, positioned participation in the sphere of choral music as "socializing music" and choral music thereby as "closely related to the public". By prioritizing the singing of music by Japanese composers in the organization he founded—the National Music Association—and in the competitions that organization would hold from 1927, he was also providing a means by which composers could be "closely related to the public." The means has remained in place: through the All Japan Chorus League that was founded after the war and to the present by the (renamed) Japan Choral Association. (Tsutsumi 2007: 18)

Although the goals were social, competing would become the most effective mechanism for fostering choral singing. Statistics from that first choral competition of November 1927 reveal its modest beginnings: eleven choirs participated in three sections: six men's glee clubs, two women's glee clubs, and three mixed-voice choirs (Tsutsumi 2007: 10). The format was quickly taken up by others. In 1932 a Children' Song Competition was founded by Kajo Norisugi, principal of the Tokyo Music School. In that competition, elementary-school children sang in unison and the best elementary-school choir—called a "choir," though the music was sung in unison—in each of twenty-two prefectures was selected, and concerts were broadcast on the radio. That competition attracted the cooperation of the National Music Association as well as sponsorship by NHK in 1934, and in 1935 the newspaper *Asahi Shimbun* threw in its support (Tsutsumi 2007:

11–12). In effect, the major institutionalizing forces for the propagation of choral music—government, education, the publishing industry, and individual initiative—were all at work. Adult choruses—men's, women's and mixed—as well as children's were attracting a growing number of people. World War II interrupted the choral competitions, but they would resume immediately after the war. Not surprisingly, Kosuke Komatsu would be active in restarting them.

WORLD WAR II

During World War II, as it had been in the modernizing process, music was a useful tool for the government. The establishment of a National Chorus by the NHK in 1943 initiated a practice that was taken up more widely:

> The groups sang two-part choral pieces on the radio for ten to fifteen minutes before eight o'clock in the evening. The Taisei-Yōsan-kai (Political Association) enlarged this project and developed the National Singing Movement. Its goal was to raise the morale of the Japanese people through the singing of patriotic songs. . . . The choirs in Tokyo also visited factories and farm villages in local areas and sang Japanese choral pieces and popular songs. As a result, the National Singing Movement prompted social music. Brass bands, harmonica bands, accordion bands, and choirs were established to increase productivity. . . .
>
> During the war, the competitions were discontinued; however, a new singing movement occurred. To increase fighting spirit, many patriotic songs were written and sung and to increase productivity, many company choirs were organized. Social music was spread nationwide by singing groups. . . . People were forced to sing war songs. This wartime musical activity was the base on which regional choral associations formed immediately after the war. (Tsutsumi 2007: 13–14)

Some composers, of course, took up the affordance offered by this governmental infrastructure to create patriotic music.

THE POSTWAR PERIOD

When, after the war, choral activity burgeoned, it served different needs—but needs nevertheless. According to Michiyuki Tanabe, of the Japan Choral Association: "Many choral groups formed after the war. There were not enough instruments, but there could be choruses. People were depressed, and they wanted to keep their spirits up" (personal communication, May 30, 2008). It is difficult now to imagine the conditions under which these determined groups met; in 1948 rehearsals of the Waseda University Music Association Choir in Tokyo, for instance, were held in the evenings in the storehouse at the school, where there was no light. The conductor conducted practices with lit (rationed) tobacco (Tsutsumi 2007: 31–32).

Another postwar psychological perspective can be gained from the story of the founding of one of the country's leading children's choruses, the Boys Choir of Tokyo, which, as the Little Singers of Tokyo for both boys and girls, celebrated its sixtieth anniversary in 2011. This is the second example I shall give of the propagation of choral singing in Japan through the combination of a determined individual and an institution that person fostered; in this instance, too, we see a positive Japanese response to a European musical sphere of participation. Because the conductors of the Little Singers have commissioned some new pieces from Japanese composers, I interviewed Saeko Hasegawa, co-director of the chorus now and daughter of the founder. She related the history of the chorus to me as she had learned it from her father. In addition to demonstrating my point, the story reveals how gradual the process of the enculturation of Western musical practices has been in the modern era. The history takes us back to between the two world wars.

There was an international connection for the Hasegawa family, Saeko said. Her father went to America as a young man, traveling by ship around South America to New York, as was necessary then:

> In a terrible storm, all his possessions were lost, leaving him without any personal documentation. "You can't go through immigration," he was told by another passenger. "You'll have to swim in the middle of the night down the Hudson River. Go to a place with a cross on it." That he did, and stayed in New York for ten years. By the time my father returned to Japan, his family had moved to the northern island of Hokkaido, where a Christian society flourished, and they had become Christians. The family would not let their son pursue his career of choice—music—so he moved to Tokyo. There he discovered Gregorian chant, finding "a basic soul of melody." Wanting to study historical European music, to read neumes, etc., he found a priest; from Father Anouilh, he received a recording of a French boys' choir that astounded and inspired him. He started studying Purcell, Palestrina, and other composers. This was right after World War II—in 1946, '47, '48. Tokyo had been destroyed; everywhere he saw little boys who lacked nourish-

> ment and suffered from bad nosebleeds. People needed each other, he felt, more than the old social borderlines tended to permit. They could "talk" to each other by music, connect by music, and it would help them to survive.
>
> With Father Anouilh's help he formed a choir. But it was not an easy process; many things had to change, both socially and musically. Before the war children sang *dōyō*—a repertoire of new songs composed expressly for children [see below]. The songs had a small range, and boys at that time sang in a very strong chest voice. If they were to sing Palestrina as Hasegawa intended for them to do, that would have to change; boys needed to be able to produce a head voice. However, a head voice was the sound of female singers; boys were being asked to produce a female sound. But a female sound invoked associations of female urban entertainment music that were undesirable. Hasegawa encountered reluctance on the part of both young boys and girls—not to mention their parents—to associate in any way with the music of females who sang in public, as the children would be doing. Hasegawa persisted, however, and the Little Singers of Tokyo has a well-established, fine reputation for performances throughout Japan and abroad. (Saeko Hasegawa, personal communication, June 1, 2004)[7]

The infrastructure of modernity reappeared in a further postwar development, namely, the formation of company choirs:

> After the war, the government urged democratization, and the union activity took wings. Choruses were a part of their cultural welfare work. Because of the economic development of the country at the time companies were hiring many employees and supporting the employees' activities outside their work in order to boost the company's image. As a result, many company choirs were organized. Out of this situation, Hideo Akiyama emerged. (Tsutsumi 2007: 28)

Considered the first professional choral conductor because he earned his living in that way, Akiyama conducted no fewer than twenty-four choirs. Enumeration of a selection of them conveys the nature of the permeation into Japanese daily life of the practice of choral singing: the National Railway Company, the Mainichi Newspaper Choir, the Ministry of Agriculture and Forestry Choir, the Aji-no-Moto Company Choir, the Kawasaki Heavy Industry Choir, the Matsuzakaya Department Store Choir, and the choir of the Long-Term Credit Bank of Japan. Company choirs were accommodated in the competition system (resumed in 1948 when Zen Nihon Gasshō Renmei [the All-Japan Chorus/Choral League] was founded) with a section of their own.

In the postwar period, two government initiatives caused further growth of choral activity among adults—specifically, women. Not surprisingly, the first occurred during the American occupation (1945–52) and the second immediately after:

> In 1948, the Ministry of Education had encouraged the establishment of the PTA (Parent-Teacher Association) at elementary, junior-high, and high-schools. . . . Two years later, ninety-five percent of the schools had a PTA. One of the organization's goals was to achieve children's happiness and healthy growth. In order to accomplish this aim, the teachers and parents joined together to organize choirs and sports clubs. As a result, a number of PTA choirs were founded after the war.
>
> Because of strong economic growth in Japan after the war, the government founded the Japan Housing Public Corporation in 1955 to promote urbanization. From 1955 to 1965, numerous *Danchi* (apartment complexes) were built in the suburbs. The majority of inhabitants were young married couples; from these residents, mothers' choral groups consisting of housewives emerged.
>
> By the 1960s, women were attempting to find their identity outside of their family. The PTA choral groups and apartment complex choral groups [were flourishing], and other mothers began to form choruses as well. In these groups they enjoyed music and established friendships. By the 1970s, radio and television included performances by mothers' choruses in their programming and thereby contributed to the mothers' chorus boom. (Tsutsumi 2007: 72–73)[8]

For women's groups as well, a discrete section was designated in choral competitions.

In 1967, as part of the twentieth anniversary celebration of the All-Japan Choral League, a national Mothers' Choral Festival was held. In subsequent years the festivals for women's groups would continue, referred to first as the Housewives' Choral Festival, then the Mama-san (Mom) Choral Festival, and back to Mothers' Choral Festival in 1980. This last name change was made because, according to Kan Ishii (Kuwakabe, Ishii, Yamamoto, Nakamura, and Mari 1996: 57–64), *mama-san* suggested the image of a lady who runs a bar in the Ginza area of Tokyo (home to a number of high-class bars).

In my fieldwork experience, the term "mama-san chorus" still prevailed, but it was being complemented by the more generic term "*josei* chorus" (female chorus) in recognition of the huge number of women who now work outside the home and see themselves as having identities in addition to or other than that of mother. Neither term is universal in chorister' thinking. For instance, in conversation with members of a volunteer group, Chorus Toreppe, which is made up of singers from several Nara-area choruses and performs at hospitals, I was told that the term *mama-san* now really means young women in general who can meet during the day, whereas josei can meet during the evening, implying older women (personal communication, April 23, 2005).

After the war, supporting and reflecting the burgeoning number of choruses, choral associations were formed in all regions of Japan. Some were sponsored by the newspaper *Asahi Shimbun*, whose important role in the sphere of choral music continues to this day.

It must be noted that, in the material of this chapter to this point, reference has been made to professional choral conductors, but not to professional choruses. Choral singing in Japan has always been and remains primarily an amateur musical activity. Almost everyone with whom I spoke insisted to me that in all of the huge metropolitan area of Tokyo the number of professional choruses is very small—the number cited is invariably 3, "2½," 2, or only 1; while that is a dramatic exaggeration, it is a fact that very few choruses are fully professional.

Professional choruses were another postwar development. Most important among them is the Tokyo Philharmonic Chorus, founded by Nobuaki Tanaka. It and he are the third example I give of the propagation of choral singing in Japan through the combination of a determined individual and an institution fostered by him or her. In this instance, too, we see a positive Japanese response to a European musical practice, but with a different result. Whereas the name "San Francisco Symphony Chorus" implies correctly that the chorus is an arm of the symphony, Nobuaki founded the Tokyo Philharmonic Chorus as an organization independent of any orchestra.

In our conversation, Nobuaki Tanaka took me back to the immediate post-war era. In 1956 he graduated as a singer from Geidai—the ubiquitous institution that would become the Tokyo National University of Music and Fine Arts. His teacher was an Austrian specialist in nineteenth-century romantic music with whom he learned many German-language lieder. But he emerged from school thinking that the Japanese music world needed good Japanese songs—solo songs and choral works in the Japanese language. Not the kind of music some Japanese composers had written especially in the Taisho era (1912–26) on German models, but contemporary music—music that was stylistically new. "There just wasn't any," he said, "so there was a *real need*" (personal communication, June 7, 2004; emphasis in original). To meet that need, he founded the Tokyo Philharmonic Chorus, made up at first of Geidai graduates.

At present, Japanese enthusiasm for choral singing continues unabated. It seems from my field research that the reasons an individual would join a chorus beyond high school lie on a continuum from totally social to utterly musical. While discussing a choral work she was writing, I asked the composer Haruna Miyake why she thought so many people participated in a chorus. "For the joy of singing," she responded, "a pleasant time, like karaoke":

> You don't have to talk to each other. You can avoid difficult conversations, avoid arguments, conflicts. Chorus is like PTA; PTA groups are close, yet people come from various places and members can be a little freer than in a small, district type of community. It's everyday life but a bit "out." A Japanese mother or wife can get out of the house for something cultural. Chorus is music, yet not music. (Haruna Miyake, personal communication, June 2, 2000)

Singers can pick and choose from any number of choruses. Amateur mixed choruses, which meet on weekends, are likely to include married couples, giving them a cultural activity to share (Mikio Itoh, personal communication, May 11, 2001). A member of the mother's chorus La Mère in Suginami-ku (Tokyo) whose rehearsal I visited explained to me that she sings in two choruses because of the different repertoires she enjoyed; the mother's chorus sings Japanese works, and the International Chorus, with both Japanese and foreign members, that meets in the internationally lively Tokyo suburb of Omote Sando, sings only European choral works by such composers as Gabriel Fauré and Charles Gounod (personal communication, May 11, 2001).

The vocal expertise a potential member brings to a group might or might not be a criterion for the chorus's welcoming that person. Fumiaki Kuriyama, who conducts more than ten choirs, does not hold auditions for any of them. "When you go to practice four times, then you can be a member. It almost never happens that someone is sent away. If the person's voice is terrible but members want the person to remain in the chorus, the members help them—encourage them, tell them to be a member. If not, nothing is said. If no one speaks to encourage them, the singer understands" (Emi Tanaka and Takuya Yokoyama, personal communication, May 16, 2006).

A chorus can function socially (or not) to the extent that members want it to. A regular part of the chorus experience for two women's choruses whose rehearsals I attended was lunch together in a nearby restaurant. This social time was more organized in one of the choruses than the other, in that each week a member would bring a gift dessert for all to share after lunch. As for men's choruses, the conductor Nobuaki Tanaka sees them as a continuation of a very old Japanese social custom of men gathering to enjoy one another's company (personal communication, June 7, 2004). In a sense, *why* they meet is less important than *that* they meet, because a huge number of Japanese are keeping music making in their lives.

For some choruses, of course, vocal quality and musicianship are extremely important; as with amateur instrumental groups, the "amateur" label does not necessarily imply a lower level of musical competence. Think of Toshio Hosokawa's *Hiroshima Requiem* (1989), for three reciters, four or eight vocal soloists, mixed chorus, children's chorus, tape (ad lib.), and orchestra, which was composed for amateur groups—the Chorale OMP (an adult mixed choir) and the Little Singers of Tokyo (see above): the two choral movements, Preludio "Night" and "Death & Resurrection," Hosokawa later incorporated into the five-movement *Voiceless Voice in Hiroshima*.[9]

THE PRACTICE OF COMMISSIONING

Notable in the chronological tracking of the widespread dissemination of and positive reception to the practice of choral singing of Japanese people were responses of individuals to need—the initial need for school songs, the need for social solace, the need for Japanese-language repertoire. For Nobuaki Tanaka to address the need he felt that the Japanese music world should have good Japanese solo songs and choral works in Japanese language, it was necessary for him to commission new works from Japanese composers. Since 1956 he has been commissioning five or six works annually for the Tokyo Philharmonic Chorus. This has greatly expanded not only the repertoire of his professional group, but the potential repertoire for good amateur choruses as well.

What began as need, however, seems to me to have turned into an expectation for new music. Even in newer editions of songbooks that are still being published by the Ministry of Education, Culture, Sports, Science, and Technology, the supply is constantly renewed. For a conductor or chorus to want to find new music for a group to learn to sing is one thing, but for a conductor or chorus to undertake to cause new music to be created is quite another. Significantly for Japanese musical culture, that is not a practice just of professional choruses, but of amateur choruses as well. A variety of reasons, I think, are shared among them. I shift now to reasons that other conductors and choral groups would want to commission new music. Needless to say, the expectation that new music will continuously be created in the sphere of song and choral music has afforded abundant opportunities for composers.

One motivation for commissioning was pointed out to me by the orchestra conductor Ken Takasaki: "For choirs there is not so much repertoire from the European romantic and classical periods" (personal communication, May 26, 2008). This insightful remark was made in the context of my observation to him that, compared to orchestras and chamber groups, there was far more commissioning of new works in the choral sphere. He was acknowledging the preference on the part of Japanese audiences for repertoire from those two periods of European music history over new music of whatever style. That can hardly be separated from a final reason that Takasaki cited, however—the predominant Christian purpose of most European choral music, to which I will return below.

One reason behind the desire for new choral music could be a conductor's interest in having unique music for a group to perform. Saeko Hasegawa explained the commissioning of pieces for the Little Singers of Tokyo even as she stressed that ultimately it was up to the parents of the choristers because they would bear the expense. Here are the notes I took on that conversation:

> She always liked contemporary music. . . . When she came back to Japan from music studies at Clark College in the US (after Geidai high school), the American Cultural Center was sponsoring contemporary music activities [see chapter 3]. In the 1970s–'80s she went to concerts such as Takemitsu's Music Tomorrow. Before 1984 she never thought of commissioning. The Little Singers were doing pieces such as Britten's *Ceremony of Carols* and others; Hungarian composers had written for children—the range was not high, but rhythm was important. Because

> the works of Bartók and Kodály were based on folklore, for her they somehow seemed related to Japan—there was somehow an affinity. So they did Bartók's music. Time passed. At the time of the Little Singers' celebration of thirty-five years, she heard that John Cage had written a piece for children; to find it, she turned to Toshi Ichiyanagi, who had studied with Cage and therefore 'must know it.' That information turned out to be wrong, but the inquiry ultimately resulted in a piece by Ichiyanagi—"Two Movements Based on the Series 'Frogs'" (1987).
>
> A few days later Saeko Hasegawa met Yori-aki Matsudaira at a concert for the first time. Someone said to Matsudaira: "It would be wonderful if you wrote for the thirty-fifth anniversary." At intermission, Matsudaira was writing something and showed it to her—a radical idea. "Great!" responded Hasegawa, so he sent *Perpetua Mobile for Little Singers* (1987) to her approximately 10 days later. Not notes—it was instead a story of how to do this seven-part piece. It used only four notes—a tetrachord—but not all together. Hasegawa commented, "Whereas Japanese kids learn how to follow, not stand out, Matsudaira asked each one to think and do it, so it was a good learning experience" (Saeko Hasegawa, personal communication, June 1, 2004; emphasis in original).

The competitions and festivals organized by the Japan Choral Association are a powerful motivation for the commissioning of new music: "The All Japan Choral League has commissioned pieces for their competitions since they were founded in 1948. . . . The composers have been encouraged to write Japanese choral pieces. One of the most notable composers is Osamu Shimizu (1911–1986) who was one of the founders of the AJCL in 1948 and the fourth president of the organization from 1964 to 1970. He wrote more than five hundred choral pieces" (Tsutsumi 2007: 24). All divisions of the competitions (junior high, high school, university, women, company, and private) at national and prefectural levels allow for free pieces, and Japanese compositions constitute most of those. Many of these have been commissioned by the chorus that presented it. The expectation for new music is reinforced by the requirement for the compulsory pieces performed by the choral groups that make it to the national competitions: a group's selection of a compulsory piece must come from the Popular Song Series published by the Association in that fiscal year. It comprises twelve pieces of varying levels of difficulty selected that year; two of these are European Renaissance and baroque pieces, but the rest are by Japanese composers. One of the pieces will be from an award-winning suite that has won the Asahi Composition Award, initiated in 1990 (Tsutsumi 2007: 122, 157).

A poem by a member of the amateur woman's chorus La Mère served as the motivation for requesting one new piece. In this instance, "commissioning" is the wrong word, because it implies payment. When I visited La Mère, I came to understand that the request for new music might or might not involve remuneration for the composer. That is to say, many conductors, like La Mère's conductor, Mikio Itoh, are expected to compose new music for the group just as part of the job. Extra compensation—a bonus—may be given if a particularly good composition helps the group in one of the choral competitions in which they might compete. I attended a rehearsal held in a local Ishikawa prefecture community center, and then the competition itself for which La Mère had prepared a new piece by Itoh. The performance began with a recitation of the poem by the chorister author; the entire presentation had to come in under the time limit of four minutes. With their performance and that piece, they won the competition at the prefectural level.

By far the most consistent reason I have been given for the commissioning of new choral music is the model established by one man: the conductor Nobuaki Tanaka, whose activities with the Japan Philharmonic Chorus are now familiar. The point here is that Tanaka not only commissions works for the Tokyo Philharmonic Chorus, but also encourages commissioning by the amateur choruses that he also conducts. One example is *A Little Friend with a Big Forehead*, composed in 1972 by Akira Miyoshi to a text by Taizo Oki; it was commissioned by the Hibari Children's Chorus, which Tanaka conducted at the time. Before playing this piece in his lecture at the 2005 World Chorus Symposium in Kyoto, Tanaka explained: "This piece is set with five sections, and this one is the third section, entitled 'A Dream.' The lyrics go, 'I had a fearful dream. I was a black child of some country far, far away. Many people died every day around me. Everybody was starving, but their tummies stuck out. They ate nuts, grasses, snakes and lizards, but still they starved.'"

Most to the point is that the example Tanaka set with amateur choruses is being followed by hundreds, if not thousands, of amateur choruses on a regular basis, even though they cannot often afford to offer commissions to composers who demand a substantial fee. A number of those choruses are conducted by musicians who sang in a chorus conducted by Tanaka or otherwise experienced his influence. Just one example is Fumiaki Kuriyama, the distinguished conductor of the Tokyo Broadcasting Children's Chorus, who conducts a number of other choirs and teaches in several places in Tokyo. As a former member of Tanaka's Tokyo Philharmonic Chorus, Kuriyama considers it an important part of his job to commission new pieces (Emi Tanaka and Takuya Yokoyama, personal communication, May 16, 2006).

Significantly, commissioning is sometimes part of an organized effort beyond the purview of a particular conductor or particular chorus. From Kaori Tanaka Nakajima, for example, I learned about two organized groups, each with offices throughout Japan, that, although completely independent from each other, follow the same system. New works are commissioned each year, paid for by members' dues; in return, members receive a copy of the manuscript score and a CD of the premiere of each piece. One of the groups, Atarashii Uta wo Tsukuru Kai (the New Songs Creation Society), established in 1994, commissions solo songs, small ensemble pieces for two or three singers, chamber operas, and theatrical pieces for solo singer and small chorus. The second group, Tsukuru Kai (the New Choral Pieces Creation Society), established in 1990, commissions choral pieces (Kaori Nakajima, personal communication, September 15, 2012).

Summer choral camps and festivals are other organized venues through which participants commission new music (see below). Typically, singers of all ages come together for three days to learn new compositions, and on the fourth day they hold concerts.

PUTTING COMPOSERS BACK INTO THE PICTURE

Earlier in this chapter I cited the expression of need felt by Kosaku Komatsu for choral singing "to harmonize public spirit and to smooth our lives." In the case of other early composers, need segued not into expectation, but into desire. That is to say, it was in terms of a desire for different music for children that a compositional development in the Taisho era was explained to me by Mikio Itoh, the business manager of the Japan Association for Children's Music (personal communication, April 13, 1999). In the early years of the twentieth century there was a reaction on the part of individual composers against the pedantic quality of the primary-school songs and against the use of texts (patriotic and Meiji-moralistic) so far removed from the children's world. A countermovement gathered outside of the school system on behalf of "good music" for children.

> In Taisho 7 [1917] there was a famous composer called Suzuki Miekichi, and he organized a group called Akaitori Undo. Top-class composers,

> such as Hakushu Kitahara and Kosaku Yamada, and top-class poets belonged to the group. They wanted to compose and offer to children more beautiful and emotional songs than the popular and school songs. Those people thought that the *Monbushō shōka* [school songs] were not really good, artistic songs for children. That was the most important thing. Those people didn't make the songs *for* children, to amuse the children. They made songs that they thought were good, artistic children's songs. (Mikio Itoh, personal communication, April 13, 1999)

> The Taisho era lasted only fifteen years. But the Taisho era was in between Meiji and Showa. There was *Taisho romanha*—more cultural thinking, appreciation of literature, romantic feeling. In Showa we went into the war period. In the Taisho era we could have the literature, etc. It was a very short but very romantic period. (Mikio Itoh, personal communication, June 5, 2000)[10]

In her article on the composer Kosaku Yamada (whom Itoh mentions), the musicologist Mamiko Naka stresses his desire to make his music communicate with Japanese audiences and thus his turn to Japanese poetic expressiveness in his choice of song texts. Privileging the text led him to a particular compositional style for song that was influenced by his having studied abroad, where he gained this perspective: "In Germany, it is said that to speak dexterously is to sing. . . . The foundation for proper pronunciation is to know dexterously the way to combine pure clear vowels and distinctive consonants. To put it in the simplest way, the most natural pronunciation fits best to singing. The word 'distinctive' never implies exaggeration."[11] Naka concludes: "Already here, we can see his endeavour to make his works intelligible to common Japanese audience. As a matter of fact, his associations with contemporary poets helped change his creative attitude into something Japanese or ethnic, thus resulting in the simplistic manipulation of the tonal materials. Perhaps for this reason, he became involved in composing new songs for children's appreciation" (Naka 1991: 564).

Often referred to as the "father of Japanese art song" (*kakyoku*, the Japanese counterpart of German lieder), Kosaku Yamada composed dōyō, lyrical tonal songs for children (with piano accompaniment), many of which are included in the series *Yamada Kōsaku dōyō hyakkyoku shū* (*100 Children's Songs by Kosaku Yamada*), published in 1927. The style of text setting is consistent from one piece to the next, and the music is very accessible.[12] Calling for proper, natural pronunciation of carefully selected texts, lyrical melody, and simple manipulations of tonal materials, the songs of Kosaku Yamada established a style of Japanese song that would endure.

Intersections: Song and Choral Music, for Children and Adults

While no longer popular with children, dōyō are still appreciated by older Japanese. Furthermore, as Itoh indicated, they are sometimes presented in solo vocal recitals by professional adult singers; I attended one such concert in the Tokyo Bunka Kaikan. New dōyō are still being composed with the same artistic goals, fostered by the Nihon Dōyō Kyokai. In our conversation at the office of the Kyokai, the director, Mikio Itoh, commented on this intersection between songs for children and for adults: it results, he remarked, from the fact that a great deal of new *dōyō ongaku* (children's music) is actually conceived of as music for mothers of young children; the reason he gave was need.

BW: Who will sing this dōyō? [I was being shown the score of a new song.]
MI: I will choose a singer. We have special adult singers only for children's songs, for recordings, for concerts.
BW: Are you composing the songs for children to sing?
MI: Good question! When a baby is born, the first song that he or she hears is what the mother sings. So mothers should know children's songs. . . . Nowadays young mothers don't know children's songs [lullabies], so they cannot sing songs to their children. This is a very big problem now. Mothers my age, they have many songs. But now mothers know only J-pop, Japanese popular songs. So it's very important to give songs not only to the babies, but to the mothers too. So composers have to think for children and mothers alike. (Personal communications, April 13, 1999, and June 5, 2000).

An intersection between solo and choral performance of the same works also surfaces with the compositions of Kosaku Yamada. They are relished in the repertoire of some adult choruses, particularly women's groups, who will sing them either in unison as choral songs or in multipart arrangements.

Like Kosaku Yamada, Yoshinao Nakada (1923–2000), Japan's most successful of composers of song since World War II, wrote songs for both children and adults that are sung both solo and by choruses. Until his death, Nakada was an active member of the Japan Association for Children's Music. A student at the Tokyo Music School during the war (1940–43), Nakada served in the army for a short period, then became active as a pianist and composer starting in 1946. "A period of concentration on piano music and songs was followed by an extensive output of choral works, children's songs and incidental scores for radio and television. His music follows the tradition of the Romantic *lied* and *mélodie*, making no use of later developments. The lyricism of his songs and his successful handling in them of Japanese texts have brought them great popularity within Japan" (Kanazawa 2001: 596). At a rehearsal of an amateur woman's chorus in 2001, I observed the nostalgic pleasure that the members derived from singing (not rehearsing), from memory, songs by Nakada, who had recently died; they knew them in three-part arrangements. Strikingly, one of those the group selected to sing was a children's game song.[13]

The artistically flexible contemporary composer Joji Yuasa has, like Kosaku Yamada, written artistic and interesting music for even very young children. Adults can enjoy hearing and singing them; the piano accompaniment can be artistic (albeit diatonic).[14] There are at least two kinds of children's songs, Yuasa commented: those enjoyable to sing by children themselves, and songs one can enjoy by hearing, not singing. "It was difficult to compose songs for children from kindergarten to the middle years of primary school; the melodic line has to be simple, and the text easy to understand. For older children, it is not necessary for the meaning of the words to be quite so simple" (Joji Yusa, personal communication, June 1, 2011).

Having composed music for children since the 1950s, Joji Yuasa has thought quite a bit about what that demands of him as a composer and explained his experience to me . Need on the part of the government media dovetailed with personal financial need for him in the late 1950s and 1960s when, since he was not earning any money as a teacher, he began to write music for radio and television programs. As a member of the Jikken Kōbō (Experimental Workshop) in 1954 he had been commissioned to write music for a ballet for very young children, between about six and twelve years old; *Circus Variation* was composed for two pianists and staged ballet (tape was not available). The director of children's programming, a woman, came to see it and decided to broadcast the ballet as a television special, the children's hour not yet having been regularized. After that he was asked to write a good deal of music for television. Some years later the director planned a program featuring newly composed children's songs, and he was asked to write for it. Yuasa told me that two of the songs he provided are still in circulation, and he remembered that one day on the train in Japan he heard two children singing his "Shinkansen Song" and knew that a song for children about American Indians was being disseminated throughout kindergartens in Japan. He has composed for children from time to time over the years: "In a way I'm proud of myself that I have done music for infants up to advanced avant-garde" (personal communication, June 1, 2011).

Whatever the reason for the creation of a new song or choral work, the primacy of the text, the desire for communication, and the musical means of assuring it that were established by Kosaku Yamada and continued by Yoshinao Nakada and others have continued to be powerful aesthetically. Words articulated syllabically in choral unison are all the clearer. (I cannot help but think of the syllabic setting of the "Ode to Joy" text in Beethoven's Symphony no. 9—the iconic song for the Japanese end-of-year celebrations.) Inclusion of portions or passages that are to be sung in choral unison can be quite dramatically juxtaposed with (an)other texture(s) in the music.

In striking contrast with the melismatic rendering of texts in much Japanese traditional music and some traditional folk-song styles, syllabic setting of the text prevails to a remarkable degree in choral music. The setting of the poems in Hayashi's drama *Scenes from Hiroshima* (see below) are entirely syllabic. When I mentioned to the composer Tokuhide Niimi composers' apparent preference for syllabic text setting, he suggested that it might be due to the style established by the Christian hymns through which multi-part choral singing was introduced to Japan, or perhaps to the style established by Kosaku Yamada, for whom clarity of text was primary (personal communication, May 13, 2002). Niimi had not noticed the consistency in syllabic settings of choral music (including a good deal of his own) before I made this observation to him, and upon pulling out a few scores he discovered that it might indeed be the case. Exceptions do occur, of course—as in Niimi's superb 2005 composition *Bone no utau* (*Corpses Sing*) for mixed voices, in which melismas sung on vowels.

After my conversation with Niimi, I noticed that, in published collections of choral compositions, the name of the poet is given primacy of place over the name of the composer. Thus the importance of the clarity of the text should always be kept in mind when considering Japanese choral music. If the text is not kept clear, we should ask why not.

Some Composers' Criteria and Choices for Texts of New Works

Other than on occasions of sociopolitical constraints on song texts, the choice of text for a choral work (or song) usually lies with the composer. In this section, I demonstrate the range of criteria and choices made by some composers.

The extent of Michio Mamiya's interest in Japanese folk song as material for new choral works is unmatched by that found in any other contemporary composer. His creative output was greatly affected by his early life. His experience with choral music began as a child when his father, a teacher, instructed children in piano and singing at their home every Sunday (personal communication, May 14, 2006). He was exposed to Japanese folk culture when, after the family's home was destroyed in the firebombings of World War II, they moved to Aomori prefecture, where they lived on the second floor of a fisherman's cooperative association.

> In the summer, at the time of the *Nebuta* Festival, a singing contest in which men and women from all over would display their skills took place in the fish market. The stage was almost directly across from the second floor window of our home, so we had first-class seats. Nearer the stage, thousands of people who had come from the countryside would eat their lunches and drink sake as they applauded and shouted, enjoying the performance along with the performers on stage. In those days there was still a close tie between the lives of the people and the folksongs being performed. . . . The folksongs of Japan are still something very important to me personally. (Mamiya 1971, as cited in Herd 1987: 116–17)

Mamiya said that his subsequent involvement with folk song came after he graduated in 1952 from the Tokyo School of Music (later Geidai). For three years he worked with the singer and musicologist Ruriko Uchida as an accompanist, and in 1955 she asked him to compose songs with accompaniment for her. From Uchida's suggestion that he collect folk songs, Mamiya undertook two major projects. Together they went to the NHK to listen to the fabulous collection of recordings there from all over Japan: "We listened to thousands of songs," he said, "and selected twenty-four of them" (personal communication, May 14, 2006).[15] Mamiya described their collaboration:

> In the period when NHK Radio Station Tokyo was in Uchisaiwaicho near Hibiya Park, in the afternoon every Sunday, there were two people playing old S.P. recordings and eagerly listening to them in the corner of the music library of the radio station. One of the two was Ruriko Uchida, an alto singer, and the other was Michio Mamiya, a composer. Their labour started in January 1956 and continued for about 18 months. After about a ten-year interval, Mamiya continued the work alone for about two more years (1968–69). (CD booklet, p. 13, Fontec CD, FOCD 3481, [n.d.])

Together as well they thoroughly researched folk songs from the Tōhoku (northern Honshu Island) region. In May 2006 Mamiya told me that he was still working with the NHK collection.

In the late 1950s and 1960s Mamiya's interest in Japanese folk music dovetailed with that of Nobuaki Tanaka, who in 1956 had founded the Tokyo Philharmonic Chorus. Mamiya's *Konsei gasshō no tame no konpojishyon* (Composition for Mixed Chorus, 1958) was among the first Tanaka commissioned in pursuit of his determination to stimulate the production of new works by Japanese composers.[16] Mamiya was not the only composer invited by Tanaka to compose works based on folk songs. Influenced by Bartók, Francis Poulenc, and Zoltán Kodály, Tanaka asked Japanese composers to write pieces for a series of concerts he held in 1960 titled "Japanese Choral Compositions on Japanese Folk Music" (Tsutsumi 2007: 25). About this interest, Tanaka explained on the occasion of the World Chorus Symposium at Kyoto in 2005:

> In the late 1950s, the Tokyo Philharmonic Chorus sent out a questionnaire to composers all over Japan. The question we asked the composers was this: if you were to arrange Japanese folk songs into choral music, what kind of music would you compose? To our surprise, the answer came back to us in the form of more than fifty new pieces.
>
> In the 1970s a number of excellent compositions were created, and many of them were rooted in Japanese tradition. I think the increase in numbers come from the fact that the postwar composers were in their forties—the prime of their lives. Since then, there hasn't been anything comparable to this concentrated "rooting" in the Japanese culture.
>
> The composers of that generation are still active in the center of the Japanese music scene. I think the shock of the war experience during their youth keeps stimulating their creativity. I'm from the same

generation, and I remember I used to yearn to have such pieces in our repertoire. (Translated by Mika Kimula)

What has become the signature feature of Mamiya's choral compositions since 1958 is his fascination with and use of *hayashi kotoba* (vocables) of various sorts as text: "They have a special character—so many *hayashi kotoba.* The syllables originally had meanings, but that is forgotten. Sometimes there is an imitative rhythm between drum and flute—*kuchi shōga*—for learning as if they are words" (personal communication, May 14, 2006). Not only the vocables from work songs but also those from lullabies, children's game songs, and other types of Japanese songs have interested him. Mamiya has also listened to jazz and its scat singing. The ethnomusicologist Fumio Koizumi (1927–1983) was of considerable help to Mamiya in his search for vocable traditions. When African musicians came to Japan, Koizumi had them recorded, and he also gave Mamiya recordings of Middle Eastern and Inuit music. Mamiya himself traveled to meet singers of the indigenous Sami of Arctic Scandinavia; from them he heard traditional songs with words. For him the words and the melody could be separated, and he subsequently based some of his works on Sami melodic lines, using vocables to substitute for words. Notably, with vocables as text, Mamiya does not need to be concerned about communication via language, and his works can be and are appreciated by choruses throughout the world.[17]

Most of Mamiya's choral pieces have been composed for a "good group," as he put it, such as the professional Tokyo Philharmonic Chorus or amateur Kyoto Echo. He has also written for a chorus from Hosei University. And "in Japan we have good children's choirs: NHK Children's Chorus, the Odawara Children's Choir, Kanazawa, Shizuoka" (personal communication, May 14, 2006).

For his *Mantra of the Light,* for female chorus and orchestra (1993), the composer Akira Nishimura chose a language that very few people in the world would expect to understand, thus skirting the desideratum of a communicable song text. Having been inspired by hearing Pandit Bhimsen Joshi, a vocalist of North Indian "classical" music, Nishimura selected a mantra in the classical language of South Asia—Sanskrit. The mantra text is intoned seven times in this seven-section, twenty-eight-minute work. The voices and the instruments "ooze" in and out relative to one another (as the CD booklet suggests) and are highly integrated; the text syllables might as well be vocables. A beautifully shimmering, mystical effect is lent by abundant, sustained high sounds; a pitch selection close to the oriental scale occurs at (infrequent) moments. The piece calls for single or unison voices, or sometimes juxtaposed different vocal pitches; there are no chords. One wants to listen for what is coming; it is cohesive but not predictable—to my sensibility, beautiful.[18]

Not surprisingly for Japan, in which Buddhism has been a living religion for nearly a millennium, Buddhist texts have attracted several Japanese composers of choral music. An example that I consider to deserve special mention is *Metta Sutta-jikyo* (1996), by Yuji Takahashi. The melody, which sounds like the sutra chanting style from Sri Lanka, is heard in a cluster of voices that narrate the translated sutra. Known in many cultures, this sutra is one that Theravada Buddhists chant every day. The word *metta* signifies mercy, love, or affection. It is a prayer for happiness and peace for everyone in the world. Through musical choices, Takahashi makes the text one that is meaningful far beyond Japan.[19]

The composer Atsuhiko Gondai expresses spirituality that for him is personal, and to do so he uses the languages of two world religions. In *Agnus Dei/Agnus Mundi II*, commissioned by Tanaka for the Tokyo Philharmonic Chorus, the Latin text, from the Catholic mass, is sometimes clear but by no means consistently so, for it is dominated sometimes by the piano and percussion, sometimes by a baritone soloist counting in German from 1 to (at most) 13 at different paces. This counting is an approach to death, and 13 is the vanishing point, Gondai has explained. In the final minute, in German, the words "Es sind noch Lieder" are sung weightily, to unpitched percussion; this is a reference to a poem by the Jewish Romanian poet Paul Celan, who, having survived the Holocaust, started to write poems: "Es sind noch Lieder zu singen jenseits der Menschen" (May 25, 2011). This is dramatic and skilled writing of contemporary choral music.[20]

Gondai has shifted from drawing on poems by Celan to Buddhist texts. His interest in Buddhist practices is manifested in his 2004 work *A*, introduced by Nobuaki Tanaka in his lecture for the 2005 World Chorus Symposium in Kyoto:

> The piece is a mandala—the symbolic diagram painting of Buddhism—described with sounds. Gondai practiced Buddhist meditation . . . and from this practice he was inspired to compose this piece. Contemplating a mandala, one understands that the cosmos exists within us, and the universe, whose vastness is spread all around us, is connected to everything.

> Gondai has always been very particular with sound patterns that follow a certain rule. For example, in this piece the rhythms are in 9/8 for nine bars, 8/8 for nine bars, 7/8 for nine bars . . . and so on. It's a piece for three small choruses, soprano solo, tenor solo, and percussion. (Translated by Mika Kimula)

That his interest in Buddhism continues is manifested on *A Millennium of Resonance in Europe 2002* (Fontec CD FOCD 9183, [2002]).

Gondai's deeply felt choral expression of Christian faith is exceptional; in fact, avoidance of the Christian content of much of the choral music composed in Western cultures has been mentioned to me as another factor in the need and desire for the creation of new works. Such major works as the Bach B Minor Mass are certainly performed, but their popularity appears to stem from the popularity of Bach's music itself; in Japan as well as elsewhere, such Christian masterworks are performed as concert music rather than as explicitly religious music.[21] Otherwise, "Japan doesn't have so many churches, and sacred music is not so popular. There are more commissions for chorus than for orchestra because choruses want new music" (Ken Takaseki, personal communication, May 26, 2008).

In selecting a text for a commissioned work, composers might need to take particular circumstances into consideration. This was certainly the case with Toshio Hosokawa's choice of the Latin requiem text for *Singing Trees—Requiem for Toru Takemitsu* (1998). While working on a new work commissioned by the Little Singers of Tokyo, Takemitsu died, and Hosokawa turned the piece into a requiem for him. Reference to the Latin requiem text—which expresses grief and a hope for peace but is not a statement of Christian belief per se—was an appropriate choice for that particular choral ensemble. A Latin text is also the basis for Hosokawa's Tenebrae (1993), for the Little Singers, whose history made that text appropriate. Notably, these two very challenging works have very adult content for a children's chorus. They are both recorded by the Little Singers on their label, along with selections of Gregorian chant.[22]

Rather than necessarily being associated with Catholicism, a text in Latin is seen as "universally communicative," according to Shin-ichiro Kobayashi, producer and general manager of the Tokyo Philharmonic Chorus: "The chorus commissioned Murray Schaefer for a piece in Latin because the chorus does international tours and everyone will understand it immediately" (personal communication, May 26, 2008). This is indeed practical, because tours often take performing organizations to many countries, such as France and Germany, and preparing a contemporary

Japanese work in Latin covers the potential need for repertoire in multiple languages other than Japanese. The composer Tokuhide Niimi, who is well respected for his choral works, agrees that Latin is like a universal language in that audiences will hear that a chorus is not singing in Japanese and understand that a non-Japanese language has been selected to reach out to audiences particularly in Europe, with its many romance languages (personal communication, June 2, 2011).

The expression of Japanese sentiments in contemporary music for chorus appears to be paramount in the selection of texts by most composers, and these contribute to keeping composers of choral music "close to the people." Because poets have always been so highly valued in Japanese culture, their texts provide endless possibilities for musical settings—texts ranging from the earliest of Japanese court collections, to the haiku of the seventeenth-century poet Basho, to contemporary poems by such luminaries as Shuntaro Tanikawa. The tragedy of war is given considerable choral expression.

Thirteen years after the atomic bomb was dropped by the United States on Japan, Hikaru Hayashi (b. 1931), an associate of Michio Mamiya's in the postwar composers' group Yagi no Kai (see chapter 4), began a work titled *Scenes from Hiroshima* that addressed his nation's traumatic experience. In 1975 Hayashi wrote:

> I wrote "Give Me Water," the first part of "Scenes from Hiroshima," in 1958, and the second part, "Twilight," and the third part," Night," in 1971. Thirteen years passed in the interim, and twenty years if you count the time since 1951, when I first read Tamiki Hara's "Scenes from Hiroshima" [*Genbaku shōkei*], the poems that inspired my work. It is depressing to think that a single composition required twenty years from conception to final completion, but I nonetheless feel privileged for the experience.
>
> I say "final completion," but in fact I have not been able to realize my original plan. I originally intended to compose an epilogue based on the poem "Green Everlasting" and that remained my intention even as I was completing part three. But in 1971, just before the first performance of the finished work, I wrote, "'Green Everlasting' remains uncomposed." At the time, I felt that I was bidding farewell to "Scenes." . . . But I have begun to think that the terrifying contemporary historical drama that is "Scenes from Hiroshima" properly ends, can end, with a singing of "Green Everlasting":

> May eddles [*sic*] of young leaves envelop the Hiroshima delta. May prayers of goodness permeate the remembrance of death and flame.
>
> But today, when the terror of nuclear weapons has not diminished in the slightest, how can one compose music for the phrase, "May eddles of young leaves envelop the Hiroshima delta"? About once every other year for the past fifteen years, I have sat down and begun composing, only to find that question standing in my way, preventing me from continuing. Of course, I am aware and believe with all my heart that finding an answer to that question is the fundamental responsibility of the artistic imagination.
>
> Nevertheless . . .[23]

But finish it Hayashi did, and, appropriately, the world premiere took place on August 5, 2001, at the Aichi Global Peace Festival (the Tokyo premiere was held four days later, on August 9), in a program titled "Hayashi Hikaru—Tokyo Philharmonic Chorus August Festival." For that program, the composer wrote:

> I began composing *Scenes from Hiroshima* when I was 27 and completed it this past summer when I was well into my seventieth year. I have been writing it, that is, for virtually my entire life as a composer.
>
> "Give me Water" was written in 1958 when I was 27, and, although there are some atonal transitional phrases, for the most part it maintains a B-flat minor tonality.
>
> "In "Twilight" and "Night," which were completed in 1971, the style changes, and tone clusters coexist with free-atonal (but not serial) music. The introduction of a five-tone scale similar to that used in the music of Noh keeps these pieces from becoming completely abstract, however, and they unfold like hell scrolls—or like the paintings of Hieronymus Bosch or Picasso's *Guernica*.
>
> Then in "Green Everlasting" which was composed in 2001, a tonal world reappears. This piece, which begins with an approximation of a gentle Gregorian chant, is not simply a return to "Give Me Water" but is rather a transcendence or sublation of that earlier piece using an inverted or complementary tonal palette.
>
> While the form of the four pieces that make up the finished *Scenes from Hiroshima* may have changed over the course of my evolution as a composer, their spiritual contents have remained constant throughout.[24]

Works for Chorus and Orchestra

That some works would put the orchestra and chorus together is not surprising, given the popularity of choral singing, the preeminence of the orchestra among European-type instrumental ensembles in Japan, and the cultural space devoted to Beethoven's Symphony no. 9. Here I wish to mention just a few examples. Bear in mind that the bulk of choral music written in Japan calls for either a capella performance or piano accompaniment.

Michio Mamiya's *Composition for Chorus no. 4, "Children's Field"* (1963) was written in response to an appeal in 1962 from the ethnomusicologist Fumio Koizumi, who, with his research team at the musicology department of Tokyo Geidai, had carried out research into *warabe uta* (children's songs) that had been handed down "from of old" and sung by primary-school children in the Tokyo metropolis. Wrote Mamiya: "One day in the year, that huge collection [of some two thousand tunes], which had been notated together with words, was delivered to me accompanied by a message from Koizumi saying, 'Would it be possible for you to compose a new piece by pumping up the children's vital power heard in these tunes?'"[25]

> The collection included a wide variety of traditional game songs, such as hand-ball songs, beanbag songs, drawing songs, counting-out songs and teasing calls. Moreover, not a few of the newest things, fashionable words and even some names of sumo-wrestling stars were perceptible in the collected words. . . . The tradition of warabeuta was well preserved, and further, they were getting reborn every day at that time. . . . About 50 tunes or their fragments from the warabeuta collection are heard in "Composition for Chorus No. 4." (Mamiya 1996: 10)

Not only the texts but also the modalities of the melodies are referentially "Japanese," with tetraphonic organization of motives, but tetrachords with varying intervallic content (among them the suggestive E–G–A and E–F–A arrangements). Even so, the musical material is by no means stereotypical of "Japanese music"; this is ingenious contemporary music.

The Fontec recording of *Composition for Chorus no. 4* features, suitably, the Tokyo Metropolitan Symphony Orchestra; the featured chorus, the Tokyo Broadcasting Children's Chorus Group, is, equally suitably, associated with the NHK, which broadcast the premiere of the piece and whose archives of Japanese folk songs have been so important for Mamiya.

The Tokyo Broadcasting Children's Chorus Group is also featured in the recording of Akira Miyoshi's *Kyōmon*, for children's choir and orchestra (1984). It was premiered in an important annual event, the Min-On Contemporary Music Festival, featuring the Tokyo Philharmonic Orchestra—the oldest orchestra in Japan, but one that is nevertheless known for having fostered contemporary music through the decades. *Kyōmon* begins with the chorus focusing on the pitch sequence A–B–A–G–E, with lots of unison singing and with repetition of motives integrated into the instrumental texture. It gradually expands tonally and to a number of voice parts, gathering dynamically with prominent brass and percussion complementing a choral progression whose register climbs. The ensuing quiet comes not suddenly, but over time. The vocal line is pitched lower than before, but the same sort of motivic repetition continues—A–G–E–A–B; A is the central pitch, but in the end it dies to E. The brass picks back up for a blast against quiet chimes, and quiet vocal unison. The piece just ends, without any obvious musical preparation.[26]

Teruaki Suzuki's *Hymnos*, for double choir and orchestra, was commissioned for the Min-On Contemporary Music Festival of 1990. Suzuki was born in Sendai but went to Tokyo for his composing education; he was a student of Akira Miyoshi at Toho Gakuen University and finished with a graduate degree in 1984. As a young composer Suzuki garnered a number of prizes for orchestra and chamber music, not only in Japan but also in Germany. Writing for chorus followed. He wrote of *Hymnos*:

> A voice in this piece is treated as part of a whole body of sounds without being separated or projecting from an orchestra, not the two interacting as independent forms, or the work being a concerto with voices and an orchestra. . . . The chorus is equally divided into two groups, and by making each part basically individual, it is planned to diversify sources and/or directions of sounds. I also had an idea of finding a three-dimensional quality and the perspective of the chorus section by making both groups respond or link each other.
>
> In this piece, I grasp the whole from a viewpoint of an accumulation of group structure, so that every instrument or every section forms independent groups at a time in many places and repeats on and off. The simultaneous progress, centralization and diffusion of many organic ensembles create a macroscopic chaos-like situation, in which I imagined a super-nova-like phenomenon, so to speak, where highly dense energy is treated perpetually.

> There is a strong image of "fire . . . one of the Five Elements." (CD booklet, p. 18, Camerata CD 32CM-190, 1991)[27]

The text comprises extracts and reconstructions of a poetic text on the subject of fire; in this contemporary composition, clarity of text is not an aesthetic principle.

COMPOSERS AND CONNECTIVITY WITH "THE PEOPLE"

Composers are integrated into the choral sphere in various ways. Here I suggest a range of them.

From 1960 to 1977 the All-Japan Choral League held national workshops for conductors (and singers) that included sessions by composers who taught their own pieces to the participants. Restored in 1990, the format of the national workshops was resumed. The location rotates among the prefectures, and the study of the music of the host regions—likely including sessions devoted to compositions by local composers—has been one of the attractions for the participants. The organization and spirit of these choral events must be understood as important for the buoyancy of the choral sphere in the country. One example will illustrate the point.

In 1990 the AJCL choral conductors' workshop was held in Gifu prefecture in the heart of Honshū Island, slightly northwest of Nagoya:

> [The event was held] from May 3 to 5, which was during Japan's Golden Week, a week of successive holidays from the end of April to early May. The Agency for Cultural Affairs [of the national government] subsidized the project. The slogan of this workshop was "Let's Soak in Chorus!" The workshop was opened not only to conductors but also to people who were interested in chorus. One thousand and five hundred people participated. They stayed in three Japanese style inns. The first day the participants attended one of four two-hour sessions: a rehearsal for a mixed choir, a rehearsal for a female choir, a lecture on polyphony, or a session on administration of choirs. A social gathering was held in the evening at each inn. The second day, a male choir rehearsal was held in place of the administration class. In the afternoon, the composer Tokuhide Niimi [born in nearby Nagoya] spoke to all the workshop participants on his works, including his new piece "Divertimento of Sea." In the evening, three hundred people attended a reception and sang songs from the standard repertoire—"Zao," "Soshun (Early

> Spring)," and "Daichi Sanko (Praise Earth)" by Makoto Sato—without music scores. During the morning of the third day, the pieces taught in the seminars were performed in the Gifu Civic Hall, and the three hundred people attending the event sang favorite songs under the direction of Nobuyoshi Yoshimura without rehearsing. (Tsutsumi 2007: 64–65)

In 1991 in Shizuoka Prefecture the workshop included two new lectures—"Gregorian Chant" and "How to Read Latin in Religious Music"—and the composer Ryohei Hirose discussed his piece *Umidori no uta* (*Song of Birds in the Sea*). In 1992 in Hiroshima the Latin class continued; Shinichiro Ikebe was the guest composer, speaking on his pieces *Folksong of the Orient* and *Ibun Bochan* (based on the story "Bochan" by the prominent writer Soseki Natsume). In subsequent years Akira Miyoshi, Minoru Miki, Ko Matsushita, and other composers participated.

Another choral association, Ongakuju, founded in 1996 by the conductor Fumiaki Kuriyama, produces a weeklong (at least) series of events with a similar format, one that encompasses concerts and seminars. Called the Tokyo Cantato, it is held in several cities, with Tokyo as the center. Top international and Japanese guest conductors and musicians are invited with the aim of providing a better quality of choral music. In 2001 I was invited by the composer Tokuhide Niimi to attend the final session at Zero Hall in Nakano, Tokyo, when participants gathered for the culmination of the week's activities. About 800 people dispersed themselves on the main floor and balcony of the hall (capacity 1150). I arrived during the performance of three pieces by a mixed chorus of thirty-five men and forty-four women who sang with piano accompaniment. The style was tonal with some dissonance, with syllabic text setting; portions scored for unison singing subdivided one of the pieces into sections.

Niimi, who was in charge of the session, then spoke from the stage, announcing the next item. In what followed, he made the point that the same piece could be performed by different forces. We heard it in succession by a male soloist, two women as a duet, and a women's chorus—each accompanied on piano; then Niimi performed it, accompanying himself on piano; it was also rendered as a solo piano piece and as one for piano four-hands. Niimi's song was a very lyrical one, in 6/8, with a syllabic text setting. By the end of Niimi's demonstration, everyone in the hall (including myself) knew the song well. Despite much repetition, it was a very engaging, pleasant experience shared by all.

Then Niimi conducted a women's chorus who sang a capella with unembellished vocal production. Of three sweet songs, one was homophonic and in a minor key; another was fast and syncopated; and the third was much more challenging to sing. Applause followed the set of three pieces.

Next, a woman conducted a children's chorus—fifty-four children dressed every which way. The first row, presumably the youngest, singers wore shorts, while the back two rows were young boys and girls in jeans. All had on some shirt under an open overshirt, giving a very informal, "we're here to enjoy ourselves" effect. They sang with absolutely rapt attention, to piano accompaniment. Their third song was jazzy, and the singers moved, snapping their fingers; that piece ended with a third verse sung by the eight oldest boys, who came to the front to sing in unison while the chorus accompanied them on scat. This piece drew applause out of turn. The remaining three songs were obviously fun to sing—a really zippy, jumpy tune, then a sweet one, and another lively one to end. Those children had been ready to perform and did so superbly.

To end that event, the afternoon, and the week of the Tokyo Cantato, everyone joined in the song that we had all learned with Niimi, in which the word *sayōnara* was rendered with considerable feeling. Onstage were the children and an adult group. Most of those in the audience who wanted to sing remained seated or stood either at their seats or in the aisles. All had scores of a multi-part arrangement. The joy in this choral experience was palpable throughout the hall.

Composers are embedded in the choral world in other ways as well. For the opening of the Japan Choral Music Center and Library in Ebisu, Tokyo, in 1979, a choir under the direction of Akira Yuyama sang *Utaibito no furusato* (*Home for Singers*), which had been composed for the occasion. Created by the composer Kan Ishii (1921–2009; brother of the composer Maki Ishii, 1936–2003), the center and library function as a reference source for information about choral activities in Japan. The center and library also encourages and coordinates choral activities with other countries such as the Asian Pacific regional meeting, the Japan tour of the World Youth Chorus, and the world symposium held in Kyoto in 2005. For the organization's twentieth anniversary celebration in 1999, a symposium was held in which three composers—Yori-aki Matsudaira, Akira Miyoshi, and Tokuhide Niimi—discussed the theme "Future Japanese Music from a Cultural Point of View"; the following year a symposium held on the theme "Suggestions for Japanese Choral Music in the Future" also featured three composers—Atsuhiko Gondai, Midori Takashima, and Ko Matsushita (Tsutsumi 2007:96–101).

Since 1993 Japan's choral magazine, *Harmony* (founded in 1971 at the urging of Kan Ishii, at that time the composer and president of the All-Japan Choral League), has included articles on Japanese composers that include interviews with them and a list and description of their choral works. *Harmony* also publishes the second-place winning composition of the Japan Choral Association competition for choral pieces written by amateurs.[28] In 1998 it was decided that a composer should be added to the board of *Harmony*; Shin-ichiro Ikebe joined that year and Ko Matsushita in 2002 (Tsutsumi 2007: 121–22).

While these sorts of institutionalized involvements on the part of composers in the sphere of choral music illustrate ways in which they have been and remain "closely connected with the people," the most telling evidence lies in the music that they are willing to create. Here the artistic flexibility that I have mentioned several times comes again into play. For instance, a major decision that must be made between the commissioner(s) and the composer of a new work is the level of difficulty. "Nobuaki Tanaka commissions difficult pieces from top composers," said Toshio Hosokawa, from whom Tanaka did just that (personal communication, June 1, 2004). On the other hand, Nobuaki Tanaka spoke to me of an amateur group of approximately seventy members in Osaka in which the average age is around seventy-five. "Every other year they commission a contemporary piece. One member will meet the composer, say 'We are old,' etc. The composer listens to what they want. From Takahashi Yuji, for instance, they have commissioned ten pieces. Those pieces are always successful—not too difficult" (personal communication, June 7, 2004). Of the more than twenty-four pieces that Takahashi has composed for chorus, however, are a number commissioned by Tanaka for the Tokyo Philharmonic Chorus in a style appropriate for that group (Yuji Takahashi, personal communication, July 28, 2012).

Whether or not the piece will be tonal or "contemporary" is another matter. That the members of La Mère prefer tonal music became clear over a lunch discussion, when Mikio Itoh told them that I was interested in *gendai ongaku*; to them that meant difficult and atonal music (personal communication, May 11, 2002). (It never became clear whether "atonal" automatically made it difficult or they separate the two characteristics.) Shin-ichiro Ikebe, a leading public intellectual in Japan, has written many works for amateur chorus—over one hundred suites, he reported to me: "About 10 percent of them are contemporary music; 90 percent tonal music" (personal communication, May 25, 2008).[29] What matters is not the composer's skill or musical preference, but his or her willingness to accommodate the preferences and capabilities of the commissioner. Attitudinally, this is artistic flexibility.

SUMMARY

In the environment of European spheres of musical participation in musical modernity, the practice of choral singing has been taken up as an activity—primarily amateur—by many, many Japanese. In this chapter I have traced the history of the practice as a governmental tool for modernization and nation building in Meiji-era schools and also in that period as a university-level activity fostered initially by Christian missionaries, as a personal response by a leading composer to interwar political tensions, again as a governmental tool during World War II, as psychological comfort in the terrible conditions of the immediate postwar period, as social activity in burgeoning urban, industrial, and commercial contexts of the second half of the twentieth century, and—all along and since—as a modern expression of Japanese sentiments.

Along with individual musical leaders and "the people," composers have throughout the history of choral singing in Japan been willing partners as needs, expectations, and desires have driven the positive response to choral singing and afforded them the opportunity to create a huge amount of new music. In the choral sphere, competitions as well as (or more than) concerts have been a significant part of this mode of musical participation, with composers in the thick of it, artistically flexible and thereby remaining "connected with the people." In this way as well as in other ways discussed in this book, Japanese composers have continued to maintain the historical social role of music in their culture.

Conclusion

In this book, I have taken Japan's musical modernity to be a condition, historically produced over approximately a century and a half of introduction to and enculturation of Western music, wherein a role of composer emerged in response to what Gluck refers to as elements in a common "grammar of modernity" that exists around the globe in processes of change that have not ended yet (2011: 676). The elements she identified—the nation-state and the insistence on national political participation, subjection to the forces of capitalism and industrialization, incorporation into the reigning geopolitical world order, and social shifts in massified urban and disrupted communal life—have all been considered through affordances they have (or have not) offered for the creation of new music by both composers and their counterparts in the sphere of traditional music, that is, performer-composers.

When the Meiji oligarchy purposely disrupted communal life as it had existed in pre-nation-state Japan, music was selected as a potentially effective tool for the opposite force—for constructing new, shared cultural space. The decision to select Western music—seen to be utilitarian for military discipline, disassociated from local social connotations, and thus potentially expressive of a united, modern nation-state—was a pragmatic one. Adoption of a musical system that was new for everyone came to be connected with the development of infrastructures of modernity, that is, a public school system, industries ranging from those of the mass media to manufacturing, and also commerce in the sphere of music—all of which afforded composers opportunities for creating new music, if they achieved competences in the new knowledge and practices. This resulted, I think, in the perception of and expectation for composers that they will be individuals who will make tangible contributions to their culture.

Among those expectations is that the work of composers would contribute to national political agendas: the very role of composer emerged with the need for someone to write school songs. As noted, there have been moments since when music was invoked in the national interest: the invocation of "tradition," including traditional music, as part of Japan's cultural essence against the West in the political tensions of the 1920s through World War II; the political pressures on composers during the interwar years; and nationalistic expectations during World War II. Other government-involved actions were less overtly political: in the 1950s, when the NHK became a publicly supported institution, the organization made efforts to bring performer-composers into the shared cultural space of modern broadcast media and at the same time hired composers from government-supported Geidai to provide music for documentary films, for the social section, and the political section. In 1966 the founding of the National Theatre put into place an institution that from the 1970s to 1990 would foster indigenous traditions by commissioning composers to write new music for traditional instruments. Japanese nonprofit law and support from the Ministry of Education, Culture, Sports, Science, and Technology have been important in the sphere of music, including for composers.

Looking back at the 140 years since new music was adopted, it is clear that music did indeed prove to be an effective tool for creating shared cultural space in modern Japan. Whether the music is in the sphere of concert music, jazz, or popular music, whether it is seriously studied or informally absorbed, all Japanese share a base level of knowledge and sensibility that is universally held across the population, unlike the people's knowledge and sensibilities of the various traditional practices. It is that shared cultural space of Western music that has provided a place wherein composers, performer-composers in traditional-music spheres, and performers on both Western and Japanese instruments might intersect in the creation of new Japanese music. This was seen, for instance, in the appointment in 1930 of the performer-composer Michio Miyagi to the faculty of the Tokyo School of Music, with results that continue to be felt to the present owing to the initiative of such creative individuals as the performer-composer Tadao Sawaii and leading hōgaku performers who commission new works from composers.

Significantly, the shared cultural space does not exist only within Japan. That the music chosen by the Meiji era leaders was Western—from cultures in positions of power in the nineteenth century and beyond—has continued to be an advantage, for it situated Japanese composers and other musicians to participate in, benefit from, and contribute to global cosmopolitan culture—specifically in the sphere of concert music.

Two marking moments emerged as particularly meaningful in the history of music in Japan in the twentieth century—the immediate postwar era, and from 1970 on. In the immediate postwar era the participation of many Japanese in musical activities burgeoned, as choruses and wind bands were formed as clubs in the schools. This was especially the case with choruses, through populations in venues as diverse as urban housing projects and companies. Spurred by the organization of competitions, composers were afforded opportunities to supply new music. Commissions offered to composers by Nobuaki Tanaka for the Tokyo Philharmonic Chorus reinforced expectations for new music for excellent amateur choruses. The 1950s and 1960s also saw the founding of orchestras, a number of which would start as amateur performing groups and then turn professional. For composers, amateur participation in the various European ensemble types that are present in Japanese culture would come to constitute a major affordance.

With the country's sense of urgency to rebuild after the devastation of the war, with the end of the American occupation in 1952 and strong conservative figures in music no longer in control, with determination prevailing to reconnect internationally but on an individual's own terms, the creative interests of individual composers went in multiple directions—from engagement with traditional music to experimentation with international modernist and avant-garde styles. Younger composers found themselves in an extraordinary cultural climate and circumstances, afforded a plethora of locally grounded possibilities for creative choices within the two deeply cultivated, historically grounded complexes of traditional Japanese and Western musics.

After Expo '70 in Osaka—the second cultural moment, which also marked the climax of intermedia arts and the avant-garde movement in Japan—composers continued in strikingly different stylistic directions. In fact, the composer Akira Nishimura dates the effort of Japanese composers to make more serious attempts to "find [their] own voice" to the 1970s (2008: 170). The pursuit of strikingly different stylistic directions by individual composers continues unabated.

One issue for Japanese composers I have left to this conclusion to address.

In the May 1984 issue of the leading music journal *Ongaku Geijutsu*, the composer Ikuma Dan published an interview with Toru Takemitsu in which Takemitsu expressed his inferiority complex in the face of Western composers and spoke of the difficult position of Japanese composers who work with European music. Since 1999, when I began to speak with Japanese composers and listen to their music, I have been watching for indications of that feeling and encountering less and less of it. Yes, Japanese composers face challenges in competing in international venues, but all composers do. It seems to me that, particularly since the death of Toru Takemitsu, who became an iconic figure, more and more Japanese composers are gaining a hearing outside of Japan and—to the point here—they are proceeding with a well-earned high level of confidence with regard to their competence and the degree of creative freedom with which they might navigate the global cosmopolitan shared space of Western concert music, should they desire to do so (not all do).

It seems appropriate to acknowledge that for many Japanese composers the situation need no longer be regarded as dichotomous, that is, as Japan and the West. With respect to the sphere of concert music, I have come to agree with Timothy Taylor: "Perhaps a better term than globalization is 'glocalization,' a word that originated in Japanese business in the late 1980s and was quickly picked up by American business. Glocalization emphasizes the extent to which the local and the global are no longer distinct—indeed, never were—but are inextricably intertwined, with one infiltrating and implicating the other. Indeed, it may now be difficult or impossible to speak of one or *the other*" (Taylor 2001: 120; emphasis added). "Glocalization" also makes a space for the engagement of composers with the traditional musics of Japan—something that is happening not infrequently in the creative work of non-Japanese as well as Japanese composers and is a very modern way of proceeding. As Gluck summed it up: "A fresh study of the modern past is . . . a means to imagine the way to a better future, not only our own but that of a globe that is now beyond the end of *elsewhere*" (Gluck 2011: 687; emphasis added).

The composerly attitude that I have addressed repeatedly in this book is that most (but not all) professional Japanese composers live their creative lives with an attitude of flexibility—not only in terms of how they will earn their living (i.e., for whom they will write music, or who and what they will teach, if they teach), but also artistically, in terms of the styles of music they are willing to write. Even the most distinguished of composers (with a few exceptions) are willing to write for both amateurs and professionals, music complex or simple, music comfortably resting in some tradition or resulting from the modern desire to find one's own voice. That is to say, despite interest on the part of some composers in learning about modernist musical theory and practices of the postwar era, with the exception of a very few individuals, I have not found that Japanese composers have bought into the high-modernist stance of the "autonomous artist," concerned only with art for art's sake, regarding the work as the only real reason for composing.

Perhaps the most telling example of this attitudinal flexibility on the part of many Japanese composers is their willingness to write music for children. In one of her essays for the *Nagasaki Shimbun*, the composer Keiko Fujiie commented that, while some composers are offended by requests to write music for children, she is not, because successful works for children in music and literature (for example, C. S. Lewis's Narnia books) can be extremely complex. This is because it is extremely difficult (but crucial) for an adult to view children on their own terms, rather than as assets or investments for the future (Fujiie 2005: 108).

Composer Reiko Arima (who was head of the Composition Department of Tokyo College of Music at the time of my conversation with her) lent her perspective on the matter of composing music "for children"—not so much music to be played or sung by children, but music to be played by an adult for children.

RA: I don't think that children have only their own world. Both adults and children share the same world, so I think we should offer music we adults think is good and try to educate their senses. Think of Schumann: He used the children's story, but the music itself was adult music.

BW: And Peter and the Wolf . . .

RA: I wrote a trio for violin, cello, and piano and a piano concertino for piano and orchestra that are pieces intended to be played by an adult that can be heard and appreciated by children from about ten years old. (Reiko Arima, personal communication, June 1, 2000, and July 13, 2012)

The primary reason for this attitude of flexibility, I suggest, is historical: the very role of composer was created by the processes of modernization that engendered the need for creative individuals who would meet the diverse demands of the developing infrastructures of modernity. The means by which professional composers might earn a living were therefore diverse from very early in the modern era. The nature of the educational system for achieving musical competence, wherein composers do not necessarily hope for or want to earn their living as a full-time appointee in an academic institution, reinforces the practice of taking advantage of affordances in other spheres of musical activity that have emerged since Western music first began to be systematically introduced in Japan. In order to take advantage of those affordances, composers must be attitudinally flexible. Significantly, neither in their own minds nor in Japanese contemporary music culture is the artistic distinction of even the most respected of composers diminished by that flexibility.

Finally, I have argued in this book that, by responding to the diverse affordances and creating new music with an attitude of flexibility, most Japanese composers have maintained a relational role in their society. In addition, after World War II, when the country's morale as well as its economy needed rebuilding, rather than retreat from the public and avoid emotional expression in their creative work, as a number of prominent Western composers did, most Japanese composers responded to the expressive needs of their fellow citizens. That, I suggest, kept composers connected with the people—in a different sort of socially relational position than the performer-composer of premodern Japan was in, but socially relational nevertheless. I see that continuing to the present. Indeed, most Japanese composers have been and are grounded in the social—they indeed remain connected to the people.

CHRONOLOGY

TOKUGAWA SHOGUNATE (1600–1868)

MEIJI ERA (1868–1912)

1869	Satsuma clan forms first brass band
1871	Official military band formed
1872	Decision to adopt Western music in primary schools
1879	Ministry of Education ratifies plan for music education; predecessor of Tokyo Music School established
1883	German musician Franz Eckert comes to teach at the Tokyo School of Music
1889	Japanese composers begin to go to Europe to study; Christian missionaries teach hymns at the Methodist Kwansei Gakuin University
1889–91	First Ministry of Education songbooks; agreement to extend music education to secondary schools
189[6]	*Tōzan ryū* group founded in Kansai by shakuhachi player Nakao Tozan
1901	First glee club established at Keio University
1906	Gakuenka, association for presentation of opera, founded by Kosuke Komatsu
First decades of 1900s	Specialist music journals begin to emerge

TAISHO ERA (1912–26)

1914–18	World War I
1918	Group of composers begin to write *dōyō* (lyrical songs for children)
1920s	New Japanese Music movement of performer-composer kotoist Michio Miyagi and his contemporaries
1921	Michio Miyagi, father of modern koto music, invents the seventeen-stringed koto

SHOWA ERA (1926–89)

1926	NHK founded as a national radio broadcasting monopoly (publicly supported beginning in 1950)

1926	New Symphony Orchestra founded (name changed in 1951 to the NHK Symphony Orchestra)
1927	First choral competition organized by the National Music Association, founded by Kosuke Komatsu
1930s	Flourishing of *nihonjinron* (ideological promulgation of Japanese uniqueness)
1930	Kotoist performer-composer Michio Miyagi initiates instruction in Japanese traditional music at the Tokyo School of Music
1930	Kosuke Komatsu founds the Newly Rising Federation of Composers
1931	Founding of the music publisher Zen On Music
1931	Japan begins Asian imperialist expansion by invading Manchuria
1932	Mainichi Nihon Ongaku Konkur (the Music Competition of Japan) established for a work for orchestra and chamber music in alternate years
1934	First professional orchestra for Western music founded—the Osaka Municipal Symphonic Band (a wind band)
1935	Name of Newly Rising Federation of Composers changed to Japan Society for Contemporary Music
1936	Founding of the Association of Contemporary Japanese Composers (later renamed the Japan Society for Contemporary Music, or Gen On)
1937	Kosaku Yamada founds the first professional orchestra—the Tokyo Philharmonic Society Orchestra; ensemble lasts only one year
End of 1930s	Institutional instruction in French music begun by Tomojiro Ikenouchi
1939	All-Japan Band Association (AJBA) initiates nationwide competition
1941–45	World War II; composers' collectives disbanded
1943	National Chorus established by NHK
1945–54	Japan occupied by the United States
1946	Founding of Toho Symphony Orchestra; name changed in 1951 to Tokyo Symphony Orchestra (TSO)
1947	NHK initiates projects for Japanese traditional music, with performer-composers and composers
1948	Founding of the Toho Gakuen Music for Children program
1949	Founding of the Tokyo University of the Arts (Geidai), successor to Tokyo Music School, renamed from Tokyo National University of Fine Arts and Music
1950	Founding of Toho Gakuen (School of Music)
1950s	NHK, now publicly supported, hires Geidai composers to write music for programs
1951	NHK assumes support for New Symphony Orchestra; ensemble becomes the NHK Symphony Orchestra
1951	NHK founds the Tokyo Broadcasting Children's Chorus
1951	Little Singers of Tokyo (children's chorus) founded by Shinichi Hasegawa
1951	First postwar Japanese composer, Yoritsune Matsudaira, awarded the International Society of Contemporary Music Prize
1951–57	Jikken Kōbō (Experimental Workshop) flourished
1952	Otaka Prize (for an orchestral piece) established
1953	Composers' cooperatives Yagi no Kai and Sannin no Kai formed

1956	Founding of the Kyoto Symphony Orchestra, the Japan Philharmonic Orchestra, and the Tokyo Philharmonic Chorus
1959	Coining by NHK of the rubric *gendai hōgaku* (contemporary music for traditional instruments)
1960s	Gendai hōgaku boom
1960	Founding of Tokyo Kosei Wind Orchestra
1961	Inauguration of the Sapporo Symphony Orchestra
1961	Opening of the first major concert hall, Tokyo Bunka Kaikan
1962	Founding of the Yomiuri Nippon Symphony Orchestra by the newspaper *Yomuri Shimbun*
1962	First commission for a composer of *gendai Nihon ongaku* (contemporary Japanese music) from NHK
1962	Founding of the Japan Federation of Composers (JFC)
1964	Cofounding of Nihon Ongaku Shudan (Ensemble Nipponia) by composers Minoru Miki and Katsutoshi Nagasawa
1964	Tokyo Olympics present Japan in a new international light
1965	Founding of the Tokyo Metropolitan Symphony Orchestra
1965	Seiji Ozawa appointed music director of the Toronto Symphony Orchestra
1966	Founding of the National Theatre of Japan, the purpose of which is to foster traditional music
1967	Premier of Toru Takemitsu's *November Steps* by the New York Philharmonic
1969	Debut of twenty-stringed koto by Keiko Nosaka
1970	Osaka Expo '70; founding of Tokyo Concerts, Inc., and Fontec (recording company)
1972	Founding of the Sendai Philharmonic Orchestra and the Hiroshima Symphony Orchestra
1974	Founding of ALM RECORDS
1975	Founding of Music From Japan (New York City) by Naoyuki Miura
1977	Premier of Karlheinz Stockhausen's *Hikari* for dancers and gagaku ensemble (later expanded, reorchestrated, and retitled *Licht—Hikari—Light*)
1977	Shakuhachi instruction added to the hōgaku curriculum at Geidai
1978	Founding of the recording company Camerata Tokyo
1980s	Founding of international music festivals in Japan
Early 1980s	Founding of the Federation of Women Composers (FWCJ) in Japan
1981	Irino Prize established for works for orchestra and for chamber music in alternate years
1984	Founding of the Saito Kinen Orchestra by Seiji Ozawa
1986	Opening of Suntory Hall, the second major concert hall in Tokyo
1988	Founding of Orchestra Ensemble Kanazawa

HEISEI ERA (1989–)

1990	Opening of Izumi Hall in Osaka
1991	Akutagawa Memorial Prize (for a work for orchestra) initiated

1994 Founding of Tokyo Sinfonietta

1995 First woman composer, Keiko Fujiie, awarded the Otaka Prize

1996 Founding of the Ensemble Nomad for contemporary music

1997 Opening of Tokyo Opera City Concert Hall: Takemitsu Memorial and initial year of the Takemitsu Composition Award for a work for orchestra

1999 End of the National Theatre commissioning project of *gendai Nihon ongaku* works from composers

NOTES

INTRODUCTION

1. In addition to commentary through this book, for a good tracking of the reasons and the process for the introduction of Western music, see Galliano 2002. For an introduction to traditional musics, see Malm 2000 and Wade 2005.

2. The exchange rate was 360 yen to one U.S. dollar, but the yen was not yet a negotiable currency in international markets. We had to spend our earnings or lose them.

3. Personal names can be challenging even for Japanese because of the multiple possibilities for the reading of the Chinese characters. In Japanese the family name is customarily given first, followed by the individual's name: Takemitsu Toru, for instance. Japanese authors writing primarily for non-Japanese readers will often distinguish the family name by writing it in all caps: TAKEMITSU Toru. Non-Japanese authors writing primarily for non-Japanese readers often choose to write names as personal name followed by family name—Toru Takemitsu—and that is the form in which the person will probably become known in international circles. I have chosen to follow the last practice primarily because Japanese producers of recordings market their products with composers' names cited as they will be recognized internationally. Herein, to avoid confusion, I have mentioned names as in the order of personal name followed by family name even in quotes from conversations in which the name would have been spoken in Japanese order. I do not indicate long vowels in names because they will not be meaningful to the non-Japanese-speaking reader.

In conversation, individuals will usually be referred to by family name plus a title: *-san* (Mr., Miss, or Mrs.), *-sama* (the honorific for *-san*), *sensei* ("respected authoritative person"). In direct quotes from conversations, I have retained that usage because it indicates the relationship of the speaker to the person mentioned.

4. My focus within North Indian music has been on elite spheres both historically and in the twentieth century. Except when citing comments or printed material in which "classical" is used with regard to the common use of the word internationally, I do not use the term "classical music" herein because *kurasiku* (classical) in Japan refers specifically to the repertoire of canonic European composers in the period of Bach,

Haydn, and Mozart. I am personally uncomfortable with the term "concert music" because of the numerous varieties of concerts that are held and the numerous varieties of repertoire one can hear at them. When I use the term "concert music," it refers to the sorts of music at performances of which audiences are expected to sit quietly and listen.

5. There has been interest on the part of ethnomusicologists in composers of other East Asian countries, particularly China and Korea. See, for example, Stock 1996, Finchum-Sung 2002, Everett and Lau 2004, and Howard 2006.

6. Unless I specify "unconfirmed," direct quotes from individuals as they appear in this book have been checked by them. I wish to thank Fukiko Shinohara, who accompanied me to some appointments, for also assisting with the checking process.

7. In this book, whenever a translator is individually acknowledged, it is because I am citing an entire item rather than some details from a source, or an item that was given to me already translated by the person who thought it might be helpful to me.

8. Among the prominent ethnomusicologists who have delved into modernity have been Erlmann 1999 and 2004; Bohlmann 2008 and 2012; Moehn 2008; and Bohlmann and Petković 2012. On the sociological side, a valuable compendium on social theory and late modernity is Hall, Held, Hubert, and Thompson 1996.

9. For the introduction to affordance theory, I am grateful to Miki Kaneda, who, when she was a Ph.D. student in ethnomusicology at Berkeley, was also enrolled in the Designated Emphasis in New Media Studies program; she therefore knew this theory and had found it useful in her dissertation on avant-garde music in Japan in the 1960s.

10. DeNora appears to be almost totally unaware of the ethnomusicological literature, which she would surely find rich in examples of studies that explore how music is used by people for feeling, thinking, and action. A specific focus on the analysis of musical events began in the 1970s under the rubric of "the ethnography of musical performance" under the leadership of John Blacking, Marcia Herndon, and Norma McLeod. The focus became so embedded in ethnomusicological practice that it ceased fairly quickly to be distinguished by a rubric.

CHAPTER 1

1. Western music was actually introduced twice in Japanese history, through events two hundred years apart. As in the second instance just presented, a bold exercise of power determined its fate in the island culture. In the first instance, in the mid-sixteenth century, secular and sacred music was brought both unintentionally and intentionally by Portuguese sailors, traders, and priests and was made accessible to everyone by Jesuit and other Catholic missionaries (Harich-Schneider 1973: 447). Scholars have estimated that by 1580 Gregorian chant, European church modes, and intervals were familiar to at least one-fifth of the entire population, having permeated all social strata (ibid.: 460). In 1614, however, the rising tide of Christianity in the country was deterred by Ieyasu Tokugawa, the founder of the Tokugawa shogunate, who issued an edict against it and, through decades of persecution, pursued the martyrdom of the faithful and the destruction of churches, schools, instruments, and other items, effectively obliterating Christianity's influential presence in Japanese culture. Not until the third Tokugawa shogun, Iemitsu (1623–1651), would Christianity and all its cultural activities

be finally extirpated—or driven underground. In the 1680s most of the surviving Christians withdrew to the Gotō islands, where "up to this day the creed is handed down orally" (Harich-Schneider 1973: 484). Recordings have been made, and there is no doubt of historical survival to the present. Interestingly, a theory circulates with increasing attention that the melody and structure of the Credo of the Mass is the origin of the melody and structure of "Rokudan," the canonic sixteenth-century piece for koto. For scholarly arguments on this question, with musical illustrations performed by Keiko Nosaka, see *Rokudan and Gregorian Chant "Credo"* (Japan Victor CD VZCG-743, 2010).

2. The Primary School Ordinance of 1900 established the foundation for the elementary school system that is in place today. In 1907 the government increased the length of compulsory education from four to six years in response to advances being made in the nation's economy, and today's six-year program of elementary education dates from that time. During the 1930s the government planned to revamp the system and increase the number of years of compulsory education to eight to reflect social changes and modernization. World War II intervened, however, and the changes were postponed. In the postwar period of democratic reforms, compulsory education was increased to nine years—six of *shōgakkō* (elementary school) and three of *chūgakko* (junior high school). Under the newly standardized system, more than 90 percent of elementary-school-age children attended public schools.

3. With apologies to Mr. Goto, I lost track of his name card and have not been able to trace his personal name.

4. Shimbo also explained that "in the 1990s, there were around three hundred children enrolled in the Toho Music for Children program. However, the number has been gradually decreasing. More sports. And parents now recognize that music is expensive and time-consuming, and there are few jobs, Now parents think: What kind of junior high school should my child attend at age twelve or thirteen? Then they stop music training to go to *juku* [preparatory study of other subjects]" (Kimiko Shimbo, personal communication, May 31, 2008).

5. A polyphonic composition in which a melody appears both as composed and in reverse, similar to a palindrome.

6. http://en.wikipedia.org/wiki/Tokyo_University_of_the_Arts, accessed July 23, 2011.

7. An exception is the recent appointment of Ichiro Nodaira. It has often been explained to me that a composer who is a full-time professor in an educational institution is not likely to have much time to compose owing to heavy administrative duties. There are of course exceptions to that, including Akira Nishimura, who is sometimes described as "the most prolific composer in Japan" and is also widely acknowledged for his leading role in the building of the composition faculty at the Tokyo College of Music.

8. Miyoshi is among the very few musicians who have received the title of Geijutsunin, which carries with it a lifetime pension from the government (Kimiko Shimbo, personal communication, May 9, 2002). Commending artistic achievement in this manner is one of the purviews of the Minister of Education, Culture, Sports, Science, and Technology, under which the Agency for Cultural Affairs functions. The organization

of the agency as of April 1, 2001, is laid out in a website that is updated regularly: http://www.bunka.go.jp/English/2002-index-e.html. Although the website was established in 2002, when I accessed it in June 2011 it referenced changes in 2010.

9. It is not unusual for a school concert to be presented at a civic or other public hall in Tokyo; the halls need to rent the space for such events, and the facilities are much better for the performances than school facilities.

10. Akio Yasuraoka is now working regularly at Tokyo Geijutsu Daigaku (Geidai).

11. Ichiro Nodaira now teaches contemporary music at Geidai.

12. Harada considered the need for instruction in analysis at Toho and other schools to be great. Miyoshi had taught analysis at Toho, asking students to analyze his pieces. But in the period when he was teaching, there were not too many teachers who could teach analysis; Minao Shibata was one who did. It was her belief that the kind of teaching of analysis at the Paris Conservatoire scarcely existed in Japan. Yoshio Irino taught it independently at his foundation. When Ichiro Nodaira returned from France, at first he independently gave open lectures—"real analysis." Harada herself took analysis as a student at Toho, but she remembered it as being completely different from what Nodaira did. When she began teaching there, because she had not found fourth-year college students who knew about expressionism, she created a course in which she started with Boulez: "structure," total serialism (which was the clearest thing for them to begin with), numbers, and matrix (Keiko Harada, personal communication, June 2, 2008).

13. As Hebert points out, "The *iemoto* model appears to have influenced the institutionalization of Western music in Japanese schools, particularly in terms of emphasis placed on pedagogical lineage and authority associated with Japan's 'prestigious' conservatories" (2012: 112).

14. Mamoru Fujieda, whose earned his Ph.D. from the University of California, San Diego, has a position at Kyushu University—a national university—but not in music.

15. Strikingly, none of the many composers with whom I have spoken has mentioned offering this instruction to potential students themselves. I have not been able to ascertain whether it is no longer done, or is too insignificant an activity to be worth mentioning, or is something one does not mention, or something else.

CHAPTER 2

1. "At the beginning when we were trying to think up a name for it, we came up with 'Electone' because the sound is produced by electricity. At first it produced a weird sound as if it were broken. . . . But we kept on improving it. Then we used vacuum tubes, which heated up and malfunctioned frequently, so the lifetime was short. Then transistors came along, and we used them although they were expensive, and things improved. Yamaha was the first in the world to establish techniques for making sound with transistors. We were also the first in digital sound, and today's semiconductor ICs came out of this" (Kawakami 1987: 276).

2. For an unofficial English translation of the Nonprofit Law of 1998 and the 2003 amendment provided by the Japan Center for International Exchange Website, see http://www.jcie.or.jp/civilnet/monitor/npo_law.pdf.

3. In Japan, dates are given according to the number of years the current emperor

has reigned. Emperor Hirohito's era was Showa, so in 1943 he was in the nineteenth year of his reign. The first modern period was Meiji, followed by Taisho, Showa, and now Heisei, the reign of Emperor Akihito.

4. Other Western piano methods are certainly available in the music stores in Japan—Bartok's *Mikrokosmos*, Kodály's method, and others. One that might be widening the crack in the Beyer armor among the imports is the Bastien method, developed by the Americans Jane and James Bastien. The Bastien method has been energetically advocated in Japan since about forty years ago, when the aspiring composer and entrepreneur Yasuko Fukuda (1933–2001) visited America to investigate other potential piano teaching methods. From the more than ten different methods she researched, Fukuda selected the Bastien method, which is published in San Diego, California, and promoted it through the activities of the Piano Teachers' National Association (PTNA), founded by Fukuda, and through To-on Kikaku, a sub-publishing company of which Yasuko Fukuda was the president. The Bastien method features a relational approach to teaching that is congenial in the Japanese context. The beginning student's part is complemented by a second part that is intended to be played by the teacher, mother, or a sibling—someone who joins in the child's learning and offers musical encouragement. As Fukuda described it, the Bastien method originated from a sense of play (Yasuko Fukuda, private communication, June 2, 2000; and Eriko Sugano, private communication, July 13, 2012).

5. A CD of *The Zoo in the Sky: The Piano Pieces for Children for Small Hands* is available (BMG Japan/RCA CD BVCC-1094, 1997), played by the eminent pianist Ikuyo Nakamichi. Another series by Karen Tanaka for Edition KAWAI, *Children of Light* (1999), is an homage to endangered animals and to the planet, and a message to the children of the future, entrusting them with the protection of the natural environment. Also played by Ikuyo Nakamichi, it can be heard on *Children of Light: The Piano Pieces for Children* (BMG/RCA CD BVCC-37200, 2005).

6. Details of the Miyoshi method are given in Hayase 2006.

7. A third music publishing company, Ongaku no Tomosha, has also commissioned piano music from Japanese composers. Mieko Shiomi, who had taught children piano for years and thus knew that what was needed was "pieces you can play after finishing Beyer" (Mieko Shiomi, private communication, June 12, 2000), composed for them an album of contemporary music. Titled *A Waltz in the Shape of a Star*, the collection "elaborated on the total elements of music" (private communication, August 7, 2012). Recently, Mieko Shiomi has been composing piano pieces for the great left-hand pianist Izumi Tateno.

8. So distinguished a composer was Ikuma Dan (1924–2001) that in 2000 the Japan Foundation supported a number of performances of his works—two operas, music for modern dance and ballet, and much else.

9. The original system was established under the provisions of Article 34 of the Civil Code enacted in 1896 and provided for "academic, artistic, charitable, ritual, religious, or other [corporations] whose purpose is the public interest," under the jurisdiction of central government ministries and agencies and the governments of Japan's prefectures. The new law, enacted in 1998, was amended in 2003 owing to concern that some organizations were misusing their status. The changes are in boldface type on

the website cited in n. 2. Every organization incorporated under nonprofit status was required to reapply, and I heard great worry expressed that organizations such as orchestras, cultural foundations, and the Japan Composers Federation, for example, would get caught up in the official accreditation process for the new system and lose their tax advantages. As of 2011 I had not heard of that happening.

10. The management and operation of the New National Theatre are administered by the New National Theatre Management Foundation. For more about the National Theatre, see chapter 4.

11. Agreeing to work with Takemitsu on the opening programs were Esa-Pekka Salonen, Oliver Knussen, Kent Nagano, and Simon Rattle, along with the Japanese conductors Hiroyuki Iwaki, Kazushi Ono, and Hiroshi Wakasugi.

12. This practice was very helpful economically for me, since I needed to attend many concerts, and ticket prices usually start at three thousand yen. At the 2011 exchange rate of approximately eighty yen to one U.S. dollar, that came to around $37.50 per ticket. Whenever someone told me they were "inviting me" to the concert, I knew that a ticket would be left for me at will call. I was fortunate to be the recipient of a great deal of this kind of generosity.

13. Saegusa and more than fifty other composers resigned from the Japan Federation of Composers in 2009 over a serious disagreement about staff compensation. Many of those have joined the Japan Composers and Arrangers Association.

14. This is an annual event, held on December 31, when the subways run on an extended nighttime schedule. Concerts go from 3 or 4 P.M. to 12:30 A.M. A ticket is good for all the symphonies, and one can come and go as one pleases. At first this concert was held at Suntory Hall; then it was moved to the much larger Ikebukuro Geijutsu Gekijo (1,999 seats). Usually there are three orchestras and three conductors. In 2005 Maestro Hiroyuki Iwaki, the leading Japanese conductor, conducted them all (Kimiko Shimbo, private communication, May 9, 2006).

15. The *Heike monogatari* is a twelfth-century prose epic that narrates struggles between two powerful clans—the Taira (Heike) and Minamoto (Genji)—at the end of the long and largely peaceful Heian period (794–1185). The Taira were finally defeated at the naval battle in March 1185, but the saga continued with internecine struggle between the two Minamoto brothers, Yoritomo and Yoshitsune.

16. On June 1, 2011, the Roppongi Men's Chorus teamed up with the Yale University Alley Cats for a concert in the Suntory Small Hall in Tokyo.

17. See http://www.sarah.or.jp/index_e.html.

18. In 2011 JASRAC received 69 million yen to distribute to its members.

19. I am grateful to Satoshi Watanabe, deputy general manager of the General Affairs Bureau of JASRAC, for informing me about SARAH and SARVH and also for clarifying and updating some details concerning JASRAC (private communication, August 9, 2012).

20. This comment was made in response to an inquiry I made of JASRAC officers with whom I was meeting about what I perceived to be a relative lack of pieces by Japanese composers in two contexts—in performances by Japanese orchestras (see chapter 5) and in the requirements of piano competitions, both of which would greatly benefit composers through royalties. In the 1999 Piano Competition Repertoire list (solo and

duo) for the PTNA competition, for example, there is just one Japanese composer listed for each category of entrants at each level up to twelfth grade. The male composers are Mitsuo Miyakawa (before grade-school age), Hirayoshi Takekuni (up to second grade), Akira Yuyama (solo: up to sixth grade; duo: primary level), Atsutada Otaka (up to eighth grade), Mitsuhiro Hanamura (up to twelfth grade), Naohiko Terashima (duo: middle level); the female ones are Karen Tanaka (up to fourth grade), Reiko Arima (up to tenth grade). For the two competition levels beyond the twelfth-grade level, the competitor can choose to play a piece in a category called "New Music," with the requirement that one piece be from a Japanese composer. Founded in 1968 by Yasuko Fukuda in the interest of improving piano teaching and also fostering Japanese composition, the PTNA began with a lecture series featuring Japanese composers such as Haruna Miyake, Hiroshi Hara, Akira Yuyama, Masanobu Kimura, and Makoto Moroi. Fukuda established the popular PTNA Piano Competition in 1976 so that Japan would have a fair competition system, one that challenged the teacher-prestige problem of other performance competitions (Yasuko Fukuda, private communication, May 13, 1999). Concern with fostering Japanese composers has given way to a focus on piano methods and connections with international artists; Fukuda explained the sparse representation of Japanese composers on the competition list by citing the expense of having to pay royalties to composers.

21. From "A Guide to JASRAC," which I received at the time of my visit to JASRAC in 2006.

22. They would benefit more if the production companies were to make recordings available in digital format. I was very surprised when I inquired of the American Naxos staff in November 2012 about the possibility of expanding the selection of contemporary works by Japanese composers in the Naxos Music Library and was told that they had never heard of any of these three companies but an inquiry would be made.

23. Between five hundred and a thousand copies are made of each CD, and if one sells out, in 2004 the policy was to reprint. Indeed, I noted that in my fourteen years of forays to stores in Tokyo FONTEC recordings remained available. This is very important for composers. That FONTEC sees its market as "nationwide"—i.e., targeting domestic sales—is clear from their website (https://www.fontec.co.jp). That is unfortunate for composers but understandable given the small market for contemporary music. For the production of some CDs, FONTEC has received support from the Nomura Foundation (of the Nomura Securities Company).

24. An editorial at the end of the magazine ("Desk Side," p. 276) seeks to respond to the question of when gendai ongaku and "difficult" came to mean the same thing. The unidentified writer argues that perhaps the resistance to gendai ongaku simply reflects a narrow aesthetic scope. To change that situation, the feature article took up "relatively young composers" in order to expose the depth and variety of their aesthetics and to "seek new ways to enjoy music." Joji Yuasa, now in his eighties, should be greatly flattered.

CHAPTER 3

1. Nobu Koda was a member of the Iwakura Embassy, a Japanese diplomatic journey undertaken in 1871 by the Meiji leaders for the purpose of observing various aspects

of European and American cultures. Just as diplomatic embassies had been crucial for the introduction of Chinese, Korean, and other Asian musics to Japan in the seventh century, embassies sent by the Tokugawa shogunate and the Meiji government were crucial for Japan's modernization. The Iwakura Embassy "had a profound impact on the development of both western music and education in Meiji Japan" (Hebert 2012: 30).

2. The American Cultural Centers were scaled down in 1970 by the Nixon administration in prosperous countries that could henceforth support exchanges themselves (Havens 1982: 75).

3. For comment on the 1969 edition of the Festival, see Galliano 2002: 172. For more on the American Cultural Center, see Y. Watanabe 2008 and Ishihara 2008.

4. In 1987 she was awarded the Gaudeamus Prize at the International Music Week in Amsterdam, and the same year she signed with Chester Music and Novello in London (G. Schirmer in New York) for publication of her works for orchestra and large ensemble, solo instruments including piano, and other media—an arrangement that continues. A complete list of works can be found on the G. Schirmer website.

5. A performer of avant-garde piano works (including Cage premieres) and then a composer, David Tudor (1926–1996) was musical director of the Merce Cunningham Dance Company after Cage's death in 1992.

6. The Sōgetsu Arts Center and this avant-garde movement in Japan are receiving scholarly attention. See, e.g., Havens 2006, Everett 2009, and Kaneda 2012.

7. For a complete list of works she has premiered, including those she commissioned, and also for a complete list of her own compositions and their availability, see Keiko Abe's website at www.Keiko-abe.com/englishindex.html.

8. A superb example is *Tree* (1991, 45:08 min.), by Yuji Takahashi for MIDI piano, trombone, and computer performance system. Haruna Miyake is featured on MIDI piano, George E. Lewis on trombone, and Yuji Takahashi on electronics. The work is found on the album *Iki to ishi: Acoustic Instruments with Computer Music Systems*, vol. 1 in the series Music from Japan (Classic Masters CD CMCD-1027, 1992).

9. The Asian Cultural Council has supported a residency in the United States for several Japanese composers, among them Mamoru Fujieda, Keiko Fujiie, Shin-ichiro Ikebe, Tokuhide Niimi, and Somei Satoh. As such, it should be counted among the significant cultural institutions that foster international artistic connections. The Council establishes priorities for funding for a block of time. In 1999 when I talked with the director of the Tokyo office, the American George Kochi, about the recent opportunities for Japanese composers through the ACC, he explained that currently the Council was focusing on dance through a Triangle Arts program, connecting artists from Indonesia, the United States, and Japan with rotating residencies in the three countries. They were also sponsoring a museology program for professional curatorial training (personal communication, April 14, 1999).

10. Brass playing has improved greatly since that conversation, probably owing to burgeoning participation in student wind-band clubs and competitions organized for them; see chapter 5.

11. Four years before this conversation, Keiko Fujiie had been the winner of the Otaka Prize '95 for orchestra composition—the first woman to be so honored. Her piece was titled *Omoidasu: Hitobito no shigusao*; the Western-language title is *Beber*

(Spanish, "to drink"). Fujiie took the title from the poem written by the Chilean Nobel laureate Gabriela Mistral, whose work she admires.

12. Both of her parents are legally blind, and her mother had some health problems at a crucial moment. Sachie stopped going to Germany after a very dangerous accident there in 1997.

13. From his base in Germany, Toshio Hosokawa has become one of if not the best-known and most frequently performed Japanese composer of his generation throughout Europe. See the review of his opera *Matsukaze* at http://www.nytimes.com/2011/08/07/arts/music/matsukaze-opera-by-the-japanese-composer-toshio-hosokawa.html?pagewanted=all.

14. In addition, he performed with the New York Philharmonic as guest conductor on numerous occasions between 1961 and 1971. Those appearances included conducting on tour in Japan and elsewhere, subscription concerts, Young People's Concerts, and various special concerts. To see his complete performance history with the New York Philharmonic, see their performance history search at http://historynyphil.org/nypwcpub/dbweb.asp?ac=a1 (Richard Wandel, personal communication, March 5, 2012).

15. According to the 2005 annual report of the Association of Japanese Symphony Orchestras, the Japan Philharmonic Orchestra was founded in Tokyo in 1956 by the NHK. An important role was played by its first principal conductor, Akeo Watanabe. When Fuji Television was established in 1959, it was for a time the resident orchestra of the two broadcasting companies. Recent annual reports of the Association make no mention of the orchestra's early association with broadcasting and stress instead, in the brief historical account, its association with the Suginami-ku ward of Tokyo.

16. When we last spoke, on May 25, 2011, Gondai shared with me how very much it meant to him that, while Ozawa has directly fostered *very* few Japanese composers, the renowned conductor had commissioned from this young composer a work to open the 2010 concert in Carnegie Hall of his Saito Kinen Orchestra. Gondai was very disappointed that, owing to ill health, Ozawa had not been able to conduct the premier of *Decathexis*.

17. A useful CD for a recording of *November Steps* as well as for Takemitsu's first piece for traditional instruments, *Eclipse* (1966); Makoto Moroi's *Five Dialogues for Two Shakuhachi* (1964); and Ryohei Hirose's *Aki for Two Shakukhachi* (1969) is *Contemporary Music for Japanese Shakuhachi Instruments*, Precious Selection 1000, no. 24 (Tower Records/RCA CD TWCL-2028 , 2005).

18. See *Eurasian Trilogy: Minoru Miki Selected Works IV* (Camerata CD 15CM-223–4, 2001). The trilogy is comprised of *Jo-no-kyoku: Prelude for Shakuhachi, Koto, Shamisen and Strings* (1969), performed by Kifu Mitsuhashi (shakuhachi), Nanae Yoshimura (20-stringed koto), and Yumiko Tanaka (shamisen) with the Tokyo Metropolitan Symphony Orchestra conducted by Hiroshi Wakasugi; *Ha-no-kyoku*: Concerto for Koto and Orchestra (1974), performed by Keiko Nosaka (twenty-stringed koto) with the Tokyo Philharmonic Orchestra; and *Kyu-no-kyoku: Symphony for Two Worlds* (1981), with the Leipzig Gewandhaus Orchestra conducted by Kurt Masur and the Pro Musica Nipponia.

19. Miki completed a series of nine operas on Japanese history: *Shunkinshō* (1975); *Ada, an Actor's Revenge* (1979); *Jōruri* (1985); *Wakahime* (1991); *Shizuka to Yoshitsune*

(1993); *The River Sumida/Kusabira* (1995); *Genji monogatari* (1999); *Ai'en* (2005); and *The Happy Pagoda* (2010).

20. *Mantra; Stabat Mater*, New Albion Records NA-016 CD, 1988. On the New Albion website, Satoh's works at the Arts at St. Ann are attributed as follows: "Satoh has collaborated twice since 1985 with theater designer, Manuel Luetgenhorst in dramatic stagings of his music at The Arts at St. Ann's in Brooklyn, New York." See http://www.newalbion.com/artists/satohs/ (accessed April 13, 2013) for information on recordings.

21. Artaud recorded *Miyabi* on *Pierre-Yves Artaud, Flauto*, Rusty Classica CD RUS555019.2 DDD, 1993.

22. The Arditti Quartet compilation of quartets by four composers is available on *Arditti String Quartet Plays Hayashi, Miyoshi, Nishimura, Hosokawa* (Fontec CD 2534, 1997): Hayashi's *Quartetto "Legende"* (1989), Miyoshi's String Quartet no. 1 (1967), Nishimura's *Heterophony* (1975/87), and Toshio Hosokawa's String Quartet no. 2, *Urbilder. Heterophony* was also included on *Arditti String Quartet plays Akira Nishimura* (Camerata CD 28CM-524, 2002) along with the String Quartet no. 2, *Pulses of Light* (1992); the String Quartet no. 3, *Avian* (1997); *Monologue* (1995), for solo violin, played by Irvine Arditti; and *Threnody* (1998), for solo cello, played by Rohan de Saram.

23. This account I am paraphrasing is from Fujieda 2009, although I also heard it directly from him in the course of my field research. Fujieda first studied with Yuasa when he was a student in the early 1970s at the Tokyo College of Music: "After college, Yuasa-sensei at the University of California, San Diego, said 'Come,' so I went" (personal communication, April 29, 2005). Fujieda completed his Ph.D. in 1988.

24. It is only an imbalance if one presumes that modern Japanese musical culture should not let Western practices dominate or that equal space should be given to indigenous traditions. For the ways in which Japanese composers engage with Japanese traditional musics, see chapter 4.

25. The portrait CD is *After the Winter* (Cypres CD CYP5605, 2001); the work is *Heavy Wood* (1998), for five players.

26. The only works Schott Japan publishes for sale are for Western instruments. Others they rent—Takemitsu's *In an Autumn Garden* for gagaku ensemble, for instance. Joji Yuasa pointed out to me that Schott will not publish his choral scores (personal communication, June 1, 2011).

27. In alphabetical order, they were Tetsuji Emura, Dai Fujikura, Atsuhiko Gondai, Keiko Harada, Naoko Hishinuma, Sunao Isaji, Hiroyuki Ito, Motoharu Kawashima, Yukio Kikuchi, Tomiko Kohjiba, Noriko Koide, Masahiro Miwa, Misato Mochizuki, Hiroyuki Natsuda, Masakazu Natsuda, Masaki Norikura, Yumi Saiki, Toshiro Saruya, Yutaka Takahashi, and Izumi Yamada.

28. All aspects are underwritten by the Foundation, which supports and oversees the cultural events at the huge performing complex Tokyo Opera City Plaza.

29. The judges have been Henri Dutilleux (France, 1997), György Ligeti (Hungary, 1998); Luciano Berio (Italy, 1999); Louis Andriessen (Netherlands, 2000); Oliver Knusse (United Kingdom, 2001); Joji Yuasa (Japan, 2002), who was designated by Ligeti; George Benjamin (United Kingdom, 2003); Magnus Lindberg (Finland, 2004); John Adams (United States, 2005); Akira Nishimura (Japan, 2007); Steve Reich (United States, 2008); Helmut Lachenmann (Germany, 2009); Tristan Murail (France, 2010); Salvatore Sciar-

rino (Italy, 2011, but postponed on account of the earthquake to January 2012); and Toshio Hosokawa (Japan, 2012). Adams withdrew late under pressure to complete his opera *Dr. Atomic*, which led to the cancellation of the competition in 2005. In 2006, instead of the award a special event devoted to Toru Takemitsu's achievements commemorated the tenth anniversary of his death. The advisory committee has been made up of the conductors Hiroyuki Iwaki (until his death in 2006), Hiroshi Wakasugi (until his death in 2009), Kent Nagano, Kazushi Ono, and Simon Rattle; and the composers Oliver Knussen and Esa-Pekka Salonen.

30. This message is modified somewhat each year. The name of the judge is updated in the second sentence, and the last phrase is shortened to "the performances of talented musicians as the excellent interpreters of contemporary music." In 2003 the final sentence read: "We hope you will come and experience with us a cheerful enjoyment of contemporary music at Tokyo Opera City."

31. That year the performer-composer Nosaka's recital featured works by herself, Ryohei Hirose, and Akira Ifukube; three of the five works were U.S. premieres. Two of the six works featured in the concert "New Works by Young Japanese Composers" (those by Mica Nozawa and Toshiro Saruya) included Nosaka on twenty-five-string koto in the ensemble, while compositions by Atsuhiko Gondai, Keiko Harada, Sunao Isaji, and Misato Mochizuki were for Western instruments. On the Saturday I presented a preconcert lecture on Keiko Nosaka and the twenty-five-string koto; on the Sunday the discussants who participated in the postconcert forum were Julia Wolfe, composer and director of Bang on a Can; and Kyle Gann, composer, music critic, and writer. See the citation of remarks in the forum in chapter 4.

32. In 1994 Music From Japan established the Resource Center for Japanese Music, featuring a composer database and Music From Japan's twenty-year collection of recordings, scores, and other source materials. Although it features mainly Japanese composers, the composer database also includes several non-Japanese composers related to Music From Japan. It can be accessed at www.musicfromjapan.org. Requests for information (at no charge) may be emailed to mfjrc@aol.com or mailed to the Resource Center for Japanese Music, 7 East Twentieth Street, Suite 6F, New York, NY 10003–1106.

CHAPTER 4

1. Preceding that by three years, Japan's oldest professional orchestra for Western music was founded—a wind orchestra, the Osaka Municipal Symphonic Band. In 1934 the Osakashi Ongakudai (Osaka Band Corps), which had been an army-affiliated band since 1923, was brought under the authority of Osaka City. It has existed continuously to the present (Hebert 2012: 45). The Tokyo Philharmonic Society Orchestra, on the other hand, lasted for less than a year.

2. This would not be published until after World War II (Mitsukuri 1967); see Galliano 2002: 67–70. For a close stylistic analysis of works by Mitsukuri and further commentary on the political context of the interwar years, see Pacun 2012.

3. Most of Miyagi's compositions, however, fall into the range of traditional music—sufficiently so that "there was probably no one who felt his music to be very alien. . . . [For repertory to be enriched] in the traditional hogaku music world, there

must be acceptance and widespread performance by many people. This demands that the new pieces must contain sufficient 'newness' to be able to attract attention, but conversely it remains necessary that the listening audience be made to feel at ease and unreserved" (Kamisango 1981: 147).

In 1974 Japan Victor released a set of recordings of his works, *Miyagi Michio daizenshū*, many played by Miyagi himself, along with two pamphlets containing information on each piece and the song texts, and his scores were compiled and published (see Miyagi and Miyagi 1977–78). Prescott's dissertation (see Prescott 1997) is available on microfilm.

4. The year 2012 marked the twenty-first anniversary of Miyagi's creation of the seventeen-stringed koto. The distinguished kotoist Teiko Kikuchi wrote to me that there are now almost forty pieces composed for the instrument and that in October 2012 a series of three concerts would be held featuring pieces from this repertoire (personal communication, August 30, 2012).

5. Possibly influential in this appointment was the support Michio Miyagi had, beginning in the 1910s, from Hisao Tanabe (1883–1984), one of Japan's leading musicologists, who specialized in both Western music and Japanese music and dance and who embraced the hybridity of *shin nihon ongaku* within the spirit of the *wakon yōsai* ideology (Japanese spirit, Western technique). Tanabe's role in Japanese imperial politics in the 1920s into the war era is detailed in Hosokawa 1998.

6. Analogous to this was the government's use of Buddhism. "With the emergence of Japan as a military and colonial power in Asia, the 'foreignness' of Buddhism became an asset. . . . Buddhism's status as the cultural heritage of all Asia allowed the Japanese to affirm their cultural and spiritual solidarity with the peoples of the Asian continent, while at the same time claiming Japanese spiritual and moral superiority . . . precisely at a time of heightened imperial ambitions and military adventurism (Sharf 1995: 110–11).

7. Performance of music from Allied nations was officially banned. For commentary on the wartime situation for jazz musicians, see Atkins 2001.

8. The Department of Japanese Music was established at the Tokyo Music School in 1936. Kikuchi informed me that, at the time of our conversation, a few other places had a koto major: at Tokai University, where a department for koto training was established in 1976 and where Kikuchi is an emeritus professor; Osaka Ongaku Daigaku; Sakuyo Ongaku Daigaku; and Takazaki Geijitsu Tankidaigaku (a two-year school). In fact, there is instruction in traditional music in quite a number of private institutions, including Toho Gakuen, where Keiko Nosaka offers instruction specifically in contemporary koto music. A comment by Teiko Kikuchi about her own students explains why a koto instructor would need to be hired specifically for contemporary repertoire: "They must come to me to study because the pieces are mostly not published, and also because students need help analyzing them. They can just play traditional pieces, but contemporary pieces need explanation. The teacher is essential" (personal communication, May 4, 2001).

9. Name changes have made the recounting of the history of this institution confusing. On April 1, 2008, the university changed its English name to the Tokyo University of the Arts. According to the website for the Tokyo University of the Arts, the

graduate school opened in 1963 and began offering doctoral degrees in 1977. See http://www.geidai.ac.jp/english/about/history.html (accessed July 9, 2011).

10. Galliano describes Kitahara Tozan as someone who "had taken courses in traditional music run by NHK" (2002: 240); this program of training courses in traditional music—the NHK Hōgaku Players Academy—was initiated in 1955. I find it pertinent here that the Tozan ryū was the shakuhachi group with which Miyagi had been affiliated in 1924; it must have been relatively easy for Miyagi's koto students to team up with a Tozan musician.

Teiko Kikuchi contradicts Galliano's accounting, which says that Akiko Yazaki joined Yonin no Kai "in the 1960s," replacing an original member, Akiko Tsuchihashi, and that the group was on a tour of Russia in 1957 and won a gold medal at the International Competition run by Young People for Peace (2002: 257). However, according to Kikuchi, Akiko Tsuchihashi got married and became Akiko Yazaki, the koto and shamisen player. Kikuchi does confirm the name of the competition (personal communication, August 30, 2012).

11. Herd demonstrates his compositional techniques through analyses of *Piano no tame no muttsu no zensō-yoku* (*Six preludes pour piano en forme de thème et variations* [1975]), *Bugaku pour orchestra da camera* (1961), and other pieces (Herd 1987: 149–64). Recordings of a number of his works are available in the Naxos Music Library.

12. His 1964 composition *Five Pieces for Shakuhachi Chikurai* can be heard on *Five Pieces for Shakuhachi Chikurai* (Camerata CD 30CM-303, 1997), featuring Kifu Mitsuhashi. While the five pieces (a suite, really, because the main motives of four of the pieces return in the fifth) were inspired by traditional shakuhachi music—*chikurai* meaning the sound of bamboo, of the wind blowing across the bamboo forests, and the sounds of shakuhachi and flute (CD booklet, p. 9). The melody weaves through reminders of traditional shakuhachi motivic structure. The pitch structures are original, however, and the use of staccato technique is inventive. A recording of the traditional piece *Reibo* on the same CD provides a good contextualization for the Moroi work.

13. For an enduring monograph on the nagauta genre in concert (rather than staged) form, see Malm 1963. Kineya's composition *Isshi ryōran* (*Flower Falling in Dazzling Splendor*, 1988) can be heard on *Isshi ryōran: Kazuko takada—San-gen* (Fontec CD FOCD 3150, 1991). While this piece was composed long after the period under discussion, it gives a sense of Kineya as a composer. It was commissioned by his student Kazuko Takada for her third recital.

14. The third member of Yagi no Kai was Yuzo Toyama (b. 1931); he has been permanent conductor of the NHK Symphony Orchestra since 1979 (see chapter 6).

15. For analysis of several of Mayuzumi's works, see Herd 1987. The political involvement of the third member of Sannin no Kai, Yasushi Akutagawa, did not have to do with "Japaneseness." It was his socialist leanings that were contrary to Japanese government positions at the time; interested in the music of Russian composers, he entered Russia illegally in 1954, at a time when Japan did not have diplomatic relations with the Soviet Union. Dmitri Shostakovich had a particularly strong influence on Akutagawa's music.

16. The Jikken Kōbō collective was markedly different from Yagi no Kai and Sannin

no Kai in a number of ways, most prominently in that it was a collective for intermedia collaboration. Its fourteen members were visual artists, musicians, poets, and engineers, as well as the composers Kazuo Fukushima, Keijiro Sato, Hiroyuki Suzuki, Toru Takemitsu, and Joji Yuasa.

17. A good writer, Yuasa has articulated his musical "cosmology" and the concepts of particular interest to him in several English-language articles. See, e.g., Yuasa 1989, 1993a, 1993b, and especially 1993c.

18. As Herd points out, *Lento in Two Movements* was composed four years before John Cage rediscovered the power of silence in his famous 1954 work *4'33"* (1987: 197–98). To put *ma* into perspective as a principle of Japanese aesthetics in spheres of culture other than music, see Pilgrim 1995.

19. See Nagahiro 2002 for a chronological listing of the programming from April 1964 to March 1972; it constitutes a condensed record of the history of gendai hōgaku in terms of composers and their works.

20. *Torso* can be heard on *A New Aspect of Japanese Contemporary Music 10: Works of Ryohei Hirose* (Camerata CD 32CM-59, 1989), featuring Keiko Nosaka (thirteen-stringed koto), Teiko Kikuchi (seventeen-stringed koto), Akiko Yazaki (shamisen), Reibo Aoki (shakuhachi), and Hideki Kitamoto (cello). The Concerto for Shakuhachi and Orchestra can be heard on *Clima: The Works of Ryohei Hirose* (Camerata CD 25CM-516-7, 1998), featuring Kifu Mitsuhashi (shakuhachi) with the Tokyo Philharmonic Orchestra; and on *"Ha-no-kyoku": Contemporary Japanese Music* (King Records CD KICC2019, 1990). The Music From Japan Resource Center has a good collection of Hirose scores, including this concerto.

21. To hear a work by Ryohei Hirose commissioned and recorded by Nihon Ongaku Shudan, see *A New Aspect of Japanese Contemporary Music 10: Work of Ryohei Hirose* (Camerata CD 25CM-59, 1989). *Minoru Miki Selected Works I* (Camerata CD 20CM-54, 2001) includes several works composed for and recorded by the ensemble: *Four Seasons danses concértantes I* (1973); *Hote* (1976); and *Wa* (1976). *Minoru Miki Selected Works II* (Camerata CD 25CM-55, 2001) includes *Concerto Requiem*, for twenty-stringed koto and Japanese instruments (1981); *Autumn Fantasy*, for twenty-stringed koto and shakuhachi (1980); *Hanayagi* (*The Greening*, 1976); *Sao-no-Kyoku* (*The Venus in Spring*, 1971); and *Tatsuta-no-Kyoku* (*The Venus in Autumn*, 1971), for twenty-stringed koto, featuring Keiko Nosaka (twenty-stringed koto) and Seizan Sakata (shakuhachi). Some recordings of the 1990s and later are available through ArchivMusic. From the website of Pro Musica Nipponia one can link to recordings of a number of compositions through iTunes; unfortunately, it is not possible to search by composers' names.

22. For a thorough discussion of this process and *Tennyō*, see Wade 1994. Nosaka has also had made a bass twenty-five-stringed koto, which she plays in ensembles with her daughter, Mizuyo Komiya. For a recording of commissioned selections for her twenty-third recital, see *Ballata Sinfonica: Keiko Nosaka Recital* (Camerata CD 28CM-651, 2003), which includes Ichiro Higo's *Canto Magico*; Yuji Takahashi's *While I Was Crossing the Bridge* and *Samushiro*; Takashi Kako's *Wind in the Watery Depths, Empty Trance*; and Akira Ifukube's *Ballata Sinfonica, prima ballata*: Allegro capriccioso, and *seconda ballata*: Andante rapsodico. *Tennyō*, performed by Keiko Nosaka, can be heard on *Concert: 20–21, Vol. 21* (Jikko Iinkai, ECJC 021, 2004); and Miki's *Ha-no-kyoku*:

Concerto for Koto and Orchestra (1974), performed by Keiko Nosaka and the Tokyo Philharmonic Orchestra, can be found on *"Ha-no-kyoku": Contemporary Japanese Music* (King Records CD KICC 2019, 1990).

23. Next to it, Engei Hall (now National Engei Hall) was opened eleven years later (1979) for the presentation of traditional Japanese comedy and storytelling. The National Nō Theatre (Shibuya-ku, Tokyo) followed in 1983, and the National Bunraku Theatre in Osaka (Chuo-ku) opened a year later. The New National Theatre Tokyo, next door to the Tokyo Opera City Plaza, opened in 1997 for performances of ballet, opera, and the like, followed in 2004 by the New National Theatre Okinawa.

24. For example, Smaldone 1989, Burt 2001, and Siddons 1999. Recordings can be heard on the following CDs: *In an Autumn Garden*, on *In an Autumn Garden*(Deutsche Grammophon CD ADD 0289 471 5902 5 GH, 2002); and *In an Autumn Garden*, performed by Reigakusha, on *In an Autumn Garden* (Sony Music Japan International CD SICC-85, 2002).

25. Two others subsequently received commissions, however: Lou Harrison for *Set for 4 Haishoo and Percussion* (1993) and Jean Claude Eloy for *À l'approche du feu méditant* (1983). The latter can be heard on *À l'approche du feu méditant* (Harmonia Mundi LP HMC 5155.56, 1985), a recording made during its world premiere performance by the Imperial Household Music Department ensemble at the National Theatre in Tokyo on 30 September 1981.

26. Because the contexts for performance and the degree of patronage for court music diminished beginning in the late twelfth century, when the emperor and nobles lost their income to the shogunate, most of the court musicians were dispersed to three temple locations. In time, in isolation from each other, variant performance practices developed. When, in the early Meiji era (1968–1912), the three groups were reassembled as part of the reconstitution of the imperial household in Tokyo, compromises had to be made in the versions of pieces. Much of what is heard of court music today is thus fairly recent musical practice.

27. For a discussion of her piece *Ten no yō na chi, soshite chi no yō na ten*, see Wade 2005: 143–45, with CD. Fujiie's interest in gagaku continues; her *Kasane Op. 84* (2004–6) for guitar quartet is a suite of ten movements in six gagaku melodic modes. It is performed on *Kasane* (Brinirini CD KYBR-0702, 2007), featuring Kazuhito, Koyumi, Terukaku, and Kanahi Yamashita.

28. The Shōsō-in is a fabulous storehouse of household materials of the imperial home of Emperor Shomu, placed there on the twenty-first day of the sixth month of the year 756 by the Dowager Empress Komyo; among the household materials were musical instruments. The largest additions to the storehouse were made in 950, when another warehouse was destroyed (Malm 1983: 5). Despite historic wooden buildings' high risk of fire, the Shōsō-in has survived. Its precious contents, designated as national treasures, have for some time been housed in a concrete building nearby for safekeeping. Available for viewing just once a year by designated officials, the collection remains a historical source of inestimable value that even highly respected individuals unfortunately have little chance to see.

29. The volume edited by the National Theatre dealing in detail with each of the ancient instruments reconstructed for the purpose of its concerts (see Kido 1994) was

awarded the 1998 Klaus P. Wachsmann Prize for Advanced and Critical Essays in Organology by the Society for Ethnomusicology.

30. The imprint reads: "Works Commissioned by the National Theatre, Tokyo/Contemporary Japanese Music, Volume No. X. Edited by the Japan Arts Council, Theatre Research and Library Resources Division, Research and Training Department, National Theatre." The volumes are published by Shunjūsha (http://www.shunjusha.co.jp/).

31. In 1989 the National Theatre Law was amended, and the stated main objectives of the council were updated to suit conditions in contemporary Japan: the preservation and promotion of traditional performing arts, and the promotion and popularization of modern performing arts in Japan. Major changes resulted. In 1990 the Japan Arts Fund was established, and the National Theatre was reorganized and renamed as the Japan Arts Council. Then, in 2003, the Japan Arts Council was reorganized and became an independent administrative institution. In the current list of projects there is none that explicitly benefits composers. See http://www.ntj.jac.go.jp/english.html (accessed April 8, 2012).

32. Because a number of them attend her recitals, it is a good place to meet composers. I wish to express my appreciation to Kimiko Shimbo, who, as assistant to the secretary general of the Japan Federation of Composers, invited me to Nanae's recital on April 22, 1999, at the beginning of this project and there introduced me to eight composers with whom I was able to follow up. Camerata Tokyo has issued several CDs of Nanae performing works written for her: *Voices Phantasma, Flame* (Camerata Tokyo CD 32CM-311, 1993); *On a Treetop* (Camerata Tokyo CD 30CM-426, 1996); *Taqsim: New Aspect for Japanese Instrument "Koto"* (Camerata Tokyo CD 25CM-208, 1999); *Subaru/Nanae Yoshimura Plays Takashi Yoshimatsu* (Camerata Tokyo CD 28CM-578, 2000); and *Saika—Colors of Mist* (Camerata Tokyo CD CMCD-28053, 2004). Her signature composition, *Nanae,* can be heard on *Nanae* (Camerata CD 25CM-189, 2000).

33. Of the many CDs on which Mayumi Miyata can be heard, examples of her work with non-Japanese composers can be heard on *Karas.Krähen, Palast des Schweigens: Mayumi Miyata spielt Gagaku* (Wergo CD WER 2056-2, 1999). Miyata performs on most of Reigakusha's recordings. She performs works by Toshio Hosokawa—*Cloudscapes: Moon Night* (1998) for shō and accordion, and *Wie ein Atmen im Lichte* (2002) for shō solo—on *Deep Silence: Toshio Hosokawa/Gagaku* (Wergo CD 68012, 2004). Playing accordion is Stefan Hussong. The pairing of the accordion and the shō is notable, because in a number of contemporary compositions by Japanese composers, the accordion is used to invoke the shō. A portrait CD of Ishikawa's playing and compositions is available on *Ou-no-seijaku, Stillness in Blue* (Waternet Sound CD WOCA-1004, 2004).

34. *Simoyo no kinuta* (*Stonework in Frosty Evening*) for long shakuhachi (1980) can be heard on *Shibata Minao: Music for Japanese Instruments* (Fontec CD FOCD3479, 2000). On *Five Pieces for Shakuhachi Chikurai* (Camerata CD 30CM-303, 1997) Mitsuhashi plays a selection of contemporary compositions that have become classics, including Makoto Moroi's *Five Pieces for Shakuhachi Chikurai* (1964, discussed above), and Miki Minoru's *Autumn Fantasy* for shakuhachi and twenty-stringed koto (1980). On *Selected Works, Vol. II: Teizo Matsumura* (Camerata CD 30CM-428, 1996), Mitsuhashi plays two more classics by Teizo Matsumura (1929–2007)—the first that respected

composer wrote for a Japanese instrument, *Poem-I,* for shakuhachi and twenty-stringed koto (1969), which, because of its bamboo construction, was featured as a sound suggestive of bamboo at a pavilion at the 1970 World Exposition in Osaka; and *Poem-II,* for shakuhachi solo (1972). Of an entirely different nature is Hitomi Kaneko's *Le Chant Vertical,* for shakuhachi and computer (2001), on *Spectral Matters* (Fontec CD FOCD 2557, 2004); that work was suggested by Mitsuhashi and was Kaneko's first public work following her study in France.

35. CD booklet, p. 12, for *Kazuko Takada San-Gen* (Fontec CD FOCD3508, 2004). In 2010 works by Sukeyasu Shiba were the featured program for Music From Japan in celebration of the organization's thirty-fifth-anniversary season and also in celebration of Shiba's accomplishments as a performer, composer, researcher, educator, and advocate of gagaku. For the celebration, Music From Japan commissioned *Mai fu jin 35* (2008), a gagaku piece based on the classical tradition, as well as dance segments choreographed by Stephen Pier to three movements from Shiba's *Shotorashion* (1980) suite for gagaku ensemble. Other works programmed were the American premieres of his *Guwa No. 1* (1966), *Ichigyo no fu* (1979), and *Chosa join* (1983); all were performed by his Reigakusha gagaku ensemble. The Resources Center of Music From Japan has a number of scores of his compositions on file.

36. See Takahashi's "Memento of Flowers: In Memory of Takada Kazuko," translated by David G. Goodman (http://www.suigyu.com/yuji/en-text/TakadaMemorial.html, accessed January 10, 2011).

37. CD booklet, p. 2, for *Finger Light: Yuji Takahashi* (Tzadik CD TZ 7010, 1995). This stirring recording features Kazuko Takada and Yumiko Tanaka.

38. Sony issued a ten-disc set titled *Music of Shinichi Yuize* (SRCL CD 3341-50,1973 and 1977–81). Unfortunately, it does not include the concertos. Yuize is the husband of the iemoto of the Seiha koto ryū-ha, Yasuko Nakashima, who herself composes very fine music for seventeen-stringed koto. In my conversation with Nakashima, I addressed her as a performer-composer, to which she replied self-effacingly: "Oh no, my husband is the composer" (personal communication, May 14, 1999). Nevertheless, she listed for me three other women in the Seiha school who compose—Makiko Goda, Sumiko Goto, and Sumiko Shiho.

39. Sawai plays *Gosechi no mai* on *Iris of Time: Virtuoso Koto Tadao Sawai* (Camerata CD 30CM-92, 1984). On the same CD he also plays Akira Nishimura's *Iris of Time: Heterophony for Seven Kotos and Three jyūshichigen-koto* (1987); Teizo Matsumura's *Fantasy* (n.d.) for koto; and Joji Yuasa's *Koto Uta Basho's Haiku* (n.d.) for koto.

40. CD booklet, p. 6, for *Thread Cog Wheels,* on *Yuji Takahashi Real Time 4* (Fontec CD FOCD 9387/8, 1992), featuring Tadao Sawai, koto, and the New Japan Philharmonic Orchestra. That Takahashi did not provide a score for this *Thread Cog Wheels* was characteristic of his working method through the previous decade or so.

Other Takahashi works for seventeen-stringed koto, performed by Kazue Sawai, can be heard on *The Wind Is Calling Me Outside* (ALM RECORDS CD ALCD-37, 1990): *While I Was Crossing the Bridge* (1984); *The Wind Is Calling Me Outside* (1986); "Gossamer" [song] (1988); and *Horses' Heads Were Toward Eternity* (1988).

41. CD booklet, p. 7, for *Super flumina Babylonis* (1994), for soprano, alto and chamber orchestra with string orchestra (ad lib.), on *Works by Toshio Hosokawa VI*

(Fontec CD FOCD 3420, 1997). Recordings of Hosokawa's works that call for Japanese instruments include *Utsurohi* (1986), for shō and harp (*Works by Toshio Hosokawa V* [Fontec CD FOCD 3406, 1997]); *Utsurohi nagi* (1995), for shō and string orchestra with harp, celesta, and percussion (*Works by Toshio Hosokawa VII* [Fontec CD FOCD 3441, 1998]); *Seeds of Contemplation—Mandara* (1986), for *shōmyō* (four singers) and gagaku ensemble (*yokobue*, shō, hichiriki, and *kugo*), and *Fragmente I* (1988), for shakuhachi, koto, and *sangen* (*Works by Toshio Hosokawa III* [Fontec FOCD 9117, 1997]); *Birds, Fragments III* (1990), for shō (or accordion), bass, and ottavino flute (*Toshio Hosokawa: Bird Fragments, Alter Ego* [Stradivarius STR 33689, 2006]); and *Somon-ka* (2001–2), for voice, koto, cello, and chamber orchestra (*Returning*: *Works by Toshio Hosokawa IX* [Fontec CD FOCD 3504, 2004]).

CHAPTER 5

1. The type of event with the closest total number of performances to those by orchestras was piano recitals, of which there were twenty-one (by both Japanese and non-Japanese artists). The small number is not indicative of any lack of popularity of piano recitals, because Tokyo offers many excellent performance venues for them.

The visiting orchestras, listed in the order in which they appeared on the schedule, were the Vienna Volksoper Symphony Orchestra, the Strauss Festival Orchestra Vienna, the Chicago Symphony Orchestra, the Berlin Radio Symphony Orchestra, the WDR Symphony Orchestra Cologne, the Amsterdam Baroque Orchestra, the Arnhem Philharmonic Orchestra of the Netherlands, the Lithuanian Chamber Orchestra, the Radio France Philharmonic Orchestra, the West Australia Symphony Orchestra, the Tchaikovsky Symphony Orchestra of Moscow Radio, the National Philharmonic of Russia, the NDR Radiophilharmonie (Hannover), the Warsaw Philharmonic National Orchestra, the Russian National Orchestra, the Pacific Music Festival Orchestra, the Vienna Philharmonic, the New York Philharmonic, the Bamberg Symphony, the Leipzig Gewandhaus Orchestra, the Cincinnati Symphony Orchestra, the Orchestre National du Capitole de Toulouse, the Bavarian Radio Symphony Orchestra, the Czech Philharmonic Orchestra, and the Mariinsky Orchestra. The links to Europe, which far outnumbered those to America (three) and Australia (one), are worthy of note.

2. The Kansai region, also known as Kinki, lies in the south-central part of the main island of Honshu and includes the cities of Osaka, Kyoto, and Kobe. It is the second-most populated area in Japan after the greater Tokyo region (the Kanto region), which encompasses the cities of Tokyo and Yokohama.

The Izumi Sinfonietta Osaka can be heard on *Metamorphosis: Chamber Symphony Works of Akira Nishimura* (Camerata CD CMCD 28084, 2005). Izumi Hall was planned and constructed as one of Sumitomo Life Insurance's sixtieth-anniversary projects; it opened in April 1990. In pursuit of creating an ideal sound field, the hall was modeled after the Grosser Musikvereinssaal (the Golden Hall) in Vienna, home of the Vienna Philharmonic. It is a shoebox-style concert hall with 821 seats and acoustics best suited to chamber music of the classical period.

3. Seven of the thirty-six players on the 2005 personnel roster were non-Japanese.

4. Among the twenty-five full-time professional groups, nine are in Tokyo, seven

are in the Kansai and Nagoya, and nine are in other locations around the country. In Tokyo there are the Tokyo Philharmonic Orchestra, the NHK Symphony Orchestra, the Tokyo Symphony Orchestra, the Japan Philharmonic Orchestra, the Yomiuri Nippon Symphony Orchestra, the Tokyo Metropolitan Symphony Orchestra, the New Japan Philharmonic, the Tokyo City Philharmonic Orchestra, and the Tokyo New City Orchestra. In the Kansai area there are the Osaka Philharmonic Orchestra, the Orchestra Osaka Symphoniker, the Century Orchestra Osaka, the Kyoto Symphony Orchestra, the Nagoya Philharmonic Orchestra (and Nagoya Pops Orchestra), the Kansai Philharmonic Orchestra, and the Hyogo Performing Arts Center Orchestra in Nishinomiya City. Elsewhere there are the Gunma Symphony Orchestra, the Kyushu Symphony Orchestra, the Sapporo Symphony Orchestra, the Kanagawa Philharmonic Orchestra, the Yamagata Symphony Orchestra, the Sendai Philharmonic Orchestra, the Central Aichi Symphony Orchestra (in the Nagoya area), the Orchestra Ensemble Kanazawa, and the Hiroshima Symphony Orchestra.

5. I have been told, but do not have systematic information that would confirm or deny it, that it is the rare middle school [in Tokyo] that does not have an orchestra.

6. For her research on the acceptance of Western music in Japan up to 1941, Inoue analyzed 1,560 programs for performances up until 1941 by nine student orchestras nationwide. She found the ten most frequently performed pieces and analyzed the content of print sources and recordings of the time to understand the impact of the media on repertoire formation.

7. The NHK Symphony Orchestra started out in 1926 as the New Symphony Orchestra and was briefly called the Japan Symphony Orchestra (Association of Japanese Symphony Orchestras 2008: 37). It has held subscription concerts continually since 1927, though performances were greatly curtailed during World War II. Since 1951 the orchestra has received full financial support from NHK (Nippon Hoso Kyokai, [Japan Broadcasting Corporation]); at that time the name was changed to the NHK Symphony Orchestra.

8. A second transnational string quartet is the Lotus String Quartet, which circulates between Germany and Japan. Although no one mentioned this group to me, their CD *Landscapes* (Hamburg: Teldec Classics International, 2000; dist. Warner Music Japan, WPCS-10426 [3984-25015-2]) is sold in Japan. It features Akio Yashiro's (1929–1976) *Quatuor à cordes* (1955); Akira Nishimura's String Quartet no. 2, *Pulse of the Lights* (1992); Toshio Hosokawa's *Landscape 1* (1992), for string quartet; Toru Takemitsu's *Landscape 1* (1961); and Akira Miyoshi's String Quartet no. 3, *Constellation in Black* (1992).

9. *Direction* (Camerata CD 30CM-557, 1999), by the New Arts String Quartet, features Ichiyanagi's String Quartet no. 3, "Inner Landscape" (1994); Toshiro Saruya's *Aither, the Beorht* (1996); Joji Yuasa's *Projection for String Quartet II* (1996); and Toru Takemitsu's *A Way a Lone* (1981).

10. Niimi's *String Quartet no. 2* is now referred to as *String Quartet no. 2, A.E.* The "A.E." designation was added to indicate that it was composed after the earthquake so that the natural disasters, the dangers of radiation, and resulting tragedies will never be forgotten. Niimi's *Trumpet Sonata—per una selva oscura, A.E. 18*, which was premiered in November 2012, is the eighteenth work he has composed since the earthquake.

11. *Fujin raijin* (*God of Wind, God of Thunder*), for Japanese big drum, organ, and orchestra (1997), was commissioned by Sumida Triphony Hall in Tokyo. It can be heard on *"Fujin Raijin": Concertos of Tokuhide Niimi* (Camerata CD CMCD-2805, 2006), performed by Hikotaro Yazaki conducting the Tokyo Metropolitan Symphony Orchestra. The CD also features Niimi's *Concerto for Violin and Orchestra* Cantus Vityalis (2003) and *Anima Sonito* for soprano and orchestra (2002).

12. Hosokawa 1997a: 6. *Ferne Landschaft I* was awarded the thirty-seventh Otaka Prize. In a similar spirit, for the fiftieth anniversary of the Gunma Symphony Orchestra, founded in 1945, the orchestra commissioned from Toshio Hosokawa a new piece, *Ferne-Landschaft II* (1996).

13. For a complete roster of composers in residence, see http://en.wikipedia.org/wiki/Orchestra_Ensemble_Kanazawa#Composer_In_Residence. A series of CDs featuring the Orchestra Ensemble Kanazawa performing commissioned works, entitled *Messages for the 21st Century*, has been issued by Deutsche Grammophon/Polydor. Vol. 1 is unavailable. Vol. 2 (POCG-1860, 1995) includes Keiko Fujiie, *Beber* (1994), for chamber orchestra; Joji Yuasa, *Piano Concertino* (1994); Karen Tanaka, *Wave Mechanics* (1994); and Toshiro Saruya, *Projection Orbit* (1994). Vol. 3 (POCG-1947, 1996) includes Ichiro Nodaira, *Concerto de chambre* no 1 (1995); Hitomi Kaneko, *Concerto pour flûte et orchestre* (1995); Jo Kondo, *To the Headland* (1995); and Toshio Hosokawa, *Garten Lieder I* (1995). For commentary on the ensemble and the recordings, see Kriesberg 2000.

14. That they had progressed to such a level of achievement Akira Nishimura attributed partially to Japan's good economy: "As the economy went up, amateurs could spend money on a good instrument—three million yen spent on a violin, up to 10 million. The sound of money is a great pizzicato!" he quipped (personal communication, May 17, 2006).

15. As I have pointed out several times and reemphasize in chapter 6 on choral music, Japanese composers are willing to write in whatever style the commissioner wishes, so this remark applies more to existing repertoire than to newly commissioned works.

16. Because the JFC holds nonprofit status, the composer keeps the copyright for those works that are published and recorded by the JFC.

17. By 2008, when the JFC celebrated its thirty-fifth year, more than six hundred works composed by its members had been published. The JFC catalogue is delivered to major international musical organizations, thereby helping in the global diffusion of Japanese music; it is also available upon request; the website is at http://www.jfc.gr.jp/contents/jfc/AbouttheJFC.html.

18. The recording is *The World of Narrative and Music* (JILA CD JILA-1760, 2005). Miyahara herself performed on piano.

19. The JILA label includes, for instance, CD compilations of piano music (eight works by composers, with one exception, born in 1944 or later on *The Field of 20th Century Piano Music* [JILA CD JILA-1105, 1998]; seven works including Setsuko Miyahara's *La lluvia de Madrid* on *The 2nd Field of 20th Century Piano Music* [JILA CD JILA-1107, 1999]; and seven works including Yayoi Kitazume's *Ének III* on *The 3rd Field of 20th Century Piano Music* [JILA CD JILA-1213, 2000]). *Mai* (JILA CD JILA-1320, 2000) is a portrait CD of chamber music compositions by Sumiko Minemura. *Current of Japanese Arias for the 20th Century* (JILA CD JILA-1320, 2001) features works by

seven composers. Notable on all JILA CDs is a good representation of both women and men composers.

20. I asked Matsudaira to compare the membership of Gen-On to the membership of the Japan Federation of Composers (JFC). He described the former as "serious composers" and the latter as composers of "serious and incidental music, i.e., music for TV, film, and the like" (Yori-Aki Matsudaira, personal communication, May 27, 2004). Many members of the JFC are composers in the popular-music industry (Kimiko Shimbo, personal communication, May 22, 2009).

Gen On also publishes a journal, *Gendai ongaku*, in which programs of their concerts are reproduced and biographical information about the composers is given.

21. While most of the works programmed could be categorized as chamber works, Makiko Kinoshita mentioned to me a concert of works for orchestra that was produced by herself and other members of Gen On. Each composer contributed 200,000 yen (c. $2,200) toward the costs—"not too much for orchestra" (personal communication, June 2, 2004).

22. All of the information on band music here comes from David Hebert's *Wind Bands and Cultural Identity in Japanese Schools* 2012: chapter 9.

23. For a list of Michio Kitazume's works and the professional profile of this leading composer, see his official website. *Eii-sho* (1993), for orchestra, for which he won the 1994 Otaka Prize, can be heard on *Orchestral Works by Michio Kitazume* (Fontec CD FOCD 2514, 1994), performed by the Tokyo Philharmonic Orchestra. Those interested in works for percussion and orchestra will enjoy hearing his *Shadows II* (1976) and *Side by Side* (1987), featured on the same CD.

24. For detailed information on the CD series, see the company's website (www.brain-music.asia); click on the site map and scroll down to "Band Restoration Series."

25. I learned about this event from Kimiko Shimbo, who assists with the arrangements between the composers and the publisher. On May 22, 2009, the day on which she told me about it, she called the publisher, who hand-delivered to me the same day a copy of the published anthology of scores for the year. When I accessed the website of Hustle Copy, I realized how this astoundingly rapid delivery had to have been made. To understand the work of this on-demand publisher, I suggest accessing its website at www.hustlecopy.co.jp/english/index.html.

26. *Works by Toshio Hosokawa I* (FOCD9115), *Per Sonare: Works by Toshio Hosokawa II* (FOCD9116), *Works by Toshio Hosokawa III* (FOCD9117), *Works by Toshio Hosokawa IV* (FOCD9118), *Works by Toshio Hosokawa V* (FOCD3406), *Super Flumina Babylonis: Works by Toshio Hosokawa VI* (FOCD3420), *Utsurohi.Nagi: Works by Toshio Hosokawa VII* (FOCD 3441), *Re-turning: Works by Toshio Hosokawa* (FOCD3504), and *Memory: Works by Toshio Hosokawa X* (FOCD9294).

27. See http://www.culturalprofiles.net/japan/units/2230.html, accessed April 1, 2011.

28. Tomiko Kohjiba wrote to me: "I said that composing is just like raising a child" (personal communication August 28, 2012).

29. That having been planned well in advance, the music director and conductor of the Sinfonietta, Yasuaki Itakura, was a guest juror for the competition.

30. At 80 yen to the U.S. dollar: $7,500, $3,750, and $1,875, respectively.

CHAPTER 6

1. A female vocal duet with a piano accompaniment, *Hana* (*Cherry Blossoms*), by Rentaro Taki (1879–1903), is considered the first Japanese choral piece ever written (Tsutsumi 2007: 1).

2. As I understand it in a non-researched way, unison group singing is commonplace also in folk music and as a potential element of male socializing.

3. The first book of school songs was produced in 1881 by Izawa and Luther Whiting Mason, the music education inspector for Boston; 90 percent used Western melodies to which a Japanese text had been added. In the second collection, only 80 percent of the songs were Western in origin; the remaining 20 percent used Japanese scales and melodies (Galliano 2002: 30).

4. See Tsutsumi 2007: 8. A Tōzai [Eastern and Western] Four-University Choral Association was founded in 1951 and has organized a subscription concert annually since 1952. The organization consists of two historical university men's glee clubs, Keio and Waseda in Tokyo and Kwansei Gakuin and Doshisha in Kansai (Tsutsumi 2007: 132). It is one of several such associations.

5. For this information on the history of choruses in Japan, Tsutsumi 2007 has been especially helpful.

6. Among the earliest of Japanese composers to study in France, Komatsu studied with Vincent d'Indy between 1921 and about 1924 (Galliano 2002: 76). In 1930, his loyalty to French music still strong, Komatsu was among the founders of the Shinkō Sakkyokuka Renmei (Newly Rising Federation of Composers) as a protest against proponents of "the German style"; see p. 62.

7. I am not certain how to relate this statement by Tsutsumi to the narrative by Saeko Hasegawa: "After the war, the Ministry of Education decided that children should be trained to sing using the head voice instead of the natural voice" (2007: 26). The practice of the Hasegawa's Boys' Choir of Tokyo opened the door to connections internationally with boys' and children's choirs in Europe.

8. While Tsutsumi did not make this connection to the PTAs, I was struck by Sheldon Garon's comment that American Occupation officials, determined to democratize Japanese women's organizations away from state-supported national federations and local women's associations, "encouraged the growth of clubs made up of women with similar interests, rather than residentially-based associations in which women had little choice but to join. Parent-teacher associations were established by Americans under the Occupation to enable activist women and the centrally administered schools to instruct mothers in child rearing, hygiene, and household management" (Garon 1997: 188, 194).

9. A recording of the world premiere of *Voiceless Voice in Hiroshima* (2001) performed by the Chorus and Orchestra of the Bavarian Radio Symphony Orchestra is available on *Works by Toshio Hosokawa* (Fontec CD FOCD 3491, 2001) and on *Toshio Hosokawa "Voiceless Voice in Hiroshima" (1989/2001)* (Col Legno CD WWE 1CD 20087, 2002). The latter received the Millennium Award 2000/2001 of the BMW musica viva Composition Prize and the musica viva Prize of ARD and BMW AG. See pp. 143–44 for more about this work.

10. A very pertinent example of this beyond music can be found illustrated on http://www.kodomo.go.jp/gallery/KODOMO_WEB/commentary/children_e.html (accessed April 30, 2011): "People seemed to be looking forward to the happy future that materialistic prosperity would surely bring. . . . It was the beginning of a dramatically different time when adults and the young together began sharing one new experience after another." For information on the Japan Romantic School, see Wakabayashi 1998: 252–56.

11. As cited in Naka 1991: 564 from no. 44, in *Yamada Kōsaku dōyō hyakkyoku shū* (*100 Children's Songs by Yamada Kosaku*, 1927).

12. A two-CD anthology of songs by Kōsaku Yamada is available as *Akatonbo* (Victor CD VICG 41212-13, 2005). The collection's fifty-eight tracks consist mainly of Yamada's art songs and songs for children. They are performed by Kurumi Kobato, Aiko Koori, Bonny Jacks, Kuniko Nakamura, Hiroko Nakamura, Kyoko Ito, the Tokyo Philharmonic Chorus, and others.

13. One of Nakada's children's game songs, "Chiisai aki mitsuketa" ("Found a Small Autumn"), I found so attractive that I included it on the CD for my textbook (Wade 2005).

14. See *Jioji Yuasa: Beautiful Songs for Children*, Eiko Hiramatsu, soprano, accompanied by Ken-ichi Nakagawa (MusicScape CD MSCD-0013, 2004). Further evidence of Joji Yuasa's flexibility is his *Hashire cho-tokkyu* (*Run, Super Express!*), which he was commissioned to write when the *shinkansen* (bullet train) went on its maiden journey in anticipation of the 1964 Tokyo Olympics.

15. The NHK collection with which they worked is now available as *Nihon min'yō taikan* [*Anthology of Japanese Folk Song*], with 90 CDs (Tokyo: Nihon Hōsō Kyōkai, 1992–94). Nine volumes, first issued in 1944–88, comprise field recordings with texts, staff notation, and commentaries on folk songs from all over Japan, many in multiple versions, organized by prefecture and function. The project was based on the Yoshiaki Machida's private archive of recordings of Japanese folk songs, which was donated to NHK in 1934. This book and CD set was published with the assistance of the eminent Japanese ethnomusicologist Fumio Koizumi.

16. This came to be referred to as *Composition no. 1 for Mixed Chorus* soon after Mamiya wrote his *Konsei gasshō to dagakki no tame no konpojishyoin II* (*Composition no. 2 for Mixed Chorus and Percussion*, 1961) and *Gasshō to ōkesutoru no tame no konpojishyon: "Kodomo no ryōbun"* (*Composition for Children's Chorus and Orchestra: "Children's Field,"* 1963). These three scores were published by Ongaku no Tomosha in 1959, 1966, and 1963 respectively. Mamiya has continued to write compositions for chorus. Compositions nos. 10–12 were published by Kawai, and the rest by Zen-On. Some recordings featuring the Tokyo Philharmonic Chorus are as follows: *Composition for Chorus no. 1 for Mixed Chorus*, on *Concert: 20–21, Vol. 14* (Jikko Iinkai CD ECJC 014, 2001); *Composition for Chorus no. 3 for Male Chorus*, on *Concert: 20–21, Vol. 20* (Jikko Iinkai CD ECJC 020, 2002); *Chojugiga Composition for Chorus*, on *Tanaka Nobuaki Conducts Modern Choral Music of Japan, 1* (Victor CD PRCD 5222, 1996); and *Works by Michio Mamiya* (Fontec CD FOCD 2519, 1996).

17. I have not delved into the composing of song apart from its adoption in choral singing, but on the issue of communication via language, the attention Joji Yuasa has

paid to vocal music merits special mention. In a series of works, Yuasa examines the meaning of language when the analysis of language goes in a certain sense beyond language to metalanguage. These elements include pronunciation, sound, physical space, psychological space, meaning, and nonmeaning—i.e., the nonlogical aspect of communication and language and the nonspoken aspect of communication. The subtitle of his *Observations on Weather Forecasts* (1986), for baritone and trumpet, is *Observations on Meta-Message as Nonverbal Communication, Intrinsic to the Human Activity in Language. Mutterings* (1988), for mezzo-soprano and seven instruments, features obsessive repetition and rearrangement of limited sets of words reminiscent of the schizophrenic mutterings in the poetry of R. D. Laing (1927–1989); the work is an intensive, agonized, emotional expression of metalanguage. It can be heard on *SONOR* (CRI CD 652, 1993), performed by the SONOR Ensemble of the University of California, San Diego.

18. This is available on *The Min-On Contemporary Music Festival '93* (Camerata CD 32CM-319, 1994), performed by the Tokyo Philharmonic Chorus and the Tokyo Symphony.

19. The *Metta Sutra* was chanted by Burmese Buddhist monks in a movement against the government in 2007. For comment by an ethnomusicologist, see Douglas (2010). As part of his lecture at the World Chorus Symposium in Kyoto in 2005, Nobuaki Tanaka played a recording of the *Metta Sutra* performed by the Stanford University Chamber Choir, conducted by Steven Sano. Yuji Takahashi's choral piece can be heard on *Nobuaki Tanaka Conducts Contemporary Choral Music* (ALM/Kojima Recordings CD LMCD 1599, 1999).

20. This can be heard on the *Tokyo Philharmonic Chorus Contemporary Chorus from Japan* (Fontec CD FOCD 3404, 1995).

21. For performance by ensembles specializing in early music and the works of Heinrich Schütz, the composer Hideki Chihara (b. 1957) composed two explicitly Christian choral works in Latin: *Maria Orientalis: Five Movements of St. Mary*, for mixed chorus; and *Doctrina Christan*, for mixed chorus. In the *Maria Orientalis*, reference is made to Gregorian chant, and the Latin text is gradually interspersed with Japanese translations of the text; this music, interweaving consonance and dissonance, creates an atmosphere of spirituality. These two works have been recorded by the Symphonic Collegium Osaka and the Heinrich Schütz Kammerchor, Osaka, conducted by the groups' founder, Shuichi Toma. Toma is now interested in contemporary and Japanese music and is thus collaborating with Chihara (CD booklet, p. 13, *Hideki Chihara Works 1*, Osaka Collegium Musicum OCM-019C3, 2007).

22. *Passio, ad lucem*, on *The Little Singers of Tokyo 50th Anniversary Concert Live*, part 3 (Little Singers of Tokyo LSOT 3, 2002). A third work written by Hosokawa for the Little Singers of Tokyo is *Into the Forest* (2002), recorded on *Re-Turning: Works by Toshio Hosokawa* (Fontec FOCD 3504, 2004).

23. From the program of the seventieth regular performance of the Tokyo Philharmonic Chorus, October 1975 (Hayashi 2003: ii).

24. Reprinted in the score of *The Finished Scenes from Hiroshima*, for mixed chorus *Give Me Water*, for mixed chorus with piano accompaniment, can be heard on *Concert: 20–21, Vol. 14* ([Jikko Iinkai] CD ECJC 014, [2002]), performed by the Tokyo Philharmonic Chorus. The complete work, for mixed chorus with piano accompani-

ment, is on the Tokyo Philharmonic Chorus's recording *Choral Works by Hikaru Hayashi* (Fontec CD FOCD 9186, 2003). Hiroshima has often been recalled in the social manner of a work for a group of singers. Hikaru Hayashi composed *Little Landscapes of Hiroshima,* for mixed chorus; performed by the Tokyo Philharmonic Chorus, it is recorded on *Choral Works by Hikaru Hayashi* (Fontec CD FOCD 3294, 1996). See also p. 249n9.

25. This collection was published as Koizumi 1969.

26. This can be heard on *The Min-On Contemporary Music Festival '84* (Camerata CD 32CM-296, 1993).

27. The title of this recording is *The Min-On Contemporary Music Festival '90*, by the Tokyo Philharmonic Orchestra and Tokyo Philharmonic Chorus (Camerata CD 32-CM-190, 1991).

28. The top winning piece, selected from the required suite of pieces to be a compulsory piece in the national competitions, is published in JCA's *Popular Song* series.

29. A selection can be heard on *Shin-ichiro Ikebe: Choral Works for Children* (Camerata CD 30CM-378, 1995).

GLOSSARY

AJBA: All-Japan Band Association

dōyō: Lyrical tonal songs (with piano accompaniment) for children (and mothers)

FWCJ: Federation of Women Composers in Japan (Nihon Josei Sakkyokka Renmei)

gagaku: Music for the Japanese imperial court ensemble

Geidai: Tokyo University of the Arts

gendai hōgaku: NHK programming rubric of "modern traditional music"

gendai Nihon ongaku: National Theater rubric for "contemporary Japanese music" for traditional instruments commissioned from composers

gendai ongaku: Contemporary music

Gen On: See JSCM

hayashi kotoba: Vocables

hichiriki: Vertical double-reed aerophone

hōgaku: Generically, Japanese traditional music

iemoto: Head of a school (*ryū*); authoritative transmitter of knowledge

JASRAC: Japan Society of Rights of Authors, Composers and Publishers

JCA: Japan Choral Association (Zen Nihon Gasshō Renmei)

jiuta: In Japanese traditional music, pieces by blind *shamisen* players of the *kansai* area

JFC: Japan Federation of Composers (Nihon Sakkyokka Kyōgikai)

JSCM: Japan Society for Contemporary Music (Nihon Gendai Ongaku Kyōkai)

Kansai: Western region of Japan's Honshu Island

Kantō: Eastern region of Japan's Honshu Island

koto: Zither-type cordophone, originally thirteen-stringed, now also with twenty or more strings *ma:* In Japanese aesthetics, a "pregnant nothingness"

Monbushō: Ministry of Education, Culture, Sports, Science and Technology (formerly Ministry of Education)

nagauta shamisen: Shamisen used for the nagauta genre of music for Kabuki theater

NHK: Nippon Hōsō Kyōkai (Japan Broadcasting Corporation)

nihonjinron: Ideological promulgation of Japanese uniqueness

ongaku: Generically, music, implying music based on European systems

origami: Traditional Japanese art of paper folding

PTNA: Piano Teachers National Association

ryū: Traditional teaching group; school

SARAH: Society for Administration of Remuneration for Audio Home Recording

SARVH: Society for the Administration of Remuneration for Video Home (i.e., Home Video)

shakuhachi: Vertical bamboo flute

shamisen: Three-stringed, long-necked, fretless plucked lute

Shinkō Sakkyokuka Renmei: Newly Rising Federation of Composers

Shin Kokyo Gakudan: New Symphony Orchestra (amateur)

Shin Nihon Ongaku: "New Japanese Music" movement associated with Michio Miyagi and his contemporaries

shō: Mouth organ used in *gagaku* ensembles

Tō Ondai: Tokyo College of Music (Tokyo Ongaku Daigaiku)

TSO: Tokyo Symphony Orchestra

BIBLIOGRAPHY

Adriaansz, Willem. 1973. *The Kumiuta and Danmono Traditions of Japanese Koto Music.* Berkeley and Los Angeles: University of California Press.

Akiyama, Kuniharu. 1974. "Japan," translated by Joseph Love. In *Dictionary of Contemporary Music,* edited by John Vinton, 364–67. New York: E. P. Dutton.

Association of Japanese Orchestras. 2005. *Annual Report.* Tokyo: Association of Japanese Symphony Orchestras.

———. 2008. *Japanese Professional Orchestras Yearbook 2008.* Tokyo: Association of Japanese Symphony Orchestras.

Atkins, E. Taylor. 2001. *Blue Nippon: Authenticating Japanese Jazz in Japan.* Durham, NC: Duke University Press.

Becker, Howard S. 1982. *Art Worlds.* Berkeley and Los Angeles: University of California Press.

Bohlman, Philip. 2008. *Jewish Music and Modernity.* New York: Oxford University Press, 2008.

———. 2012. *Revival and Reconciliation: Sacred Music in the Making of European Modernity.* Lanham, MD: Scarecrow Press.

Bohlmann, Philip, with Nada Petković. 2012. *Balkan Epic: Song, History, Modernity.* Lanham, MD: Scarecrow Press.

Boulanger, Richard, Roger Reynolds, Joji Yuasa, and Charles Wuorinen. 1984. "Interview with Roger Reynolds, Joji Yuasa, and Charles Wuorinen." *Computer Music Journal* 8, no. 4 (Winter): 45–54.

Bourdieu, Pierre. 1986. "The Forms of Capital." In *Handbook of Theory and Research for the Sociology of Education,* edited by John G. Richardson, 241–58. Westport, CT: Greenwood Press.

Brandon, James. 1998. *Nō and Kyōgen.* Honolulu: University of Hawaii Press.

Burnett, Henry, and Hilary Tann, eds. 1989. "Tradition and Renewal in the Music of Japan." Special issue, *Perspectives of New Music* 27, no. 2 (Summer).

Burt, Peter. 2001. *The Music of Tōru Takemitsu.* New York: Cambridge University Press, 2001.

Clammer, John. 1995. *Difference and Modernity: Social Theory and Contemporary Japanese Society*. London: Kegan Paul International.

Coaldrake, Kimi. 2004. "Traditional Japanese Music Instruments in the Concert Hall." In *Musicology and Globalization*, edited by the Musicological Society of Japan, 256–60. Tokyo: Academia Music.

———. 2008. "Miki's *Autumn Fantasy* (1990): International Japanese or Asian?" In *Performing Japan: Contemporary Expressions of Cultural Identity*, edited by Henry Johnson and Jerry C. Jaffe, 68–92. Folkstone, Kent: Global Oriental.

Currid, Brian. 1996. "Finally I Reach to Africa: Ryuichi Sakamoto Sounding Japan(ese)." In *Contemporary Japan and Popular Culture*, edited by John Whittier Treat, 69–102. Honolulu: University of Hawaii Press/Curzon Press.

Dan, Ikuma. 1961. "The Influence of Japanese Traditional Music on the Development of Western Music in Japan." *Transactions of the Asiatic Society of Japan*, 3rd ser., 8 (December 1961): 201–17.

De Ferranti, Hugh. 2004. "*Kwaidan* and *Eclipse* as Examples of Takemitsu's Approach to Biwa." In *Musicology and Globalization: Proceedings of the International Congress in Shizuoka 2002, in Celebration of the 50th Anniversary of the Musicological Society of Japan*, edited by Tatsuhiko Itoh, Keiichi Kubota, Yasuhiko Mori, and Yoshio Tozawa, 415–18. Tokyo: Musicological Society of Japan.

———. 2013. *Music, Modernity and Locality in Interwar Japan: Osaka and Beyond*. London: Ashgate.

DeNora, Tia. 2003. *After Adorno: Rethinking Music Sociology*. Cambridge: Cambridge University Press.

"Desk Side." 2000. *Ongaku no Tomo* (May): 276.

Direction: New Arts String Quartet. Camerata CD 30CM-557, 1999.

Doak, Kevin M. 1996. "Ethnic Nationalism and Romanticism in Early Twentieth-Century Japan." *Journal of Japanese Studies* 22, no. 1: 77–103.

Douglas, Gavin. 2010. *Music in Mainland Southeast Asia: Experiencing Music, Expressing Culture*. New York: Oxford University Press.

Edwards, Michele. 2004. "Constructing Identity: Interplay of Japanese and Global Elements." In *Musicology and Globalization: Proceedings of the International Congress in Shizuoka 2002, in Celebration of the 50th Anniversary of the Musicological Society of Japan*, edited by Tatsuhiko Itoh, Keiichi Kubota, Yasuhiko Mori, and Yoshio Tozawa, 291–95. Tokyo: Musicological Society of Japan.

Eppstein, Ury. 1994. *The Beginnings of Western Music in Meiji Era Japan*. Lewiston, NY: Edwin Mellen Press.

———. 2002. "Reflecting on Two Cultural 'Mirrors': Mode and Signification of Musical Synthesis in Tōru Takemitsu's *November Steps* and *Autumn*." In *A Way Alone: On the Music of Takemitsu*, edited by Hugh De Ferranti and Yoko Nasrazaki, 125–53. Tokyo: Academia Musica.

Erlmann, Veit. *1999*. *Music, Modernity and the Global Imagination: South Africa and the West*. New York: Oxford University Press.

———, ed. 2004. *Hearing Cultures: Essays on Sound, Listening, and Modernity*. New York: Berg.

Everett, Yayoi Uno, and Frederick Lau, eds. 2004. *Locating East Asia in Western Art Music*. Middletown, CT: Wesleyan University Press.

Everett, Yayoi Uno. 2009. "Scream against the Sky." In *Sound Commitments: Avant-Garde Music and the Sixties*, edited by Robert Adlington, 197–208. New York: Oxford University Press.

Field, Norma. 1997. *From My Grandmother's Bedside: Sketches of Postwar Tokyo*. Berkeley and Los Angeles: University of California Press.

Finchum-Sung, Hilary. 2002. "*Uri Saenghwal Umak*: Music, Discourse, and Identity in South Korea." Ph.D. diss., Indiana University.

Flavin, Philip. 2008. "Sōkyoku-Jiuta: Edo-Period Chamber Music." In *The Ashgate Research Companion to Japanese Music*, edited by Alison McQueen Tokita and David W. Hughes, 169–95. Hampshire and Burlington, VT: Ashgate.

Fujieda, Mamoru. 2009. "Tuning of 'Patterns of Time.'" In *Arcana IV: Musicians on Music*, edited by John Zorn, 140–50. New York: Hips Road.

Fujiie, Keiko. 2005. *Ongaku essei-shu: Kotori no uta no yō ni, tsukamaegatai vokarīzu* [Essays on Music: Like a Small Bird's Song, Vocalization Difficult to Catch]. Tokyo: Tokyo Shoseki.

Fujitani, Takashi. 1996. *Splendid Monarchy: Power and Pageantry in Modern Japan*. Berkeley and Los Angeles: University of California Press.

———. 1993. "Inventing, Forgetting, Remembering: Toward a Historical Ethnography of the Nation-State." In *Cultural Nationalism in East Asia: Representation and Identity*, edited by Harumi Befu, 77–106. Berkeley: Institute of East Asian Studies, University of California, Berkeley.

Galliano, Luciana. 2002. *Yōgaku: Japanese Music in the Twentieth Century*. Translated by Martin Mayes. Lanham, MD: Scarecrow Press.

———. 2012. *The Music of Joji Yuasa*. Edited by Peter Burt. Newcastle upon Tyne: Cambridge Scholars Publishing.

Garon, Sheldon. 1997. *Molding Japanese Minds: The State in Everyday Life*. Princeton: Princeton University Press.

Gibson, James J. 1977. "The Theory of Affordances." In *Perceiving, Acting, and Knowing: Toward an Ecological Psychology*, edited by Robert Shaw and John Bransford, 67–82. Hillsdale, NJ: Lawrence Erlbaum Associates.

———. 1979. *The Ecological Approach to Visual Perception*. Boston: Houghton Mifflin .

Giddens, Anthony. 1990. *The Consequences of Modernity*. Cambridge: Polity Press.

Gluck, Carol. 2011. "The End of Elsewhere: Writing Modernity Now." *American Historical Review* 116, no. 3 (June): 676–87.

Gottschewski, Hermann. 2004. "Europe, America and the National 'Music' of Japan at the End of the 19th Century." In *Musicology and Globalization: Proceedings of the International Congress in Shizuoka 2002, in Celebration of the 50th Anniversary of the Musicological Society of Japan*, edited by Tatsuhiko Itoh, Keiichi Kubota, Yasuhiko Mori, and Yoshio Tozawa, 296–99. Tokyo: Musicological Society of Japan.

Guide to Three Seasons Annual Competitions of Orchestral Composition: Toru Takemitsu Composition Award 2007/2008/2009. 2005. Tokyo: Tokyo Opera City Cultural Foundation.

Guignard, Sylvain. 1991. "Art as a Survival Means: Some Considerations about Western and Traditional Music in Japan." In *Tradition and Its Future in Music: Report of SIMS Osaka 1990*, edited by Masakata Kanazawa, Makoto Ohmiya, Mari Shimosako, Akiko Takamatsu, Yosihiko Tokumaru, Tuneko Tukitani, and Osamu Yamaguti, 337–40. Tokyo and Osaka: Mita Press.

Guignard, Sylvain, ed. 1996. *Musik in Japan: Aufsätze zu Aspekten der Musik in heutigen Japan*. Munich: Ludicium Verlag.

Hall, Stuart, David Held, Don Hubert, and Kenneth Thompson, eds. 1996. *Modernity: An Introduction to Modern Societies*. Oxford: Blackwell.

Harich-Schneider, Eta. 1973. *A History of Japanese Music*. London: Oxford University Press, 1973.

Harootunian, H. D. 1998. "Figuring the Folk: History, Poetics, and Representation." In *Mirror of Modernity: Invented Traditions of Modern Japan*, edited by Stephen Vlastos, 144–59. Berkeley and Los Angeles: University of California Press.

Hattori, Kazuhiko. [1997]. CD booklet, *The Third Japan Contemporary Music Festival*. Japan International League of Artists, JILA-1002.

Havens, Thomas. 1982. *Artist and Patron in Postwar Japan: Dance, Music, Theater, and the Visual Arts, 1955–1980*. Princeton, NJ: Princeton University Press.

———. 2006. *Radicals and Realists in the Japanese Nonverbal Arts: The Avant-Garde Rejection of Modernism*. Honolulu: University of Hawaii Press.

Hayase, Takako. 2006. "A Comparison of Akira Miyoshi's Miyoshi Piano Method with Nancy and Randall Faber's Piano Adventures Based on Royal American Conservatory Examination (RACE)." DMA thesis, University of Cincinnati, College-Conservatory of Music.

Hayashi, Hikaru. 2003. Preface to the score of *The Finished Scenes from Hiroshima*, for mixed chorus, translated by David G. Goodman, ii. Tokyo: Zen-on.

Hebert, David G. 2001a. "Hoshina and Ito: Japanese Wind Band Composers." *Journal of Band Research* 37, no. 1 (2001): 61–77.

———. 2001b. "The Tokyo Kosei Wind Orchestra: A Case Study of Intercultural Music Transmission." *Journal of Research in Music Education* 49, no. 3: 212–26.

———. 2005. "Music Competition, Cooperation and Community: An Ethnography of a Japanese School Band." Ph.D. diss., University of Washington.

———. 2012. *Wind Bands and Cultural Identity in Japanese Schools*. Dordrecht and New York: Springer.

Herd, Judith Ann. 1987. "Change and Continuity in Contemporary Japanese Music: A Search for a National Identity." Ph.D. diss., Brown University.

———. 1989. "The Neonationalist Movement: Origins of Japanese Contemporary Music." *Perspectives of New Music* 27, no. 2 (Summer): 118–63.

———. 1994. "Piano Industry in Japan." In *Encyclopedia of Keyboard Instruments*, edited by Robert Palmieri, 1:186–90. New York: Garland.

———. 2001. "Shinohara, Makoto." In *The New Grove Dictionary of Music and Musicians*, edited by Stanley Sadie and John Tyrrell, 23:269. London and New York: Macmillan.

———. 2004. "The Cultural Politics of Japan's Modern Music: Nostalgia, Nationalism, and Identity in the Interwar Years." In *Locating East Asia in Western Art Music*, edited by Yayoi Uno Everett and Frederick Lau, 40–56. Middletown, CT: Wesleyan University Press.

———. 2008. "Western-Influenced 'Classical Music' in Japan." In *The Ashgate Research Companion to Japanese Music*, edited by Alison McQueen Tokita and David W. Hughes, 363–82. Hampshire and Burlington, VT: Ashgate.

Hirakawa, Sukehiro. 1998. "Japan's Turn to the West," translated by Bob Tadashi Wakabayashi. In Bob Tadashi Wakabayashi, *Modern Japanese Thought*, 30–97. New York: Cambridge University Press.

Hitomi, Kaneko. 2004. CD booklet, *KanekoHitomi: Spectral Matters*. Fontec CD FOCD2557.

Hiyama, Rikuro. 1977. *Gakki Gyōkai* [The Musical Instrument Business World]. Tokyo: Kyōiku-sha.

Hosokawa, Shuhei. 1998. "In Search for the Sound of the Empire: Hisao Tanabe and the Foundation of Japanese Ethnomusicology." *Japanese Studies* 18, no. 1: 5–19.

———. 2001. "Seikaino burasubando, burasubandono seikai" [Wind Bands of the World, the World of Wind Bands]. In *Burasubando no shakaishi* [Social History of Brass Bands], edited by K. Abe, S. Hosokawa, Y. Tsukahara, M. Touya, and T. Takazawa, 55–81. Tokyo: Seikyusha.

Hosokawa, Toshio. 1994. "The Pattern and the Fabric: In Search of a Music, Profound and Meaningful." In *Ästhetik und Komposition: Zur Aktualität der Darmstädter Ferienkursarbeit*, 74–78. Mainz: B. Schott's Söhne.

———. 1997a. CD booklet, *Works by Toshio Hosokawa II*. Fontec FOCD9116, 1997.

———. 1997b. CD booklet, *Works by Toshio Hosokawa IV*. Fontec FOCD9118, 1997.

———. 1997c. CD booklet, *Works by Toshio Hosokawa VI*. Fontec FOCD3420, 1997.

———. 2002. CD booklet, *Works by Toshio Hosokawa VIII*. Fontec FOCD3491, 2002.

Howard, Keith. 2006. *Creating Korean Music: Tradition, Innovation, and the Discourse of Identity*. Surrey: Ashgate.

Hsu, Francis. 1975. *"Iemoto": The Heart of Japan*. New York: Schenkman.

Hughes, David W. 1993. "Japan." In *Ethnomusicology: Historical and Regional Studies*, edited by Helen H. Myers, 345–63. New York: W. W. Norton.

Ichiyanagi, Toshi. N.d. *An Ancient Resonance in Contemporary Music*. Translated by Gavin Frew. Published privately.

Inoue, Tokiko. 2009. "Senzen Nippon ni okeru gakusei ōkesutora no kyokumoku sentaku ni kansuru jissyōkenkyū" [Empirical Research on the Selection of Works by Student Orchestras in Prewar Japan]. *Journal of the Musicological Society of Japan* 55, no. 2: 53–67.

Ishida, Kazushi. 2002. "Japan: Japanese Composers." In *Asian Composers in the 20th Century*, edited by the Japan Federation of Composers, 222–38. Tokyo: Japan Federation of Composers.

Ishihara, Mari. 2008. "Amerika bunka senta setchi no nerai: Kanagawa kenritsu toshōkan shozo Amerika bunka senta no shiryo no bunsetsu o tōshite" [The American Cultural Center: The Motives for Its Establishment; An Analysis of the Kanagawa Prefecture Archives of the American Cultural Center Resources]. In

Mita Toshōkan Jyohogakkai kenkyutaikai happyoronbunshu 2008, 45–48. Tokyo and Osaka: Mita Toshōkan Jyoho Gakkai.

Ivy, Marilyn. 1995. *Discourses of the Vanishing: Modernity, Phantasm, Japan*. Chicago: University of Chicago Press.

Iwabuchi, Koichi. 1999–2000. *International Journal of Urban Labour and Leisure* 2, no. 2. http://www.ijull.org.uk/.

———. 2002. *Recentering Globalization: Popular Culture and Japanese Transnationalism*. Durham, NC: Duke University Press.

Jameson, Fredric. 1998. *The Cultures of Globalization*. Durham, NC: Duke University Press.

Japan Musicians Who's Who: Composers and Conductors. 1985. Tokyo: Ongaku no Tomosha.

Japan Society of Rights of Authors, Composers and Publishers. N.d. *A Guide to JASRAC*. Tokyo: Japan Society of Rights of Authors, Composers, and Publishers.

Japan Victor. 1974. *Miyagi Michio daizenshū*. Set of 26 LPs: nos. 1–25, SJL2141-M–SJL2165-M; no. 26, K3. Pamphlets edited by Kikkawa Eishi and Miyagi Kiyoko. Tokyo: Victor Ongaku Sangyo Kabushiki Kaisha.

Johnson, Henry M. 1996. "*Koto* Manufacture: The Instrument, Construction Process, and Aesthetic Considerations." *Galpin Society Journal* 49: 38–64.

———. 2004a. *The* Koto*: A Traditional Instrument in Contemporary Japan*. Amsterdam: Hotei.

———. 2004b. "The *Koto*, Traditional Music, and an Idealized Japan: Cultural Nationalism in Music Performance and Education." In *Japanese Cultural Nationalism at Home and in the Asia-Pacific*, edited by R. Starrs, 132–64. Kent: Global Oriental.

———. 2010. *The* Shamisen: *Tradition and Diversity*. Leiden: Brill.

Kakinuma, Toshie. 1984. "Wadaiko in Ishii Maki's 'Monopris.'" *Ongaku Geijutsu* 42, no. 9 (September): 51–53.

Kamisango, Yuko. 1981. "Traditional Elements in the Compositions of Miyagi Michio." In *International Symposium on the Conservation and Restoration of Cultural Property: Preservation and Development of the Traditional Performing Arts, 6–9 August 1980*, edited by the Organizing Committee of the International Symposium on the Conservation and Restoration of Cultural Property, 143–47. Tokyo: Tokyo National Research Institute of Cultural Properties.

Kanazawa, Masakata. 2001. "Yoshinao Nakada." In *The New Grove Dictionary of Music and Musicians*, edited by Stanley Sadie and John Tyrrell, 2nd ed., 17:596. London and New York: Macmillan.

Kaneda, Miki. 2012. "The Unexpected Collectives: Intermedia Art in Postwar Japan." Ph.D. diss., University of California, Berkeley.

Kasaba, Eiko. 1989. "Notes sur la reception de la musique de Messiaen au Japan." *Revue internationale de musique française* 30 (November): 93–100.

Kawakami, Genichi. 1987. *Reflections on Music Popularization*. Tokyo: Yamaha Music Foundation.

Kido, Toshiro. 1984. "Gagaku in Takemitsu Toru's *In an Autumn Garden*." *Ongaku Geijutsu* 42, no. 9 (September): 42–44.

———. 1994. *Reconstructed Music Instruments of Ancient East Asia.* Tokyo: Ongaku no Tomosha.

Kishibe, Shigeo. 1967. "Japanese Music—Conflict or Synthesis?" *World of Music* 9, no. 2: 11–21.

Kitagawa, Junko. 2008. "Orchestras and Their Music." In *Music in Contemporary Japanese Society,* edited by Wolgye Tsuneko, Juno Kitagawa, and Satomi Oshio, 58–71. Tokyo: Hōsō University Foundation for Education, 2008.

Kitahara, Michio. 1966. "Kayokyoku: An Example of Syncretism Involving Scale and Mode." *Ethnomusicology* 10, no. 3: 271–84.

Kobayashi, Midori. 1999. *The Lives of Women Composers.* Tokyo: Heibonsha.

Koizumi, Fumio, ed. 1969. *Warabe-uta no kenkyū* [A Study of Warabe-uta]. 2 vols. Tokyo: Warabe-uta no Kenkyū Kenkō.

Kojima, Miko. 1997. CD booklet, *Virtuoso Koto—Tadao Sawai: Iris of Time.* Camerata Tokyo, Camerata 30-CM-92.

Komatsu, Kosuke. 1957. "Choral Movement and Competition." *Gasshokai* 1, no. 7: 54–56.

———. 1965. "The Dawn of Chorus." *Gasshokai* 9, no. 4: 27–28.

Komiya, Toyotoka, ed. 1956. *Japanese Music and Drama in the Meiji Era.* Translated by E. Seidensticker and D. Keene. Tokyo: Obunsha.

Krauss, Ellis S. 2000. *Broadcasting Politics in Japan: NHK and Television News.* Ithaca, NY: Cornell University Press.

Kreyszig, Walter. 2004. "Japanese Music under the Influence of the Second Viennese School of Composition: An Example of East–West Acculturation, Globalization, Interculturality in the Post-1945 Era." In *Musicology and Globalization: Proceedings of the International Congress in Shizuoka 2002, in Celebration of the 50th Anniversary of the Musicological Society of Japan,* edited by Tatsuhiko Itoh, Keiichi Kubota, Yasuhiko Mori, and Yoshio Tozawa, 419–22. Tokyo: Musicological Society of Japan.

Kriesberg, Matthias. 2000. "Japan's New Generation of Composers." *New York Times,* February 6.

Kurabayashi, Yoshimasa, and Yoshiro Matsuda. 1988. *Economic and Social Aspects of the Performing Arts in Japan: Symphony Orchestras and Opera.* Tokyo: Kinokuniya.

Kuwakabe, Yoshihiko, Kan Ishii, Jyutaro Yamamoto, Yoshiro Nakamura, and Yoshiko Mari. 1996. "The Second Golden Age of Choral Music Came by Mothers' Power." *Harmony* 97: 57–64.

Lancastershire, Terrence. 2003. "World Music or Japanese: The *gagaku* of Tōgi Hideki." *Popular Music* 22: 21–39.

Landy, Leigh. 1987. "An Analysis of *Tayutai* for Koto (1972), Composed by Makoto Shinohara." *Interface: Journal of New Music Research* 16: 75–96.

Lejeune Löffler, Marie-Raymonde. 2004. "Musical and Musicological Globalization from an European Perspective: Exemplified in the work of Toshio Hosokawa." In *Musicology and Globalization: Proceedings of the International Congress in Shizuoka 2002, in Celebration of the 50th Anniversary of the Musicological Society of Japan*, edited by Tatsuhiko Itoh, Keiichi Kubota, Yasuhiko Mori, and Yoshio Tozawa, 423–27. Tokyo: Musicological Society of Japan.

Leppert, Richard, and Susan McClary. 1987. *Music and Society: The Politics of Composition, Performance and Reception*. Cambridge: Cambridge University Press.

Long, Stephen. 2004. "Japanese Composers of the Post-Takemitsu Generation." *Tempo* 58, no. 228: 14–22.

Malm, William P. 1963. *Nagauta: The Heart of Kabuki Music*. Tokyo: Charles E. Tuttle.

———. 1971. "The Modern Music of Meiji Japan." In *Tradition and Modernization in Japanese Culture*, edited by Donald Shively, 257–300. Princeton, NJ: Princeton University Press.

———. 1983. "Japanese Music and Its Relations to Other Musical Traditions." *World of Music* 25, no. 1: 5–15.

———. 2000. *Japanese Music and Musical Instruments*. New ed. Tokyo: Kodansha International.

Mamiya, Michio. 1962. Notes to the score of *Jū-yon no Nihon no uta* [*Fourteen Japanese Folk Songs*]. Tokyo: Ongaku no Tomosha.

———. 1971. Notes to *Nihon minyō-shū* 1955–59 [*Japanese Folk Song Collection*]. Tokyo: Zen-on.

———. 1996. CD booklet, *Orchestral Works by Michio Mamiya*. Fontec FOCD3306.

Mathews, Gordon. 2004. "Fence, Flavor, and Phantasm: Japanese Musicians and the Meanings of 'Japaneseness.'" *Japanese Studies* 24, no. 3 (December): 335–50.

Matthei, Renate, ed. 1991. *Komponisten in Japan und Deutschland*. Translated by Mariko Teramoto. Kassel: Furore-Edition.

McGrew, Anthony. 1996. "A Global Society?" In *Modernity: An Introduction to Modern Societies*, edited by Stuart Hall, David Held, Don Hubert, and Kenneth Thompson, 466–503. Oxford: Blackwell.

May, Elizabeth. 1963. *The Influence of the Meiji Period on Japanese Children's Music*. Berkeley and Los Angeles: University of California Press.

Minichiello, Sharon, ed. 1998. *Japan's Competing Modernities*. Honolulu: University of Hawaii Press.

Mitsukuri, Shūkichi. 1967. "Japanese Scales and Their Harmonic Treatment." In *The Japanese Music*, edited by the Japanese National Committee of the International Music Council, 1–11. Tokyo: Tokyo Press.

Miura, Naoyuki. 2003. "Message from Naoyuki Miura, Artistic Director, Music From Japan." In the program for the Music From Japan Festival, New York, p. 1. New York: Music From Japan.

Miyagi, Kiyoko, and Kazue Miyagi, compilers and eds. 1977–78. *Miyagi Michio Sakkyoku shū: Sōkyoku gakufu*. Fukuoka: Dai Nihon Katei Ongakkai.

Miyoshi, Masao, and H. D. Harootunian, eds. 1989. *Postmodernism and Japan*. Durham, NC: Duke University Press.

Moehn, Frederick. 2008. "Music, Mixing, and Modernity in Rio de Janeiro." *Ethnomusicology Forum* 17, no. 2: 165–202.

Mori, Barbara Lynne Rowland. 1996. "The Traditional Arts as Leisure Activities for Contemporary Japanese Women." In *Re-Imaging Japanese Women*, edited by Anne Imamura, 117–34. Berkeley and Los Angeles: University of California Press.

Mori, May. 1995. "Living National Treasures: The Japanese Government's Program for the Preservation of Traditional Art Forms." *UCLA Journal of Dance Ethnology* 19: 202–3.

Morris-Suzuki, Tessa. 1984. *Re-Inventing Japan: Time, Space, Nation*. Armonk, NY: M. E. Sharpe.

———. 1994. *Technological Transformation of Japan: From the 17th to the 21st Century*. New York: Cambridge University Press.

Motegi, Kiyoko. 1984. "Shamisen in Nagasawa Katsutoshi's *Shamisen Concerto Ongaku Geijutsu* 42, no. 9 (September): 57–59.

———. 1999. "The Creation of Tradition at the National Theatre of Japan: A Descriptive Documentation." In *Gendai no Nihon Ongaku, I, Ichiyanagi Toshi Sakukhin* [Contemporary Japanese Music: The Works of Ichiyanagi Toshi], edited by Nihon Geijutsu Bunka Shinkōkai [Japan Arts Council], translated by Steven G. Nelson, [28–32]. Tokyo: Shunjūsha.

Munroe, Alexandra, ed. 1994. "A Box of Smile: Tokyo Fluxus, Conceptual Art, and the School of Metaphysics." In *Japanese Art after 1945: Scream against the Sky*. New York: Harry N. Abrams.

Nagahiro, Hitoshi. 2002. *Chronological Table of Broadcasts of gendai hoogaku (Contemporary Music for Japanese Instruments): NHK Radio's "Gendai no nihon ongaku" [Japanese Music of the Present], April 1964–March 1972: Nihon Dentoo Ongaku Kenkyuu* [*Research on the Traditional Music of Japan*], supplement, *Bulletin of the Research Centre for Japanese Traditional Music* 1 (March).

Naka, Mamiko. 1991. "Polarity in Acculturation Process: A Composer Yamada Kōsaku." In *Tradition and Its Future in Music: Report of SIMS Osaka 1990*, edited by Masakata Kanazawa, Makoto Ohmiya, Mari Shimosako, Akiko Takamatsu, Yosihiko Tokumaru, Tuneko Tukitani, and Osamu Yamaguti, 563–66. Tokyo and Osaka. Mita Press.

Nishimura, Akira. 2008. *Magic of Classical Music: Theory of Spiritual Canonic Pieces*. Tokyo: Kodansha.

Nitobe, Inazo. 1931. "Music in Japan." In *Western Influences in Modern Japan*, edited by Inazo Nitobe, 469–523. Chicago: University of Chicago Press.

Numano, Yuji. 2004. "Some Aspects of Indeterminancy since the 1970s: The Conjunction of Eastern and Western Music via Indeterminate Notation." In *Musicology and Globalization: Proceedings of the International Congress in Shizuoka 2002, in Celebration of the 50th Anniversary of the Musicological Society of Japan*, Edited by Tatsuhiko Itoh, Keiichi Kubota, Yasuhiko Mori, and Yoshio Tozawa, 333–37. Tokyo: Musicological Society of Japan.

Nuss, Steven. 1996a. "Tradition and Innovation in the Art Music of Post-War Japan." Ph.D. diss., City University of New York.

———. 1996b. "Western Instruments, Japanese Music: Issues in Texture and Harmony in Minoru Miki's *Jo no kyoku*." *Theory and Practice* 21: 167–87.

———. 1999. "'Yes I Wrote It, but I Didn't Mean It': Hearing the Unintended in Niimi Tokuhide's *Ohju* (1988)." *Perspectives of New Music* 37, no. 2 (Summer): 51–115.

———. 2004. "The Politics of Toshirō Mayuzumi's *Essay for String Orchestra*." In

Locating East Asia in Western Art Music, edited by Yayoi Uno Everett and Frederic Lau, 85–118. Middletown, CT: Wesleyan University Press.

Obata, Y. 1974. "The Band in Japan from 1945 to 1970: A Study of Its History and the Factors Influencing Its Growth During This Period." Ph.D. diss., Michigan State University.

Ohsaki, Shigemi. 1991. "Reception of European Music in Japan: Its Problems and the Tasks of the Musicologist." In *Tradition and Its Future in Music: Report of SIMS Osaka 1990*, edited by Masakata Kanazawa, Makoto Ohmiya, Mari Shimosako, Akiko Takamatsu, Yosihiko Tokumaru, Tuneko Tukitani, and Osamu Yamaguti, 413–16. 337–40. Tokyo and Osaka: Mita Press.

Oron, Aryeh. 2002. "Saito Kinen Orchestra (Symphony Orchestra)." Fanfaire website. http://www.bach-cantatas.com/Bio/Saito-Kinen-Orchestra.htm, accessed April 13, 2013.

Oshio, Satomi. 2008. "Thinking about Japanese Music through Voice." In *Music in Contemporary Japanese Society*, edited by Tsuneko Wolgye, Junko Kitagawa, and Oshio Satomi, 142–53. Tokyo: Hōsō University Foundation for Education.

Pacun, David. 2012. "Nationalism and Musical Style in Interwar Yōgaku: A Reappraisal." *Asian Music* 43, no. 2 (Summer–Fall): 3–46.

Palmer, Anthony J. 1991. "To Fuse or Not to Fuse: Directions of Two Japanese Composers, Miki and Takemitsu." In *Tradition and Its Future in Music: Report of SIMS Osaka 1990*, edited by Yosihiko Tokumaru, Makoto Ohmiya, Masakata Kanazawa, Osamu Yamaguti, Tuneko Tukitani, Akiko Takamatsu, and Mari Shimosako, 420–26. Tokyo and Osaka: Mita Press.

Prescott, Ann Elizabeth. 1997. "Miyagi Michio, the Father of Modern Koto Music: His Life, Works and Innovations, and the Environment Which Enabled His Reforms." Ph.D. diss., Kent State University.

Richards, E. Michael, and Kazuko Tanosaki, eds. 2008. *Music of Japan Today*. Cambridge: Cambridge Scholars.

Sharf, Robert H. 1995. "The Zen of Japanese Nationalism." In *Curators of the Buddha: The Study of Buddhism under Colonialism*, edited by Donald S. Lopez, Jr., 107–60. Chicago: University of Chicago Press.

Sheppard, W. Anthony. 2008. "Continuity in Composing the American Cross-Cultural: Eichheim, Cowell, and Japan." *Journal of the American Musicological Society* 61, no. 3 (Fall): 465–540.

Siddons, James. 1999. *Toru Takemitsu: A Bio-Bibliography in Music*. Westport, CT: Greenwood Press.

Silverberg, Miriam. 1992. "Constructing the Japanese Ethnography of Modernity." *Journal of Asian Studies* 51, no. 21 (February): 30–54.

Smaldone, Edward. 1989. "Japanese and Western Confluences in Large-Scale Pitch Organization of Tōru Takemitsu's *November Steps* and *Autumn*." *Perspectives of New Music* 27, no. 2 (Summer): 216–31.

Sparrer, Walter-Wolfgang. 2001. CD booklet, *Koto Uta*. Kairos CD 0012172KAI.

Stock, Jonathan. 1996. *Musical Creativity in Twentieth-Century China: Abing, His Music and Its Changing Meanings*. Rochester, NY: University of Rochester Press.

Suchy, Irene. 1991. "Compositions of German Musicians in Japan from 1872 to 1945." In *Tradition and Its Future in Music: Report of SIMS Osaka 1990*, edited by Edited by Masakata Kanazawa, Makoto Ohmiya, Mari Shimosako, Akiko Takamatsu, Yosihiko Tokumaru, Tuneko Tukitani, and Osamu Yamaguti, 475–83. Tokyo and Osaka: Mita Press.

Suter, Rebecca. 2008. *The Japanization of Modernity: Murakami Haruki between Japan and the United States*. Cambridge, MA: Harvard University Asia Center.

Takemitsu, Toru. 2004. "Toru Takemitsu, on *Sawari*," translated and annotated by Hugh de Ferranti and Yayo Uno Everett. In *Locating East Asia in Western Art Music*, edited by Yayoi Uno Everett and Frederick Lau, 199–207. Middletown, CT: Wesleyan University Press.

Taylor, Timothy Dean. 2001. *Strange Sounds: Music, Technology, Culture*. New York: Routledge.

Thornbury, Barbara E. 1997. *The Folk Performing Arts: Traditional Culture in Contemporary Japan*. Ithaca: State University of New York Press.

Tokita, Alison McQueen, and David W. Hughes, eds. 2008. *The Ashgate Research Companion to Japanese Music*. Hampshire and Burlington, VT: Ashgate.

Tsukitani, Tsuneko. 2008. "The Shakuhachi and Its Music." In *The Ashgate Research Companion to Japanese Music*, edited by Alison McQueen Tokita and David W. Hughes, 145–68. Hampshire and Burlington, VT: Ashgate.

Tsutsumi, Mihoko. 2007. "A History of the Japan Choral Association." Ph.D. diss., Florida State University.

Turino, Thomas. 2000. *Nationalists, Cosmopolitans, and Popular Music in Zimbabwe*. Chicago: University of Chicago Press.

———. 2008. *Music as Social Life: The Politics of Participation*. Chicago: University of Chicago Press.

Vlastos, Stephen, ed. 1998. *Mirror of Modernity: Invented Traditions of Modern Japan*. Berkeley and Los Angeles: University of California Press.

Wade, Bonnie C. 1994. "Keiko Nosaka and the Twenty-Stringed *Koto*: Tradition and Modernization in Japanese Music." In *The Musicological Juncture: Essays in Honor of Rulan Chao Pian*, edited by Bell Yung and Joseph S. C. Lam, 184–98. Cambridge, MA: Harvard University Press.

———. 2005. *Music in Japan: Experiencing Music, Expressing Culture*. New York: Oxford University Press.

Wakabayashi, Bob Tadashi. 1998. *Modern Japanese Thought*. New York: Cambridge University Press.

Washburn, Dennis C. 1995. *The Dilemma of the Modern in Japanese Fiction*. New York: Columbia University Press.

Watanabe, Shuko. 1994. "Traditional and Synthesis Influences on the Solo Piano Works of 34 Japanese Composers Surveyed." DMA thesis, University of Maryland.

Watanabe, Yasushi. 2008. *American Senta: Americano Kokusai Bunka Senryaku* [*American Center: America's International Cultural Battle Plan*]. Tokyo: Iwanamishoten.

"What's Composium." 1999. *Program for the Composium 1999 (May 5–10)*, 1. Tokyo: Tokyo Opera City Cultural Foundation.

Yamamoto, Miki. 2004. "The Significance of the International Music Festival in Asia as a Form of Globalization: The Pacific Music Festival." In *Musicology and Globalization: Proceedings of the International Congress in Shizuoka 2002, in Celebration of the 50th Anniversary of the Musicological Society of Japan*, edited by Tatsuhiko Itoh, Keiichi Kubota, Yasuhiko Mori, and Yoshio Tozawa, 265–67. Tokyo: Musicological Society of Japan.

Yamakawa, Naoharu. 1984. "Tracing the Composition Activities for Traditional Instruments." *Ongaku Geijutsu* 42, no. 9 (September): 18–23.

Yano, Christine Reiko. 1998. "Defining the Modern Nation in Japanese Popular Song, 1914–1932." In *Japan's Competing Modernities: Issues in Culture and Democracy, 1900–1930*, edited by Sharon Minichiello, 247–64. Honolulu: University of Hawaii Press.

———. 2002. *Tears of Longing: Nostalgia and the Nation in Japanese Popular Song*. Cambridge, MA: Harvard University Asia Center.

Yoshida, Hidekazu. 1959. "A Review of the World of Musical Composition in 1958." In *Nihon no sakkyoku 1959*. Tokyo: Ongaku no Tomosha.

Yuasa, Joji. 1989. "Music as a Reflection of a Composer's Cosmology." *Perspectives of New Music* 27, no. 2 (Summer): 176–97.

———. 1993a. "Temporality and I: From the Composer's Workshop." *Perspectives of New Music* 31, no. 2 (Summer): 216–28.

———. 1993b. "Theater as an Environmental Medium." *Perspectives of New Music* 31, no. 2 (Summer): 192–209.

———. 1993c. "The World of *Nō* as I Perceive It: Concerning Some Problems in Music." *Perspectives of New Music* 31, no. 2 (Summer): 186–91.

INDEX